CONSTRUCTIN
FRENCH AND E

The 1980 Quebec referendum was a momentous event that redefined
Canada's nationalist ideologies. While the political implications of the
referendum have been widely analysed, this is the first sustained study of
the role played by the media in shaping and interpreting the referendum
campaign.

Robinson addresses interrelated issues in public opinion creation during
the 1980 campaign. She explores how the ideologies of Quebec and Canadian nationalism were constructed and modified by the separate French
and English networks, and how their idiosyncratic visual styles and thematic selections reinforced Montreal viewers' linguistic and political
divisions. In addition, Robinson compares French and English media professionals and discovers how their work settings and their perception of
their roles had become polarized a decade before through the imposition
of the 1970 War Measures Act. The two journalistic groups were affected
by its imposition in radically different ways, resulting in much more self-
censorship and bland programming on the part of the French media than
the English during the 1980 referendum. Finally, Robinson demonstrates
how the instant playback capabilities of television, newly developed at
the time of the referendum, have affected news discourses and turned
electoral coverage into personalized and sensationalized 'tabloid formats.'
These formats narrowed citizens' abilities to conceive of alternative
political interpretations and actions.

GERTRUDE JOCH ROBINSON is a professor and past director of the Graduate
Program in Communications, McGill University.

GERTRUDE J. ROBINSON

Constructing the Quebec Referendum: French and English Media Voices

UNIVERSITY OF TORONTO PRESS
Toronto Buffalo London

© University of Toronto Press Incorporated 1998
Toronto Buffalo London

Printed in Canada

ISBN 0-8020-0909-3 (cloth)
ISBN 0-8020-7890-7 (paper)

Printed on acid-free paper

Canadian Cataloguing in Publication Data

Robinson, Gertrude Joch
    Constructing the Quebec referendum : French and English media voices

    Includes bibliographical references and index.
    ISBN 0-8020-0909-3 (bound)   ISBN 0-8020-7890-7 (pbk.)

    1. Mass media – Political aspects – Canada.   2. Mass media and public
    opinion – Canada.   3. Referendum – Quebec (Province) – Public opinion.
    4. Quebec (Province) – Politics and government – 1976–1985 – Public
    opinion.*   5. Quebec (Province) – Politics and government – 1994–   – Public
    opinion.*   I. Title.

    P95.82.C3R62 1998   070.4'49971404   C98-930966-5

University of Toronto Press acknowledges the financial assistance to its
publishing program of the Canada Council for the Arts and the Ontario Arts
Council.

This book has been published with the help of a grant from the Humanities
and Social Sciences Federation of Canada, using funds provided by the Social
Sciences and Humanities Research Council of Canada.

To my children
Wendy, Markus, and Beren,
and in memory of
Martin and Andrew

Contents

viii   Acknowledgments

Acknowledgments

The present book was written over a period of eighteen years, during which many people influenced my thoughts and aided me in ways too numerous and varied to mention. Among those who have introduced me to the Quebec and Canadian cultural scenes and for whose help I am particularly grateful are Armande Saint-Jean, Claude-Yves Charron, René-Jean Ravault, Maurice Pinard, Carmen Lambert, Will Straw, Ron Burnett, Marc Raboy, Paul Attallah, Gaëtan Tremblay, Bill Gilsdorf, Steven Kline, and Robert A. Hackett. Colleagues from Sweden and the United States Peter Dahlgren and Joseph Gusfield, and my sister Hanni Woodbury, have encouraged me through their example and through their enthusiasm for academic research. I also must acknowledge a substantial debt to various generations of graduate students in the Graduate Program in Communications at McGill University, who helped me refine my ideas and assisted me in the detailed comparative analyses on which this book is based. Among them are Michael Bloom, Dennis O'Sullivan, Maria Luisa Casas-Perez, Diane Wells, Jane Bisel, Mark Adams, Katka Selucky, Daniel Downes, and Marie-Anne Poussart. Joseph Jackson provided expert formatting support.

Funding and institutional support for research and writing were obtained from a variety of sources. The Faculty of Graduate Studies of McGill University made the initial seed grant for taping the Montreal news coverage of selected referendum events. A sabbatical semester at Carleton University in 1983 provided me with an opportunity to begin writing early versions of what are now chapters 3 and 4. Much of the television data analysis was supported by two official sources in the three years between 1981 and 1984. The Social Science Research Council of Canada (grant #410-81/84-0398) provided support to two inter-university teams at McGill and the Université du Québec à Montréal, which analysed the referendum press and televisual coverage respectively. The second grant, from the Fonds pour la formation de chercheurs et l'aide à la recherche (FCAR) (grant #292-68), permitted us to develop a Goffmanian news analysis schema that is sensitive to the rhetorical and narrative dimensions of news texts. This schema has provided the data for the French/English comparisons on which the book is based.

In 1985 I spent a year as a visiting professor at the University of Landau (Rheinland/Pfalz) sponsored by the Deutscher Akademischer Austausch Dienst (DAAD) and the Deutsche Forschungsgemeinschaft. This stay provided me with an opportunity to try out the news schema on German television and to discover that the ARD and ZDF news rhetorics differ substantially from the Canadian schemas. This work suggested that news discourses are culture-bound, not universal as we had initially supposed; and encouraged me to think further about French/English news practices and their impact on public-opinion formation. Two McGill Social Sciences Research Fund summer grants in 1987 and 1990 provided additional monies for editorial work on the manuscript. Without this institutional support, for which I am extremely thankful, the media's role in Quebec's nationalist politics could not have been explored in all its complexity. Any errors remaining in the text are of course the sole responsibility of the author.

CONSTRUCTING THE QUEBEC REFERENDUM

Introduction

The Quebec referendum called for 20 May 1980 was a momentous political event that set in motion a process of constitutional rethinking about two options for the province's relationship with the rest of Canada. Since that date, numerous political attempts have been made to accommodate the disparate notions of French and English Canadian 'nationalism,' attempts that included the Meech Lake (1990) and Charlottetown (1992) accords. Each of these political events indicated that, from the vantagepoint of hindsight, the governing élites, both federal and provincial, were arrogantly out of touch with the popular mind – a mind that had been misread in 1980 and thereafter both by media pundits and by politicians. Strangely enough, what is remembered of the 1980 referendum – in which 86 per cent of the Quebec electorate cast a vote – is that it seemed to bring the victorious federalist side no joy. Despite Quebecers' rejection of a new sovereign yet 'associated' relationship with the rest of Canada by 59.6 per cent to 40.4 per cent, the province and the nation were caught up in the grief of René Lévesque, who stood alone on the stage of the Paul Sauvé Arena with tears in his eyes and vowed 'à la prochaine.' Though the Parti Québécois was convincingly reelected in 1981 on a platform of 'good government,' the referendum had demonstrated that its sovereigntist aspirations were not shared by the majority of Quebecers. The 1980 results, and the remarkable shifts in public mood in the past eighteen years, run counter to the conventional wisdom that all Quebecers are nationalists. What, then, is the relationship between nationalist ideology and mass belief? And what has the role of the media been in reconstructing the varied meanings of Canadian nationalism?

The Media and Political Power

Conventional political research on ideology has asserted that the elaboration of nationalist discourse has been the work of self-conscious patriots and visionaries. Interestingly, Gilles Gougeon's Radio-Canada interviews with Quebec historians in 1993 reinforce such an explanation. He claims that there is a difference between the thought of nationalist leaders and the much more fundamental state of mind of the 'people,' a state of mind that Léon Dion describes as 'the defensiveness of a threatened minority.' Supposedly, this state of mind is mobilized only in certain crisis situations (Dion, 1961: 90–3). Another popular way of explaining where nationalist ideology originates is to focus on 'class' as the determining factor that mobilizes a group into dreaming about revolutionary change. Richard Handler (1988) argues persuasively against such an oversimplification, noting that even if it were possible to explain the genesis of ideology in terms of social structure, this explanation would still be unable to tell us what the ideology *means* to those who are involved. Furthermore, class is neither an objective nor a verifiable reality, nor are the interests in terms of which class is argued transparent. Furthermore, class theory objectifies different types of ideologies as though they were separate and distinguishable, when in fact ideologies are ways of speaking about the world (1988: 25–6). Explanations that focus on the media's role in creating and sustaining ideological positions are equally unsatisfactory, in that they frequently reduce this complex social process to a question of media 'effects' that can somehow be inferred from the content.

In this book I will follow a different strategy. I will assume that the daily rituals and routines of news production and consumption were linked, albeit intangibly, to the ways in which the 1980 referendum battle was conceptualized and fought. I will then try to unravel the complex levels on which the 'effectivity' of the media (Fiske and Hartley, 1978) has manifested itself in public interpretations of Quebec's nationalist goals. I will use the term 'effectivity' rather than the more common 'effects' to explore the political power of the media, because it will help us avoid the assumption that the relationships being considered are linear and immediate and that they refer only to directly observable and measurable relationships.

Media power in postindustrial societies flows from five intertwined roles: as providers of social information; as a political link between élites and the population; as a direct influence on political actors; as a source of opinion (through editorials and commentary); and as a setter of agendas (Siegel, 1982: 15). Chapters 2 and 3 will demonstrate that by surveying contemporary society, the mass media provide the basic information on daily events that is beyond most citizen's personal experience. This surveying function includes reporting on the economy and trade, on relations with other countries, and on stock market and other business events, as well as on sports and weather; together, these frame postindustrial existence. These surveying activities constitute a considerable if unintentional source of media power, because they serve to mark out the very terrain in which other social actors and institutions must organize their activities and their explanations. The news media affect political life additionally by providing the major information link between the government and the public; it is through this link that government explains its policies. The nature of this linkage also shapes the public's involvement in the political process and in doing so helps to demonstrate the 'democratic nature' of the governmental system. Furthermore, the media's political linking function helps to popularize the major political players themselves, and to cement reciprocal relations with reporters. Since the 1970s, new video and instantaneous signal distribution techniques have changed the temporal and spacial rules of campaigning and heightened the importance of political 'image' over substance. The last chapter will speculate about the implications of this development for democratic politics in general, and for the Canadian political scene in particular.

Media–government relations provide the political framework in which democratic media function in postindustrial society; but this does not address the media's important role in public meaning creation and their ability to influence public opinion. Pierre Bourdieu (1979) and others have criticized the epistemological assumption that citizens are able to formulate opinions on any topic and that these opinions are of equal value in democratic society; it must still be said, however, that the media are virtually indispensable channels in the process of forming and expressing public opinion. As public 'sense making' institutions, the media profoundly influence the fabric of political life and everyday culture. Two aspects of this influence have been extensively documented: the media's 'agenda setting' and 'priming' powers. As early as 1963, Bernard Cohen described the media's agenda-setting power as 'telling people what to think *about* rather than what to *think*.' Evidence that people judge political issues and campaigns by what the media have emphasized, supports this efficacy (McCombs & Shaw, 1977). The discovery of the 'priming' function of television news is more recent and is explained as influencing viewers' standards of political judgment and choice. Shanto Iyengar and S. Kinder discovered that when evaluating complex political issues, citizens do not take into account all they know, but consider what comes to mind – namely, those bits and pieces of political memory which are accessible. Television is particularly powerful in determining what comes to a citizen's mind and what does not (1987: 4). Robert Hackett notes that the agenda-setting and priming efficacies of the media are part of a broader phenomenon: the media, in effect, provide their audiences with a 'frame' and a map for perceiving the social and political world beyond their immediate experience (1991, 14–15). He argues that the news helps citizens construct understandings of what is important, what is good and valuable, what is bad and threatening, and what is related to what on a given day in the 'public' domain of citizen interest. The media's frames thus have both a cognitive and an affective dimension; this will be graphically revealed in this book's discussion of referendum programming.

To understand the processes of framing happenings and transforming them into news stories, we must scrutinize the news product itself and relate it to both its conditions of production and its conditions of reception. Organizational research has successfully tied the news to its organizational settings and to the activities of news workers. Much less well understood is how the media survey the political environment and construct the frames through which political happenings are assessed by viewers and readers. Frames, according to Erving Goffman (1974), are constructed by members of a given society out of attitudes toward everyday life. Embedded in this process is the presupposition that objects of the world are as they appear – a presupposition that is shared by others and thus socially sanctioned. This 'social realism' is what enables the competent citizen to reduce the complexity of the daily environment, by directing him or her to pay attention to only a small range of occurrences (1974: 10–11). Although relevance frames are socially constructed, they remain relatively constant over time. Certainly, the political assumptions underlying Quebecers' interpretations of the six-month-long referendum period in 1980 were of this nature. News frames in turn establish what is 'pertinent' and 'taken for granted' by both news producers and viewers in the political realm beyond a citizen's personal experience. Our evidence will show that although the referendum campaign was a plebiscite, it was framed as an 'election' and thus generated a type of political reporting similar to what was produced during the 1979 federal contest. The concept of frames is thus useful in that it helps us investigate not only what is rendered visible in news accounts but also what becomes *invisible* – that is, why particular foci occur in the news product. In this way it makes sense to talk about 'ideological' framing.

However, the framing metaphor also has theoretical drawbacks. It is associated mainly with the linguistic level of news text analysis and is therefore unable to explain metatextual relationships. The Goffmanian theory of frames is incapable of explaining how different news frames affect one another, and how they change. In addition, it is unable to relate individual linguistic descriptions such as news stories to the structured regularities that news narratives seem to exhibit over time. An example of such 'regularities,' according to Gaye Tuchman (1978: 104), is the contrasting presentational styles displayed by news anchors, such as the 'fatherly' image of Knowlton Nash, and the 'sparkling' image of Barbara Frum, who was host of the CBC's *As It Happens* and *The Journal*. To deal with these types of issues, a third level, discourse analysis, must be added to the book's language and production analyses. Discourse analysis reveals the circular nature of all communication processes and documents the interconnectness of all participants in the social communication loop. Stuart Hall was one of the first to make this theoretical shift when he introduced his encoding–decoding theory in 1973. For Hall, meaning structures are the discursive rules and codes of language that allow the program message first to be produced and later, when received, to have 'very complex perceptual, cognitive, emotional, ideological and behaviour consequences' (Hall, 1980: 130–131). Hall thus differentiates between the meaning structures of producers and those of audience members, as well as between the respective frameworks of knowledge and relations of production that are involved in this process. He is also responsible for discovering the important 'transformative' processes that take place in the communicative circle when events are transposed into and out of message forms, as journalistic producers encode and viewers/readers decode news messages. These processes are clearly not symmetrical, since encoding and decoding call on very different types of knowledge on the part of producers and viewer/interpreters in the communicational circle.

Teun Van Dijk (1988) elaborates on the linguistic and social levels of news analysis clarified by Goffman and Hall to explain how news texts are ideologically 'overdetermined.' These overdeterminations, he points out, are a result of *narrative* regularities in speech and knowledge, including special logics and presentational forms that can only be charted through a third level of scrutiny, called discourse analysis. Discourse analysis helps illuminate the interpretive strategies, styles of argumentation and allocations of authority positions through which (for good example) the notions of Quebec and Canadian nationalism were constructed and sustained throughout the 1980 referendum campaign. It appears that this third level of analytic regularities is quite separate from the regularities on the other two levels; at the same time, however, it is grounded in them and mediates between them. By separating out this third level we will find it easier to clarify the idiosyncrasies of news narratives. Discourse analysis will help us pinpoint the French and English narratives' unique stylistic forms and journalistic modes of address, the ideological idioms and rhetorical figures of speech, as well as how particular forms of knowledge were validated in the news programs.

News discourses are structured ways of speaking about public issues and have developed from different traditions in print and broadcasting. Journalists do not invent; rather, they appropriate preexisting narrative styles, as Gaye Tuchman (1978) and Michael Schudson (1982) among others have demonstrated. This occurs not only through the classification of events into 'hard' or 'soft' or 'ongoing' news, but also through the types of models that are offered to explain newsworthy events. Explanations work through generalization and abstraction, and these processes change over time. Since the 1980s, for instance, explanations based on economic considerations including 'welfare fraud,' 'cost cutting,' and 'downsizing' have been used to justify the widespread social reengineering of Canadian society. Each of these explanations carries with it a particular rhetoric and tone. In the words of Peter Bruck: 'Discourses are metaphorically speaking like rivers, they are at one and the same time resources and powerful flows' for journalistic practitioners (1985: 85). Since narrative reproduction adds 'something more' to linguistic descriptions, it can be said that news discourses are 'overdetermined.'

Besides placing happenings into particular discourse flows, narrative interposition engenders a second classification process: it associates the happening with other, already discursively formed happenings, which then help form the background or substantive context for the ways in which this one will be interpreted. During the 1980 referendum campaign, 'relevant' news items such as public opinion polls and leader interviews were identified as 'belonging' to this discourse through colour coding, flags, and the repeated portrayal of the major 'dramatis personae.' Chief among them the two provincial party leaders, Premier René Lévesque and Liberal Claude Ryan. The dual structuring process accomplished by narrative forms is captured in French literary theory by the distinction between *histoire*, the story matter, and *discours*, its manner of delivery. Later we will show that the news programs on Montreal's French and English TV stations had unique stylistic forms and particular narrative fluencies, as well as unique uses of speaker roles, which in turn generated different styles of argument. We will also demonstrate that as overdetermined texts, news discourses try to 'steer' viewer/listener interpretations toward their own implicit points of view. Narrative forms thus enhance the media's ideological efficacy in the processes of political persuasion.

Some writers argue that because the media function as public 'sense making' institutions, media effects cannot be isolated from other social effects. For example, David Altheide (1985) notes that modern society is dominated by a 'media logic,' which he defines as the process through which media transmit and package information. Consequently, in the postmodern era the media themselves 'are the dominant force to which other institutions conform.' In particular, Altheide argues that the political process has become tied to the logic of media work and transformed by it (18–19). Media discourses themselves, as the referendum descriptions of the YES and NO sides demonstrate, were involved in constituting the varied notions of 'Quebec society.' They were also involved in selecting and evaluating a small number of political events as salient to the referendum campaign. French and English media descriptions of these events provided Montreal's francophone and anglophone audiences with very different maps of the political situation.

The Media's Ideological Functions in Postindustrial Society

Scholars such as Stuart Hall argue that the mass media have three major ideological functions in modern industrialized and capitalist societies. First, they provide a selective construction of social knowledge (1979: 341). By this he means that the media, through their means of signification, provide a frame of reference through which different social groups come to experience and understand their own and others' 'lived reality.' In Quebec, which had been governed by the Parti Québécois since 1976, this meant that the media were preparing the public to focus on alternative ways of conceiving the province's future in the Canadian federation. Second, because modern industrial society is pluralistic, the media strive to provide a running inventory of what Hall calls the currently available 'lexicons of lifestyles and ideologies.' On the eve of the 1980 referendum, this mapping of social groups and their political positions involved three identifiable groups: the francophones; the anglophones; and the allophone Quebecers who voted or not for the Parti Québécois. Yet even among the PQ supporters there were subdivisions: there were the radical *indépendantistes*, the *étapistes*, and the moderates, and still another group that felt no attachment to Canada at all, but nonetheless disagreed with the party's vision of the future as presented in the White Paper (Quebec 1979). To represent all of these groups, among whom a consensus on basic social and political values and goals was lacking, required enormous ideological labour on the part of the media.

The third function of the media is to create some form of consensus and consent. For the Quebec media, this was the most difficult function of all, because to make the Canadian federation narratively appealing, both French- and English-language media had to organize and once again bring together that which they had oppositionally represented and classified throughout their referendum coverage. The media engineered this consensus, which involved creating an 'imaginary cohesion' for Montreal's varied publics, by reinterpreting political platforms, and also by providing the very *forms* in which the arguments were able to appear. In Michael Schudon's scheme of things, it could be said that Montreal news programs had to find new narrative forms for talking about Quebec politics which in turn became the premise for *any* conversation about the province's future in the Canadian confederation (1982: 98).

This book focuses first on the French and English media professionals who created the referendum descriptions. We will explore their differing work settings and role conceptions. Dominique Clift suggests that during the 1970s, French-language journalists viewed their social role as more 'exalted' than their English counterparts and were more militant in protecting their professional autonomy from management (1982: 207). Such a role conception would correspond to what Johnstone and colleagues called the 'participant' stance (1976: 114). Quebec's anglophone journalists, in contrast, supposedly favoured a more 'neutral' North American stance, and prided themselves on being 'uninvolved.' Yet, as will be shown in Chapter 2, 'objectivity' and 'neutrality' are not the same thing (Lichtenberg, 1991: 229), and making these types of binary classifications constitutes an oversimplification. Arthur Siegel (1982) and Walter Soderlund and colleagues (1984) furthermore document that language determines the news agenda and thus the ideological point of view from which reports are written. While these studies provide useful insights into the different professional work contexts of French and English journalists, they fail to show how the francophone and anglophone media arrived at their different referendum framing and coverage. Our comparisons therefore will focus on the political presuppositions that contextualized French and English news coverage at Montreal stations and how these were created through in-house directives as well as by the Canadian Radio-television and Telecommunications Commission (CRTC), which laid down special referendum reporting requirements. Together, these demonstrate that working situations generate symbolic environments that have 'real' interpretive consequences.

Our analysis will show that the differences in ideological framing between the francophone and anglophone stations was reinforced through remarkably different visual presentation styles. These preexisting visual traditions affected not only the referendum accounts of French and English stations, but the ways in which their viewer groups interpreted these accounts. Differences in coverage *style* were therefore *not* the result of an individual journalist's decision to opt for an 'objective' rather than a 'participatory' reporting stance, as Johnstone, Slawski, and Bowman (1976) would have suggested. Instead, they resulted from a complex interplay of station resources and practices, network guidelines, and 'local' understandings about which types of events to select for coverage. These local understandings were co-constructed with the relevant audience groups.

The second focus of this book considers how the media transfigured and reframed the description of various referendum events and created integrative coherence around various types of nationalist discourses. Here, the platforms of the Parti Québécois (White Paper) and the Liberals (Beige Paper) will be presented, and their redefinition by the Montreal media élites will be scrutinized. In the process we will demonstrate Richard Handler's insight (1988) that there is a close resemblance between nationalist ideology and social science theory, which have interacted with each other to legitimate changing renditions of 'nationalism' over time. Thus, the PQ was promoting a version called 'Québécois nationalism' that differs from the nationalism that was espoused during the Quiet Revolution of the 1960s. Throughout the referendum campaign, we discovered, the French and English Montreal stations not only selected different events for political reportage, but also used a limited repertoire of arguments to describe the different versions of nationalism for their respective audiences. The comparisons demonstrate that media rhetorics are not neutral observations of political 'facts,' but rather narrative reconstructions that are written for specific viewer groups whose political leanings are known.

This book's third focus is on the visual news 'formats' and their efficacy in arguing for particular types of nationalist agendas. These news formats addressed socially distinct groups of Montrealers, who are described as of French, English, or allophone (Italian, Greek, or Portuguese) origin. Throughout the campaign, how these viewer citizens interpreted these messages was carefully followed by pollsters, by media commentators (through people-in-the-street interviews), and by Quebec scholars, among them sociologists Maurice Pinard (1986), Richard Hamilton (1981), and Évelyne Tardy (1980). Though our own comparative study focused primarily on the production and programming dimensions of the referendum campaign, the data about reception collected by these scholars permits us to draw tentative conclusions about how different groups of Montrealers interpreted selected aspects of the campaign.

Joshua Meyrowitz (1985) contends that contemporary television news formats have redefined our notions of public space and time, within which political behaviour is enacted. In the referendum campaign, this was evidenced by the fact that video recording devices and satellite capabilities shortened the transmission time for political reports and nearly eliminated distinctions between public and private space. Both time and the fact that statements were made in different geographic locations used to protect politicians' words and actions from immediate public scrutiny. This is no longer the case. From the 1980s onward, instant replay and voice-over capabilities have drastically altered the representational ground rules for politicians and eroded the power differentials that used to exist between themselves, and the journalistic élites who were covering them for the citizen public. In this context, the move to what has been called 'image politics,' which is heavily influenced by advertising strategies, can be explained as a defensive move on the part of politicians to protect themselves from overexposure and to partially regain control over the manner in which they and their words are represented. This demonstrates that media power in the postmodern Information Age results not only from journalists' ability to fashion the program editorially, but also from the unique ways in which television 'places' the politician in relation to the viewers/citizens. The audiovisual referendum coverage demonstrates how the public personae of René Lévesque and Claude Ryan were constructed positively or negatively in relation to a whole series of events, which would predispose different Montreal viewer groups to assess their words and actions in opposite ways. Journalists have *learned* how to produce these descriptions and viewers have *learned* how to *read* and decipher them.

Methods of Analysis and Evidence

This study of the evolution of the nationalistic discourse under the Parti Québécois, and the ways it was reshaped by media élites, is based on many disparate experiences and texts. There was our field experience of the referendum campaign itself, during which we taped relevant news programs. We also visited CBC headquarters in Toronto and Radio-Canada in Montreal for documentary evidence on these institutions' referendum reporting activities. In addition, we interviewed francophone and anglophone journalists such as André Gagnon, Elly Alboim, and Alan Handel, who had participated in creating referendum coverage both on television and in the Montreal press. We applied what has been called 'discourse analysis' and comparison to the television material in order to trace the ideological role of the Montreal media in constituting and defining the referendum plat-forms. Studying news programs as discourses – that is, as sets of conven-tions which strive to control and limit the meanings of the events they convey – has enabled us to map out the *regularities* of speech and knowl-edge, as well as the logics and presentational forms that have informed not only individual news programs, but also the referendum coverage as a whole. The highly polarized referendum campaign provided a particularly clear example of how the oppositional views of the Parti Québécois and the Liberals were narrated for the three identifiable voter groups in ethnically diversified Montreal: those who were in favour of sovereignty-association, those who were against it, and those who were neutral. The in-depth com-parison of the French- and English-language newscasts furthermore per-mitted us to relate the journalistic encoding practices to the various possible decoding positions that Montreal's linguistically differentiated viewer groups could entertain, in what Stuart Hall (1980) has identified as the circular political communication process.

We sampled five key events leading up to the referendum vote in order to acquire an understanding of the different stylistic features of the French and English referendum discourses. The events spanned the White Paper presentation containing the PQ's platform (1–3 November 1979); the referendum question announcement (21–22 December 1979); the Beige Paper presentation introducing the Liberal Party's federal agenda (9–12 January 1980); the Quebec Assembly debate explaining the advantages of the sovereignty-association option (4–11 March 1980); and the final week of the referendum, including the 'day after' account of the vote outcome (14–21 May 1980). Included were the 6:00 p.m. and 10:30 p.m. local and national news segments of Montreal's two French stations (CBFT 2 and CVTM 10) and two English stations (CBMT 6 and CFCF 12).

To guarantee the accuracy and generalizability of the French and English programming patterns, we applied a unique, three-stage audiovi-sual analysis to all of this voluminous material. Our approach was based on Goffman's 'dramaturgical' (1959) and 'frame' (1974) analysis. Goff-man points out that political behaviour can be conceived as a drama enacted on an electronic stage. The news program reconstructs this drama through its selection of actors, the roles they are assigned, and the politi-cal settings in which they appear. Together these constitute the complex symbolic web within which meaning creation in the television news pro-gram can be explained. Discourse theory links news personnel and extra-station roles (such as politicians and experts) with varied visual modes and types of reports, as well as with particular political happenings. Appendix

C details the methodological categories we employed; ensuing chapters provide additional information on how the textual comparisons are theoretically grounded.

To get at how French and English stations reconstructed their unique news genres and the 'preferred meanings' their news programs conveyed, we undertook three levels of analysis. First, we analysed the hundreds of hours of station material from the five periods as a whole, to unearth the unique audiovisual presentation styles of Montreal's French and English news programs. Then we created a 'composite week' made up of a Monday-through-Sunday selection of seven days of programming from all five periods, to analyze the themes that were developed as the major referendum events were retold. The composite-week evidence eliminated reportorial variations grounded in different stations' journalistic resources and in the unpredictability of news happenings. The French composite week covered four news broadcasts daily and provided 9.1 hours (546 minutes) of evidence. The English material covered six news programs daily and provided 16.1 hours (966 minutes) of coverage, which were used for comparison purposes.

We also explored individual program days from the composite weeks, to understand the paradigmatic (selection and categorization) and syntagmatic (combinatory and narrative) features of Montreal's French and English news programs. This comparison served to specify the unique ways in which the stations made public sense of referendum events for their linguistically differentiated viewer groups. These program comparisons demonstrate that the French and English media selected very different events, and developed very different narrative treatments of the same events, and that this resulted in audiovisual typifications and 'preferred descriptions' of people and events that were unique for the two station groups. These audiovisual typifications, which are further explored in Chapters 3, 4, 6, and 7, included juxtaposing of the chain-smoking and 'animated' Lévesque with the expressionless and 'stolid' Claude Ryan. These visual renditions were further reinforced by the use of blue and red emblems and flags, which became condensed symbol frames for the contending political alternatives of the secessionist Parti Québécois and the federalist Liberals. To further verify that the themes and arguments that we had discovered in the television coverage were also found in the print media, we compared the White Paper and Beige Paper coverage in Montreal's *Le Devoir*, *La Presse*, and *Gazette*. These widely read newspapers had been studied by researchers such as Gaetan Tremblay and Claude Yves Charron (1981), Denis Monière (1980), and Yves Gagnon (1980). Their efforts provided us with natural counterfactual examples for verifying the generalizability of our own interpretations.

From the tri-level textual analyses, this book constructs two primary readings for the two language groups. According to Clifford Geertz (1973), 'readings' can never be exact snapshots of a situation, because they incorporate a hermeneutic, interpretive element. The *quality* of readings must therefore be sought in their ability to convince, rather than in their supposed objective truth value. Such an approach, which Geertz calls the 'interpretive turn,' has introduced a fundamental debate into the social science community concerning not just its methods, but its aims. The rising interest among 1980s sociologists, political scientists, anthropologists, and communication scholars in the analysis of symbol systems poses the question of how such systems relate to what goes on in the world (Geertz, 1983: 34–5). This book, which explores the links between public action and public opinion creation, is part of this new scholarship which focuses on how symbol systems impact on social reality. As such, it also challenges four of the methodological assumptions of mainstream social science: the strict separability of theory and data; the availability of a formal language of analysis purged of subjective references; the researcher's claims to moral neutrality; and the availability of an Olympian view from which to judge the evidence.

This reconfiguration of social theorizing immediately raises questions about the quality of our interpretations and their generalizability beyond this case study. We agree with other constructivist theorists that the quality of interpretations is guaranteed not by a single set of truth values, but by the *systematic* way in which methods are employed and our interpretations fit in with the accounts of others. Our interpretations in this study meet this standard. The additional evidence we used was provided by voting statistics, governmental documents (including the White Paper and Beige Paper, and the accounts of participants, as well as the reports of political scientists and sociologists, and of the political actors involved. For example, Maurice Pinard (1983, 1986, 1997) systematically explored the implications of socio-political variables on referendum voting intentions and checked these against the public's voting practices. Évelyne Tardy (1980) contributed a more detailed analysis of the role of women voters and their particular response to the Liberal Party's 'Yvettes' campaign. Journalists such as Graham Fraser (1984), Ian MacDonald (1984) and William Johnson (1994), offered inside accounts of reportorial practices in various Montreal media institutions, and René Lévesque's (1986) and Claude Morin's (1991) memoirs documented the views of some of the participating political actors. All of these accounts provided natural 'counterproofs' to this book's own interpretation of the evidence. The impact of language on media formats is not a matter of chance, or of the polarizations generated by the 1980 referendum situation, but rather must be sought in the systemic and complex interconnections between the political descriptions offered by Canada's two media systems and the ways in which the country's political life is unfolding.

The language-based differences in reporting styles and content have been corroborated by other researchers. Arthur Siegel demonstrated in 1978 that Quebec French-language broadcasting provided more coverage of Quebec issues than of Canadian ones and deduced from this that French-speaking Montrealers were receiving very different geographical emphases from which to fashion their view of the country and its political system, than English-speaking Canadians (1978, 13). In 1981 André Caron investigated how language affected program content in Montreal stations, and discovered that English Montreal stations offered almost double the amount of news programming (26 per cent) as their French counterparts (15 per cent). The same researcher demonstrated that language also affects the presentation style of news programming, with francophone stations relying more on the 'announcer' (anchor) role than English stations, which vary the news text through the use of interview material (1983: 481). Fred Fletcher (1987) and Walter Soderlund et al. (1984) additionally confirm that the political emphases in the 1979 campaign coverage varied by language.

Our own systematic comparisons of the French and English television news accounts are grounded in Van Dijk's (1988) tri-level discourse theory mentioned earlier. This theory distinguishes between the syntactical, semantic, and pragmatic levels of news flows as well as the settings in which these discourses are encoded and the reception settings in which they are decoded by Montreal's varied viewer/listener groups. Discourse flows are characterized by unique 'styles' and 'rhetorics,' which cut across the syntactic, semantic, and pragmatic levels of the news discourse and affected how different viewer groups were able to read and make sense of referendum events. Since meaning creation and narrative forms are always constrained by the context in which they are produced and received, we utilize a 'ground-up' approach derived from linguistics (Barthes 1977) to map out these constraints and their interpretive implications.

To get at the first, 'denotative,' meaning creation level, we sampled Montreal French and English media settings as well as journalistic practices. In addition, we collected the governmental rules and CRTC directives that set out the guidelines for referendum coverage. This information was acquired through interviews with journalists at the francophone and anglophone stations and at three Montreal daily newspapers. The second, 'connotative,' meaning creation level was provided by the 'nationalism' themes contained in the White Paper and Beige Paper. Newspaper accounts from *La Presse* and the *Gazette* served as a check for the ways in which francophone and anglophone news styles were developed. The comparisons show that the YES and NO 'definitions of the situation' represented in the television coverage were grounded in the PQ's vision of 'Québécois nationalism.' We consulted the interpretations of respected Quebec historians to further our understanding of the types of arguments the 1980s version of Quebec nationalism incorporated. These historians included Jean-Paul Bernard, Réal Bélanger, Pierre Trépanier, Richard Desrosiers, and Louis Balthazar, who have written extensively on the changing meaning of Quebec nationalism and its history. Their views provided background material that helped us to understand why the two political alternatives were argued the way they were.

To get at the third, 'ideological,' level of public meaning creation, we followed two strategies. First, we performed a rhetorical analysis to compare the two sides' explanations of the referendum outcome; for this, we used the 20 May 1980 speeches of the referendum contestants – René Lévesque for the YES and Claude Ryan for the NO sides – as well as Prime Minister Pierre Trudeau's federal response. In addition, we sampled voters' interpretations of what the outcome meant by comparing twenty-nine French- and English-speaking 'vox pop' interviews, which were conducted as citizens left the PQ and Liberal Party rallies in different parts of Montreal. Together, these tri-level analyses and comparisons constitute the first-ever attempt to understand how a political campaign unfolded and how it was argued for citizens of different languages and political persuasions.

Though none of this evidence taken in isolation would provide a sufficient base for inferring the efficacy of media messages, taken together it indicates that readers/viewers do interpret media content and that their interpretation practices are related – though not linearly – to language, gender, education, and political affiliation. Reader response research confirms that 'selective viewing' does exist. Jan van den Bulck documents that both genders search out news/information programming and that higher educational level is correlated with greater interest in informational content (1995: 160–71). Our discussion of the 'Yvettes' phenomenon during the final phase of the referendum campaign confirms these correlations. Van den Bulck also points out that news texts make sense to viewers because as a 'genre' they employ specialized narrative styles, which the viewer learns to decode and which journalists learn to produce. To employ this genre meaningfully, journalists not only must follow certain professional 'rules of reporting,' but also, and more importantly, must share a political 'definition of the situation' with their viewer group. A station's referendum coverage would otherwise be unintelligible to its particular audience.

A number of key concepts, which reappear in the subsequent analysis, emerge from our interpretive approach. On the denotative level, these include the idea of unique political 'definitions of the situation' which framed the news discourses and were shared by the message producers as well as by the viewer groups they were addressing. These definitions were different for Montreal viewers who embraced the YES, the NO, and the undecided sides of the campaign. The varied political definitions in turn gave rise to an inventory of overarching 'preferred descriptions,' which placed referendum events into easily distinguishable interpretive contexts. In addition, different types of preferred descriptions resulted in distinguishable 'narrative strategies' in the francophone and anglophone news programs. In rhetorical terms, we found that these strategies were ordered into a set of arguments or 'canonical formulas,' which contained only seven evaluative elements, which were mirror images of one another, in the French and English news programs. The details of these rhetorical structures will be analysed and illuminated in subsequent chapters.

The Organization of the Book

Each of this book's eight chapters explores the interrelated questions of how different élites presented their versions of nationalism during the 1980 referendum debate; how journalistic work practices and professional demands affected program construction; and how television formats influenced public opinion among French- and English-speaking viewers. As symbolic 'maps,' media discourses also dictate how politicians are able to play their roles and what they can say on the electronic stage. In this way, the book contributes to theoretical issues in public opinion creation and news analysis, as well as to the debate about how new technologies affect the political process. News analysis research in the 1980s showed that it is the *form* rather than the *content* that accounts for television's persuasiveness, its stylistic dimensions, and its rhetorical thrust (Knight, 1989). These stylistic dimensions of the news narrative differ for the print media, for radio and for television (which is just as McLuhan predicted), and may thus be called 'media specific.' On the rhetorical level, however, the print media and television construct discourses that utilize similar argumentation styles. Through various types of quoting practices, they follow a 'pseudo-scientific' rhetoric that legitimates both the narrator and the narrator's message. These rhetorical devices help the journalistic practitioner camouflage interpretative involvement behind the stylistic criteria of 'objectivity,' 'balance,' and 'neutrality,' as Chapters 5 through 7 will demonstrate.

Besides an introduction, the book has four parts. The first part provides the historical and institutional context for Quebec's 1980 referendum campaign – that is, the historical backdrop against which the referendum was played out. Chapter 1 explores the selected historical understandings that framed the party platforms for the YES and NO sides. It is intended mainly for those readers who are not already familiar with the background to the 1980 referendum campaign. The same chapter also includes a timeline of key federal–provincial events, which provide the immediate historical context for the two versions of nationalism presented in the Parti Québécois's White Paper and the Liberals' Beige Paper.

The second chapter scrutinizes the city's media institutions, which constituted the work setting in which French and English journalists fashioned their reports. It is written by media scholar and critic Armande Saint-Jean (University of Sherbrooke), who has extensive personal experience in the Quebec journalistic milieu. The chapter illuminates how Quebec journalists' working conditions had been altered by the 1970 War Measures Act, which had turned many journalists into active nationalists. As a consequence, Montreal's newspapers and television stations had great difficulty defining the notions of 'balance' and 'neutrality,' not only for their viewers/readers but also for their own reporters during the referendum campaign. The conflicts that arose from this were most serious in French media outlets, because – surprisingly – *all* Montreal media institutions supported the NO side. The increased use of management directives, and the suspending of reporters, indicates that public opinion creation during the referendum campaign required a strong organizational effort. The directives that were circulated within some newspapers led to confrontations between management and journalists about the proper definition of professionalism and about the civic rights of media personnel.

Part II explores how television formats, on both the visual and the narrative levels, have invaded the Canadian political landscape and transformed the electoral behaviour of public officials as well as the narrative 'logics' through which public events are explained to the viewing public. Chapter 3 explores the Canadian electoral rules and how television changed them since the 1970s. On the Canadian political scene, party affiliation and regionalism used to be the two most important factors in voter decision-making. Party affiliation has since become eroded through television campaigning, in large part because leaders' local pronouncements are immediately available on the national stage. No wonder politicians seek shelter in 'image politics.' The chapter also surveys the Canadian electoral information net, which is linguistically bifurcated and utilizes two distinct visual presentation styles. These have evolved out of differences in how news presenter roles and outside locations are utilized in program formats. Francophone news programs in 1980 were constructed mainly around the in-studio anchor role, which was presented 'piece to camera.' Anglophone stations made more use of reporter and interviewer roles, which are typically accompanied by action footage from outside locations. These format differences, subsequent chapters will demonstrate, resulted in the development of different argumentation styles in the francophone and anglophone stations.

Chapter 4 explores how the political decision to cast the referendum as an 'election,' though it was really a plebiscite on Quebec's constitutional future, affected the coverage of the referendum campaign. This chapter suggests that this framing resulted in referendum events being described using standard sports metaphors, and that the political consequences in the event that Quebecers voted for sovereignty-association were downplayed as a result. The 'politics as usual' approach was reinforced by such format devices as flow and visual intercutting. It was further reinforced by the blue/red colour symbolism associated with the Quebec and Canadian flags and by the juxtaposition of the YES and NO side arguments in an adversarial manner. These stylistic features worked to structure the political alternatives into simple opposites, even though a much larger range of political attitudes was possible in the situation at hand. The comparison also demonstrates that both sets of television stations legitimated their news accounts as 'factual,' although they utilized different stylistic verification practices.

Part III contains two chapters that probe how the YES and NO sides contextualized their radically different proposals for the province's political future. These culture-specific narratives, it appears, were constructed both from incompatible ideological versions of Quebec and Canadian 'nationalisms,' and from argument strategies that legitimated journalists' voices over those of politicians in news programming. All of this in turn created spectator positions with different types of political understandings about ongoing referendum events. Chapter 5 traces the historical origins of Québécois nationalism and the meanings it assigned to the concepts of 'nation' and 'people' in the Parti Québécois and the Liberal Party documents. An analysis of Montreal newspaper coverage of the White Paper's tabling in November 1979 demonstrates how the French- and English-language press used these differential understandings of nationalism to select and highlight different aspects of referendum events.

Chapter 6, 'Interpreting the White Paper on Television,' demonstrates that three levels of sense-making are involved in the creation of an ideological position: journalistic conventions about political players; available political knowledge about the democratic process; and opposing notions of nationalism. All media, it appears, utilize a 'realist' narrative style similar to that found in classical novels. Yet the print media and television achieve this 'scientific narrative,' and handle the preferred 'neutrality,' in very different ways. On television, action footage and quotations from politicians' statements are particularly effective neutrality strategies, because they are based on familiar visual codes (photography) and because they reinforce the 'looking glass' quality of television programming.

Part IV compares francophone and anglophone public opinion creation processes and the ways that television news as a 'genre' creates its narrative scripts. The chapters in this section examine the processes by which 'imaginary cohesion' was achieved and how ideological closure was created after the emotional referendum vote of 20 May 1980.

Democratic theory legitimates four groups of actors as players on the political stage: politicians, journalists, experts, and 'people-in-the-street.' All of their voices are represented in the news narrative. Chapter 7 analyses how these groups' voices were used in explaining the referendum outcome. This chapter shows that in creating public opinion, it was politicians who were in control of 'naming' or defining what the referendum vote was all about. They not only set news guidelines for 'balanced' coverage, but also provided alternative scenarios for future party political action. The other two processes of public opinion creation, however, favoured journalists. Their production and editorial practices influenced both the 'assignment of ownership' and the legitimation of a particular view of public events. It is journalists who determine how the narrative voices of politicians, experts, and 'people-in-the-street' will be selected, hierarchized, and endowed with interpretive coherence. Media élites, the evidence demonstrates, were active players in the creation of versions of national identity; they were also interested contestants in maintaining their professional independence and in legitimating the quality of their reports.

The final chapter summarizes the book's answers to its three initial questions. The section on the media and Canadian nationalism explores how the Quebec and Canadian versions of nationalism were co-constructed over the past thirty-five years and can therefore not be treated as independent of each other. Because the English-Canadian version was articulated mainly within a context of North American hegemony, it has difficulty articulating Quebec's alternative agenda. The Montreal case study also illuminates the crucial role that journalists played in constructing the nationalist agendas. As interpreting and 'naming' élites, they resemble historians and sociologists, who use the same categories of 'nation' and 'people' to construct their nationalist rhetorics. They furthermore employ the same 'scientific' legitimation strategies to mark their news discourses as 'factual' rather than 'fictional,' though their quoting practices tend to subvert these distinctions. The final section explores how public opinion can turn into action – as happened in the 'Yvettes' phenomenon – and raises questions about the role of television news discourses in the construction of contemporary democratic practices.

Televisual formats now reach into and organize aspects of social life that were previously unrelated to the media. Media formats not only change how politicians address the public, but also circumscribe the public's *involvement* in the political process itself. The more polarized the political climate, the more salient the emotional dimensions of the television format become, because television as a medium magnifies emotions. In the 1990s, television news has not only become the primary symbolic battleground in Western democracies, but has also narrowed the spectrum of political action by utilizing narrative strategies that are emotionally charged. Image politics, with its advertising formats and commercialized visuals, has not only rearranged the time and space dimensions of contemporary electoral campaigns, but has also curtailed the meaning frameworks in terms of which voters are able to *imagine* public debates and construct alternative political solutions.

PART I

REFERENDUM ACTORS AND JOURNALISTIC PRACTICES

1

The Referendum Actors and Issues in Historical Perspective*

When the citizens of this country refuse to acknowledge their given reality, they invent another history – marked by their preconceptions – one which they imagine as their real history, even though few historians would identify it as such.

Chaput-Rolland (1987: 60)

Contrary to received wisdom, the 1980 referendum was neither the end nor the beginning of a process, but rather just another stage in the ongoing three-hundred-year history of French settlement on the North American continent. The significance of the events that constituted the referendum must therefore be sought both in terms of immediate political antecedents and the historical process of which it was a part. This process, relatively unknown to English-speaking Canadians, is about building and sustaining a unique political and cultural identity.

At issue at the time of the 1980 referendum was therefore not only the intention of the Parti Québécois to negotiate a change in Quebec's political status, but also a two-decade-old quarrel between the supporters of independence and their federalist adversaries. Clearly, the quarrel continues to this day; nothing was settled in 1980, just as nothing was settled in 1970, when Pierre Trudeau imposed the War Measures Act to stamp out 'separatism' once and for all. In retrospect, it seems furthermore that nothing was settled in 1942 during the Conscription Crisis, nor was anything settled

---

*This chapter was co-written with Dr Armande Saint-Jean of the University of Sherbrooke. I thank her very much for the unique insights she brings to the history of Quebec, which provides the backdrop for understanding the 1980 referendum.

after the defeat of the Patriots' Rebellion in 1837–8. This suggests that no subsequent political gesture was able to resolve the contradictions resulting from the 1759 conquest – not even the British North America Act of 1867. One must go back to the origins of Canada – to the first moments of coexistence between the two founding groups – if one wants to eliminate some of the ambiguity that continues to cloud the referendum of 1980 (and its replay in 1995). For what was at stake in 1980 was nothing less than the possibility for a group of people to choose a new future and to correct the past errors of its lived history. The referendum offered Quebecers the choice between accepting their political heritage within a federal Canada, and imagining a new, separate but 'associated' political existence.

To situate the 1980 referendum in historical perspective, we must therefore retrace a number of important moments that together constitute the quest for identity of the French minority in North America. According to Fernand Dumont (1993), this quest has three key elements: the origin, the state, and the French language. Collectively these three elements constitute and describe the dimensions of the Québécois collective memory, provide the basis for the current political ideology, and explain the symbolic discourses of Quebec literature. Origins, Dumont argues, create the framework for sentiments of identity. The state embodies the powers to act in the present and to determine the future, while the French language is the most visible means through which identity continues to be constructed. In the Canadian situation, according to Dumont, language continues to be the 'signature of difference' (1993: 14).

Focus on Beginnings

In this *belle province* where the motto *Je me souviens* has not prevented collective historical amnesia, few people remember that the origins of the constitutional tensions go back as far as the 1759 Conquest and the subsequent Treaty of Paris (1763). The documents codifying the Conquest legally, politically, and institutionally, foresaw the assimilation of the French-speaking majority in Nouvelle-France; it was in this context that Lord Durham arrogantly dismissed Lower Canada as an 'old static society in a new and progressive world' (in Brown, 1988: 252). Yet this assimilation did not happen. The enduring resistance against assimilation can be partly explained by the *Canadiens'* attachment to their country of origin – an attachment that manifested itself in successive generations of *Canadiens*, rural and urban, keeping alive the folkways brought from *la douce France*. Even though this homeland, France, had abandoned its colony in political terms, the French descendants in North America retained their pride in their origins. To this day, many Québécois maintain their links to the Old World, searching geneological records for the first ancestor who landed in Nouvelle-France and establishing contacts with cousins in Brittany, the Poitou, or the Limousin. The same pride resurfaced during the Conscription Crisis of 1942, when many francophones rejected joining the Canadian Armed Forces (which did not welcome them in any case), but still wished to aid occupied France. Some did this by joining the U.S. Army instead, among them René Lévesque. Echoes of this attachment to the mother country also resurfaced in the moving testimonies of those Québécois veterans of the Second World War who returned to Europe in 1994 in order to commemorate the fiftieth anniversary of the Dieppe Raid.

For all the sentimental attachment to the mother country, France as a political entity has little political influence on modern Quebec. The Québécois criticize France for its cultural imperialism and its attempts to impose a uniform French language across the globe. Both in spite and because of this stance, it is easier to understand why General Charles de Gaulle's message resonated so powerfully during his 1967 visit to Expo 67 in Montreal. When the great general made his extraordinary call 'Vive le Québec libre!' from the balcony of Montreal's city hall, he was undoubtedly aware that he was echoing a slogan that was being used by the indépendantistes, who were demanding political autonomy for Québéc.

This demand draws attention to another fundamental component in the construction of identity – namely, the role of the state. Officially conquered, the society of Bas-Canada began to develop under political institutions not of its own making; at the same time, it set about inventing means to remain at the margins of this imposed structure. This explains how Lower Canada retained a unique political and legal system that continues to this day. Politically, it has fiscal autonomy within the federation; its assembly is 'national' rather than legislative; and it once had an upper Chamber (abolished in 1960) that mirrored the federal Senate. Legally, its Civil Code is based on the Napoleonic Code and thus differs from English common law, which is used in the rest of Canada. As a province, it has initiated a number of unique legislative arrangements, opting out of the Canada Pension Plan, for example, and creating its equivalent, the Quebec Pension Plan, and running its own health and blood plans. Another manifestation of this uniqueness relates to the province's political identity as defined in cultural terms. Quebec's notion of 'nationhood' is conceived in terms of unique traditions and is inscribed in the political framework of the province, where two distinct communities, French and English, coexist side by side. The two collectivities claim different political affiliations: the anglophones of Quebec identify themselves primarily as 'Canadians'; the francophones have stopped calling themselves French Canadians and identify themselves as Québécois first and Canadians second.

These differences in political identification have resulted in antagonisms between the two communities – antagonisms that are reinforced by their élites, which promote different social projects. The formation of a number of important economic institutions since the 1960s, founded either on the co-operative system (like the *Mouvement Desjardins)* or as a collaboration between state and private capital (Caisse de dépôt, Hydro-Québec, Régie des rentes, Régie de l'assurance-automobile, Régie de l'assurance-maladie), has provided modern Quebec with the economic instruments to foster its own development. In the process, a Québécois-French bourgeoisie has emerged whose members belong to the professions and constitute the new business élite. The anglophone bourgeoisie, in contrast, maintains closer ties with business networks in Toronto and New York than with the mandarins of the Grande Allée in Quebec City, or the brokers of the rue Saint-Jacques in Montreal. These parallel networks have not been integrated, and this has created difficulties for immigrants to Quebec. Confronted with polarized identifications, these new groups tend to cling to their original national references and to sidestep the struggle for provincial identity, which after all was not of their making. Even though the concepts of 'nation,' 'people,' and 'state' continue to be contested, it is clear that the political distinctiveness of Quebec, inherited from the time of Lower Canada, has generated a sense of Québécois identity and was therefore at the heart of both referendum debates. From this perspective, the 1980 referendum may be interpreted as an attempt on the part of the provincial government to renegotiate the federal compact in order to cement Quebec's political and cultural specificity.

The third element in cultural identity formation, which has made Quebecers what they are, is the French language. That this language has survived suggests the strength of Quebecers' resistance against assimilation on a continent often spoken of as a 'melting pot.' The Royal Proclamation after the Conquest was intended to impose English laws and the English language on the *Canadiens,* whose French customs and practices, however, remained so strong that the Quebec Act of 1774 did not mention the subject of language (Laurion, 1987). Later, the Constitutional Law of 1792 divided the colony into two parts, Upper and Lower Canada, and recognized each by its customs and languages. As a result, Gaston Laurion explains, the British North America Act of 1867 could not but confirm the legal status of the French language in Quebec and in the Parliament in Ottawa; at the same time, however, it gave English – used by a minority of Quebecers at the time – special status through Article 133.

The threat of assimilation was again raised in 1961 when some census analyses suggested that the number of francophones in Canada and in Quebec seemed to be shrinking, and that the birthrate in Quebec was falling. These revelations led to a number of commissions of inquiry whose common mandate was to consider the future of Canada's political institutions. From Laurendeau-Dunton – whose conclusions stopped short of constitutional recommendations but explicitly called for the safeguarding of the rights and languages of the founding peoples – to the Pépin-Robarts Commission on Canadian Unity (1977), the Canadian political system came under recurrent scrutiny. Yet in the end, those who hoped for a political solution that reaffirmed the importance of the two founding cultures to the Canadian political project were disappointed. Some Québécois intellectuals, including Marcel Rioux, have concluded that the referendum polarized the anglophones of Canada and the francophones of Quebec in the same way that the American Civil War polarized the North and South (1990: 300). The adoption in 1977 of Bill 101, the French Language charter, by the Parti Québécois government further increased hostilities regarding the official status of the French and English languages in Quebec and, more fundamentally, the political and social rights of Quebec's anglophones. This bill, and other PQ initiatives, redefined English Quebecers – who had always considered themselves an extension of the Canadian majority in the province – as a cultural and linguistic minority. This redefinition made Quebec's anglophones feel persecuted, even though their social institutions were better protected in Quebec than those of francophones elsewhere in Canada. The domain of language continues to retain its symbolic value, because it is here, to this day, that Canada's different cultural practices and two oppositional national projects most visibly confront each other.

Contextualizing the Referendum

At the time of the referendum in May 1980, the Parti Québécois had been in power for four years. By delivering 'good government' it had garnered great popular support for René Lévesque. Quebec was respected as a modern society with a progressive social outlook. The young party had refurbished Quebec's political and social institutions, introduced nondenominational education reforms, and improved the job market for a new generation of Quebecers. By the late 1970s there was a flowering of cultural production in literature, cinema, television, and music, and performers such as Félix Leclerc, Gilles Vigneault, and Jean-Pierre Ferland were introducing Quebec culture to the rest of the world.

The referendum campaign, with its formula for sovereignty-association, was designed to appease both those who wanted an autonomous Quebec and those who wished to maintain a federal link. It is clear now that the formula appealed only to francophones who supported the Parti Québécois. Even among this group, however, there were dissenters who had visions of a Republic of Quebec with its own army, money, and flag. Since they were only a small minority, they remained relatively silent about their preferences. The Liberal federalist opposition, in contrast, was more vocal about its stance, emphasizing that the 'separation' of Quebec from Canada would have dire economic consequences and possibly cause Canada to disappear from the international map. These opposing agendas were echoed in the media descriptions, which later chapters will analyse.

Federalist concerns began to surface immediately after the PQ victory in 1976, when federal cabinet members from Quebec launched a vocal campaign against Radio-Canada, fearing that separatists were infiltrating Quebec broadcasting. Some ministers wanted to purge suspect elements and tried to enlist the Canadian Radio-television and Telecommunications Commission's (CRTC) support in guaranteeing 'neutrality,' and that the French-language service would promote Canadian unity. Radio-Canada and the journalists themselves protested loudly against such interference, contending that freedom of conscience and the civil rights of journalists were not incompatible with honest and objective reporting. Later chapters will demonstrate that the francophone media lived up to their professional ideal of 'balance' and that their referendum coverage was even-handed and competent.

Our discussion suggests that the 1980 referendum was called in a social climate full of misunderstandings on both sides of the political fence. To avoid excessive spending on the part of the federalists and to ensure a fair representation of its own option, the Parti Québécois followed British precedent for the referendum: it enacted legislation to create two umbrella commissions to represent the YES and the NO sides in the campaign. Even though this law had political advantages, it imposed and legitimated a Manichean division of people and issues – one that failed to acknowledge the varied concerns of Quebec's multiple publics. The ensuing media reporting was consequently framed by a simple notion of 'balance' that merely required the juxtaposition of *any* voices from the YES and the NO committees, rather than subdividing these further into stronger and weaker supporters of the two options.

The Protagonists

The partisans of the YES option – those favourable to sovereignty-association – were found mainly among the Parti Québécois supporters, and among former *indépendantistes* who had resigned themselves to this option by default. These PQ supporters were numerous and were present in all social domains: in the professions, among the labour unions, in the civil service, among the academic intelligentsia, and (to a lesser degree at the time) in finance and business. The party thus benefited from a solid political base; as well, its electoral machine had been honed during the 1976 electoral campaign. Even if many disliked the phrasing of the question, the party activists were used to fighting electoral battles against great odds, and viewed the referendum fight as another of these occasions. They were led by René Lévesque, who was embarking on the most important gamble of his political career. The party made him the centre of the campaign, both for strategic reasons and because he had excellent media connections.

The provincial Liberal Party was headed by Claude Ryan, former editor of *Le Devoir*, a one-time militant in the Young Catholic Movement who had succeeded Robert Bourassa after the latter's electoral defeat in the provincial election of 1976. The Liberals as a party were dispirited and at odds about their future direction. Ryan was recognized as rigorous and competent, but also as lacking charisma (of which Lévesque had a great deal). Ryan knew that he would be unable to generate popular enthusiasm for the federalist side. His role as the official leader of the NO camp was additionally complicated by the fact that the Federal government distrusted his political leadership. This made it difficult for Ryan to legitimate himself as the head of the NO forces in Quebec.

The main protagonists in the referendum campaign were therefore Lévesque and Trudeau, who had known each other for more than twenty years. They had participated in the same intellectual rebellions that had laid the groundwork for both the Quiet Revolution and the province's renewed participation in federal politics. These former allies were still polite to each other in public; nevertheless, they had become political enemies in the intervening years. This enmity became more pronounced after 1976, when all three federal parties in Ottawa recognized that a political confrontation was inevitable. Quebec MPs and cabinet members were caught in the middle of this confrontation. Torn between their Quebec roots and their allegiance to federalism, they faced difficult questions about the significance of the referendum and its consequences for Canada. It was Trudeau, not Ryan and his Beige Paper, who provided the answer to this question. He promised that a NO to sovereignty-association would mean a YES to renewed federalism. Trudeau would later honour this promise by repatriating the Canadian Constitution and adding to it a Charter of Rights. This Charter has shifted the balance in favour of collective rights, at least insofar as particularized interest groups and thus the French collectivity are concerned.

Our account suggests that the fundamental stakes in the referendum debate went well beyond the answer to the question itself. The real issue was the survival, the identity, and the future of the francophone collectivity in North America. The contrasting visions for this future were contained in two documents: the PQ's White Paper, 'D'égal à égal' and the Liberal Party's Beige Paper, 'A New Canadian Federation.'

The Parti Québécois's White Paper

The White Paper, published in November 1979, explained sovereignty-association as a new relationship between Quebec and Canada. It suggested that sovereignty-association would guarantee Quebec's existing territory, law-making autonomy, and taxing power while at the same time preserving certain links with Canada. There were to be no customs barriers at common borders, and decisions relating to tariffs on goods produced elsewhere were to be made jointly. Quebec would continue to be bound by treaties to which Canada was a signatory; travel between the two nations would be unrestricted; and if Canada consented, citizens of both nations would have dual citizenship and the Canadian dollar would circulate in both jurisdictions.

The White Paper's intent was thus not only to explain sovereignty-association, but also to show how it would be implemented. The basic concept was to establish a hierarchy of 'community' agencies similar to those foreseen by the European Economic Community. Chief among these new agencies was to be a Community Council, in which representatives of Canada and Quebec would render decisions on issues arising from the terms of association and from foreign trade agreements. Legal conflicts arising from the terms of association were to be resolved in a special court, to which judges would be appointed from Quebec and Canada equally. Finally, a central monetary authority was proposed, in which representation of both nations was to be determined by the size of their respective economies. This central authority was to direct a central bank charged with issuing currency and determining the rate of exchange used by both states. Quebec and Canada would, however, each have their own banking authority to manage their national debt and direct their financial operations.

After explaining sovereignty-association and providing for its implementation, the PQ's White Paper devoted nearly a quarter of its 107 pages to addressing anticipated objections. It argued, first, that despite the consistent refusal of the federal government and the provincial premiers to negotiate terms of association with Quebec, such an association already existed and probably would continue to exist, since its destruction would require great expenditures of time and money on the part of the federation. Accordingly, the paper asserted, the purpose of the Quebec government's proposal was neither to establish an association between Quebec and the rest of Canada, since one clearly already existed, nor even to challenge this association, but rather to 'negotiate its structures and its decision-making processes.' Thus, many of the electorate's reservations would seem to have been overcome, since the practical emphasis was on the association component of the PQ's proposal.

Sovereignty, on the other hand, was discussed in more theoretical terms that stressed the advantages of consolidating national and provincial governments. In effect, a YES victory in the referendum would amount to a mandate for Quebec to negotiate a new and more autonomous relationship between itself and the rest of Canada – one that would provide monetary benefits by reducing overlap in government services. At the same time, Quebec would continue to trade with Canada and profit from Canadian trade agreements. Following this logic, a NO vote in the referendum would not lead to a renegotiation of Quebec's standing in the federation, as proponents of the NO side promised; instead, it would be a signal to the rest of Canada that Quebecers were not particularly interested in change.

The Liberal Party's Beige Paper

In January 1980, two months after the White Paper was tabled, Quebec's Liberal Party published its counterargument. Calling the PQ's plan a 'house of cards' and its outlook 'pessimistic' and backward-looking, it emphasized the hidden political agenda implied by the 'sovereignty-association' option and the economic dislocation resulting from secession. The Beige Paper argued that Quebec was already a distinct and unique society and that it had always determined its own destiny within the framework of a federated Canada. This confederation had been advantageous for Quebec over time and would continue to be so in the future, especially if it could be made to function more effectively. In short, the paper contended that the federal system gave Quebec a dual advantage: a chance to maintain and develop its own culture while participating in 'the benefits and challenges of a larger and much richer society' (1980: 10).

Declaring federalism to be the form of government 'best suited to Canada,' and believing unification to be advantageous to both Quebec and Canada, the authors of the Beige Paper proposed that a new written agreement [a constitution] be drafted. Such a document would affirm the equality of the two founding peoples and guarantee the rights and liberties of individuals (including language rights) within a federal system of government. This 'new federalism' was conceived as a modification of the existing situation. It called for the streamlining of overlapping federal and provincial services – a problem that had also been cited in the White Paper. In addition, it envisaged an elevation of Quebec's status within the confederation. Although the Beige Paper maintained that the provinces should be equal, it conceded that 'as the primary home of the French way of life in Canada, Quebec must enjoy certain prerogatives consistent with its responsibilities.' At the same time, it cautioned, 'the constitution will never be able to take account in an explicit way of all of the differences inherent in the reality of Canada' (1980: 41).

Like the White Paper, the Beige Paper argued that many Canadian problems were the result of an ambiguous relationship between federal and provincial jurisdictions – a problem that had come to a head during the modernization drive of the 1970s. To prevent federal encroachment on provincial rights, powers, and obligations, it recommended that the federal domain be more clearly specified and that the jurisdiction of the provinces be recognized as encompassing any area not designated or named as a federal responsibility by the constitution. Thus, the provinces were to be granted authority to regulate and supervise most activities in the fields of commerce, investment, insurance services, education, culture, and public transportation, while the federal government would direct international and interprovincial matters in the same domains and attempt to equalize provincial development through transfer payments.

Generally, then, what the Beige Paper proposed was a modification of existing constitutional arrangements that would accommodate Quebec's special needs and concerns within the existing political framework. The document argued that Canadian federalism was responsible for Quebec having already reached 'a certain level of development' and that reform was consequently the joint responsibility of both governments. The Beige Paper thus implied that a NO vote in the referendum would be a vote for both Quebec and Canada, since the two were interdependent.

The Referendum Question

Since the PQ and Liberal options both addressed the perceived popular desire to enlarge the province's jurisdiction, most Quebecers were faced with a difficult decision in the May 1980 referendum. The wording of the question therefore took on added importance. For more than eighteen months it went through a series of revisions, which were tested and refined by means of frequent public opinion polls. Early formulations of the question consisted of proposals for reapportioning the powers laid out in the British North America Act so that they would correspond more closely to the principles of the sovereignty-association option. These attempts produced straightforward questions referring to proposed legislation ('Do you endorse Bill X?'). Later versions reflected the findings of public opinion polls that most Quebecers did not favour Quebec as a 'distinct country,' though they were willing to give the government a mandate to negotiate a new status for Quebec – one that was loosely based on the principles of sovereignty-association. Accordingly, as the question changed shape over time, a YES vote victory was increasingly defined as a 'bargaining position,' rather than an object in itself (Fraser, 1984: 201).

By early 1979, public opinion polls were indicating that a YES vote on the sovereignty-association issue was unlikely. Consequently, a two-stage political implementation strategy was developed with the goal of uniting a majority of Quebecers behind the movement. This strategy proposed an immediate vote on the question of whether to negotiate a new relationship with the rest of Canada and a later vote on the eventual results of those negotiations. The referendum question thus underwent yet another reformulation, emerging as follows: 'Do you give the Quebec government a mandate to negotiate with the rest of Canada a new political agreement based on the principles of sovereignty-association and equality between the two peoples of Canada?'

In December 1979, Joe Clark's Conservative government fell in a vote of no confidence on the budget; by February 1980, the Trudeau Liberals were once more in power in Ottawa. In spite of this unexpected turn of events, Lévesque announced that the referendum would proceed as scheduled, even though the final version of the question had still not been arrived at and the political situation had radically changed, pitting two 'favourite sons' against each other. Consequently, the question was once more rewritten – by Claude Morin, Louis Bernard, and Daniel Latouche – in an all-night session on 18 December 1979 (Lévesque 1986, 209–301; Fraser 1984, 205–6). In its final form, it read:

The Government of Quebec has made public its proposal to negotiate a new agreement with the rest of Canada, based on the equality of nations;
this agreement would enable Quebec to acquire the exclusive power to make its laws, administer its taxes and establish relations abroad – in other words, sover-

eignty – and at the same time, to maintain with Canada an economic association including a common currency;
any change in political status resulting from these negotiations will be submitted to the people through a referendum;
ON THESE TERMS, DO YOU AGREE TO GIVE THE GOVERNMENT OF QUEBEC THE MANDATE TO NEGOTIATE THE PROPOSED AGREEMENT BETWEEN QUEBEC AND CANADA?

This, then, was the question to which the citizens of Quebec were expected to answer 'YES' or 'NO.'

In the end, the vote went this way: 40.44 per cent for and 59.56 per cent against the government's proposition. In retrospect, it is clear that the YES and NO sides of the campaign were grounded in a set of mutually exclusive notions of Quebec and Canadian nationalism. We will explore these notions in greater detail in Chapter 5. Let it be said here that for the Parti Québécois the province was an ethnic 'homeland' for all French-speaking Canadians, wherever they lived; for the Liberal Party, Canada was the 'homeland' of all Canadians, wherever they lived and whatever their ethnic background. Chapter 5 will demonstrate that it is these contrasting 'definitions of the situation' that resulted in differing analyses of the referendum 'events' that were presented to Montreal's francophone and anglophone citizens. It will also document how the media performed what Stuart Hall (1979) calls the 'ideological labour' of fitting at least six different audience interpretations into a single set of binary oppositions.

To further contextualize the referendum debate and recall those political events which had the greatest impact on its outcome, Appendix A reproduces the major events initiated by the federal and provincial contestants in the campaign. For the sake of clarity, these events have been identified with the geographical centres of political decision-making in which they took place (Quebec/Ottawa). However, they could just as easily have been ordered according to a variety of other criteria, such as the political level on which they were initiated, their importance to the two party platforms (PQ/Liberal), and their impact on Canadian governmental structures (separatism/federalism). This indicates that at least three cross-cutting binary oppositions were reinforcing each other during the referendum. These once again called on Canadian governments and their voting publics to find a viable compromise for what Hershel Hardin calls the set of 'fundamental contradictions' that constitute Canada's political heritage. These include the contest between French and English Canada; the disparate regions against the federal centre; and Canada against the United States (Hardin, 1974: 12).

2
Journalistic Ethics and Referendum Coverage in Montreal

ARMANDE SAINT-JEAN

By the time of the 1980 referendum Quebec journalism, both francophone and anglophone, had undergone two of the most turbulent decades in its recent history. Since the 1960s newsworkers had been questioning not only their professional practices and their role in Quebec's modernization process, but also the ways in which they lived and expressed their professional ethics. Journalistic ethics are grounded in notions of duty, of individual conscience, and of social morality, and are constrained by prevailing legal frameworks. They are reflected in the collective attitudes of the profession – in the principles the media choose to abide by and in the moral positions that journalists adopt and defend. All of this came under scrutiny at the time of the Quiet Revolution of the 1960s, during which the province transformed its social and political institutions and became a modern society.

This chapter will explore how the Quiet Revolution affected how Quebec journalists conceived their role in the 1980 referendum, especially as it related to their professional ethics. Few scholarly analyses have explored the social history of journalism in Quebec, or considered the ways in which socio-political events have influenced it (Saint-Jean 1993). Yet it is this history of professional change that explains why Quebec journalists approached the referendum situation in the way they did.

The 1960s: Professional Renewal

The 1960s opened with Jean Lesage's Liberal Party winning the provincial election and setting out to transform Quebec from a conservative, inward-looking society into a modern welfare state. Within five short years, health and education were wrested from the control of the Catholic Church and an important resource industry, electricity, was nationalized. Also, large infrastructure projects were initiated during this time, giving Quebecers a growing sense of pride. Among these were the construction of the Montreal subway in 1966 and the organization of the world's fair, Expo 67, which brought millions to Île Ste-Hélène. A year later, in 1968, Manic 5, the Hydro-Québec dam, was completed, laying the foundation for electrical exports to the United States and other markets.

Renewal and expansion were also evident in the press; employment was rising and new media outlets were being created. Some analysts look back on this time as the Golden Age of Quebec journalism (Godin, 1981; Pelletier, 1986). Two forces from the previous decade propelled this renewal: the formation of journalists' unions, associated with the Fédération nationale des communications (FNC/CSN); and the advent of a new medium, television. According to Michel Roy (1980), unionization elevated the profession's social status and raised the level of professional practice. Television for its part attracted a whole new generation of highly skilled practitioners, among them Judith Jasmin and René Lévesque, whose reporting became a touchstone for colleagues in other news media. Radio-Canada's television news and public affairs programming helped open up the province to the world outside and introduced viewers and journalists to international topics. Live interviews, overseas reporting, and in-depth analyses and commentary enjoyed great popularity with television audiences.

Print journalists responded by making newspapers trendier and more dynamic. For the first time in its eighty-year existence, *La Presse* sent correspondents (three of them) overseas and readers received fresh reports from countries few had visited. New beats were created at home as well, and journalists were encouraged to specialize. Political columns and analyses began to appear on the front pages of Quebec newspapers. Investigative journalism began to be practised, and a more personal and lively writing style emerged. This 'new journalism' was more than a fad: it established new professional standards that have remained guideposts to this day. Chief among these standards was the notion that journalists should actively chronicle the political transformations that Quebec was undergoing. Roy recalls that young as well as older journalists were for the first time being introduced to such concepts as freedom of the press, social responsibility, and the watchdog role of the media in a democratic state. As a result journalists, along with teachers, university professors, civil servants, trade union leaders, artists, and writers, became part of a new class of intellectuals – a kind of rising élite within the province's growing bourgeoisie (1980: 31, 34).

Placed as they were at the centre of numerous and heated debates about the future shape of Quebec society, journalists as a group became more socially and politically involved, both individually and collectively. This call for engagement stood in stark contrast to the type of journalistic practice that had prevailed until then. Two trends consequently developed within the profession in the late 1960s and the 1970s. The first was toward professional and labour union activism, which attempted to transform the power relations within media institutions and to give journalists more autonomy in the news production process. The second was toward active political engagement, and drew journalistic talent into politics. Gérard Pelletier, Jeanne Sauvé, Jean-Louis Gagnon, and André Laurendeau left for federal politics, while others, including René Lévesque, Pierre Laporte, Yves Michaud, and (later) Claude Ryan entered provincial politics.

Specialization and higher educational qualifications also led to the development of a new type of journalist – the columnist. Except for *Le Devoir*, until the 1960s, Quebec newspapers had virtually ignored the editorial page as a place where newspapers could distinguish themselves from each other. The first columnists began appearing in Quebec papers in the mid-1960s; soon after, these new 'star reporters' began showing up in many newsrooms. At first they focused on politics, but they soon branched out to cover local politics and social and human interest stories, as well as the arts, culture, and the new medium of television. These special journalists functioned as trend setters for the profession, in terms of both the topics they covered and the reporting styles they introduced.

The 1970s: Brutal Awakening

The profession's buoyant expansion and activist social stance faced its first brutal challenge at the very beginning of the new decade: it found itself at the heart of one of Canada's most important recent political crises. In the fall of 1970, at the height of the FLQ crisis, then–Prime Minister Pierre Trudeau ordered Canadian troops into the streets of Montreal. He also imposed the War Measures Act in an attempt to crush the separatist movement and to muzzle the Quebec press. Much has been written about the October Crisis, and heated debates continue to this day. What must be documented in this context, however, is the tragic consequences the War Measures Act had for Quebec journalism.

Recall that the War Measures Act was aimed at rupturing the direct media access that opponents of the Liberal Party had established with certain Montreal broadcast stations (Raboy, 1983). Even before the crisis, various federal politicians had criticized the Quebec media for their alleged complacency regarding the FLQ's intentions and actions. One of the lingering effects of the War Measures Act was, therefore, that it muted freedom of speech in the province. Two incidents illustrate this: only one daily newspaper, *Le Devoir*, had the courage to criticize the War Measures Act as abusive; and a number of journalists were fired from Radio-Canada after protesting against the manipulation of information that the act condoned (Dagenais, 1990). Equally negative was the War Measures Act's long-term impact on professional attitudes. Many journalists testify that an atmosphere of suspicion lingered that fostered prudence and self-censorship among Quebec journalists long after the crisis had abated. Marc Raboy (1983) documents how the fear of reprisals convinced many in the labour and grass roots movements that alternative media would not be condoned in post-1970s Quebec. Furthermore, for Quebec's journalistic profession as a whole the War Measures Act forced an ideological rupture that heightened suspicion of political authority generally.

Another significant feature of the 1970s evolution of the Quebec press was that a viable, market-oriented partisan press – one that would have counterbalanced the increasing power of the large media conglomerates – was never created. The popular weekly *Québec-Presse*, which was published and financed by union activists, lasted only five years, from 1969 to 1974; while the Parti Québécois-owned *Le Jour* survived for only two years, folding just before the PQ's victory in 1976. In the jargon of the time, the profession learned that it was impossible to use the media system against the 'interests of the ruling classes' (Raboy, 1983).

During the militant 1970s, strikes at most of Quebec's dailies and broadcast outlets served notice that working conditions needed overhauling and that journalists wanted greater autonomy over the news product they were creating. The length and number of these strikes testify to the high level of activism that Quebec's journalist unions encouraged at the time. Strikes took place in 1971 at *La Presse* and in 1975 at *Le Devoir*, and reached a crescendo in 1977–78 when almost half of all unionized members of the FNC/CSN (Fédération nationale des communications) were on strike. At this time, *Le Soleil*, *La Presse*, the private network Radio-Mutuel, *Montreal Matin*, and the *Montreal Star* were all shut down. Unfortunately, the strikes at the two Montreal dailies led to their demise, which further reduced the city's information diversity. *Montreal Matin* was sold to Power Corporation. The *Montreal Star* was transferred first to FP and subsequently to the Thompson chain, which eventually shut down this venerable English-language daily on the grounds that it was unprofitable. Clearly, then, the referendum period fell into the final phase of journalistic militancy against Quebec media consolidation – a phase that ended in 1980–81, when Radio-Canada and *Le Devoir* were once again silenced.

While it failed in its ultimate objective, this militancy greatly improved working conditions for Quebec journalists and substantially increased professional salaries. It also introduced autonomy clauses into contracts and improved working conditions. At *La Presse* today, the work week is four days and overtime is commonly granted. Unionization was undoubtedly a positive development; it was, however, criticized by some for turning practitioners into 'spoiled brats' who failed to strike a proper balance between personal demands and public service responsibilities (Godin, 1981).

The inability of Quebec journalists to gain editorial control over news production and content demonstrates that commercial viability has a price: it curtails the *range* of public debate on issues of civic concern. This outcome will be further scrutinized in Chapter 8. The decade of militancy also provides another insight: the francophone Quebec print market is too small to support an alternative press of the kind found in the English-language provinces, where the proportion of newspapers to population is historically higher. A final outcome of the collapse of militancy is that Quebec journalists shifted their professional outlook so that it more closely resembled English-Canadian and North American norms (Robinson and Saint-Jean, 1997: 360–70). Journalists who work in a climate where information is perceived as a commodity that is subject to market forces, and where they are viewed as 'employees' rather than as independent actors in the public communication exchange (Demers, 1989), eventually accept self-censorship as a way of life, because it reduces pressures and reprisals. Instead of critics they become information packagers providing neutral descriptions of events.

Thus, by 1980 the institutional stage was set – a stage that is still in place today. In the 1970s chain ownership concentration increased in both the electronic and print sectors, and many independent outlets and daily newspapers were closed down. Government studies such as the Davey Committee (1970) and the Kent Commission (1981) could not stem this tide of consolidation, nor could protests from the journalism associations. By the 1980s, the Quebec press was more highly concentrated than the English-Canadian media, with three conglomerates dominating the province: Power Corporation (P. Desmarais); Québecor (P. Péladeau) and Unimédia (J. Francoeur). None of these conglomerates had existed five years earlier (Raboy, 1992). Over time, what had once been an alternative political press turned to cultural, environmental, and women's issues, further reducing editorial outlets for political opposition. Incredibly, by the time of the 1980 referendum campaign, there was no pluralism in the press: all Quebec dailies favoured the federalist NO option.

In such a setting, the profession's conception of its social role had undergone a transformation. This role had been widely debated in the seventies, with the 'activists' pitting themselves against the more neutral 'observers'; by 1980, however, Quebec journalists had become more homogeneous in their professional outlook. As the referendum loomed, they now agreed that good journalistic practice required one to be a 'witness to' or a 'critic of' the situation, rather than an active agent on the political scene. Long strikes and failed attempts at gaining more control over news-making had diminished the profession's aggressiveness. Some analysts go even further, describing Quebec journalists at the time as apathetic and close to moral collapse (Marsolais, 1992). There is agreement, however, that this professional demoralization was a result of the 1970 War Measures Act, and was amplified by fear of reprisals. In 1979 a group of federal ministers who wanted to prevent separatists from infiltrating the journalistic ranks of Radio-Canada began a campaign to mobilize the CRTC to oversee referendum coverage. This suggestion was in fact implemented, though not in the interventionist manner in which it had initially been proposed.

All of this refutes the claims that most Quebec journalists were YES partisans and that their coverage was therefore biased and self-serving. Though they were personally as interested in the referendum debate as all Quebecers, their professional ethics called for balanced reporting and thus a stance that precluded taking sides in the debate. Clearly, Quebec journalists had accepted the classic North American notion of journalistic detachment. As objective witnesses, they would present the facts; they would not carry their opinions into the news columns (Sauvageau, 1981). This approach, subsequent chapters will demonstrate, resulted in scrupulous adherence to 'balance' criteria, though differently defined in both French- and the English-language Quebec news outlets during the 1980 referendum campaign.

The Notion of Balance in the Referendum Coverage

Political opinion studies indicate that the media are a major – though not *the* major – factor influencing voters' choices. Journalists choose the topics that create the political agenda on which the electorate bases its decisions. In the case of the 1980 referendum, as in ordinary political campaigns, media descriptions provided the perspectives for political choice and delineated the topics and terms of reference that constituted the agenda for public discussion.

This choice of stories and angles of treatment does not happen in a void. News-making is circumscribed by 'knowledge in use' about routines, by technical skills, and by professional ideologies. Also, news-making is brought into context by culturally constructed meaning 'frames,' which are shared with identifiable viewer (or reader) groups and thus make particular political events comprehensible. Erving Goffman (1974) explains that such culturally determined frames provide background understanding for events. Both 'knowledge in use' and 'frames' determine which events are selected for description and how they are treated in news programs. This is a highly complex process the effect of which is to contextualize and circumscribe the ways in which the public is able to make sense of events, as a resource for either social knowledge or social action.

Since the news narrates 'reality,' *fairness* in a political democracy prescribes a rule that journalists refer to as 'balance.' This rule requires that at least two points of view be provided on any issue. The audience often interprets balance as 'objectivity' and perceives such balanced coverage as politically neutral and unbiased. News media guidelines and subsequent interviews with news personnel indicate that the idea of balance played a key role in determining the style in which referendum events were to be covered. Moreover, the media coverage was in a way 'pre-framed' through the regulations imposed by the Parti Québécois legislation, which gathered all opinion groups under one of two umbrella committees – one for the YES side and one for the NO side. This juxtaposition of opinions and activities in the referendum campaign gave the requirement for balance a legal dimension that is absent in ordinary election campaigns.

Because of their War Measures Act experiences and the professional climate of 1980, journalists viewed the balance rule as the most important ethical rule when it came to covering the 1980 referendum. They saw themselves as providing information rather than influencing opinions. Most journalists felt that they had to remain uninvolved and that they could take no active part in the debate. The only exception related to the editorial pages and opinion columns, where facts could be placed in interpretative contexts; but even here, columnists were presumed to be neutral, disengaged, and 'objective.'

Yet in the polarized conditions of the referendum campaign it was not going to be easy to create the *appearance* of neutrality. Media organizations, both print and electronic, were therefore particularly concerned about convincing readers/viewers that their coverage was balanced. Each media outlet did this in its own unique way, though all signified their concern by publishing a set of directives designed to demonstrate that balance would be observed. For example, Jean Sisto declared the following in *La Presse*: 'The paper will comport itself, as is its habit, in such a way as to provide as honest and objective an account as possible ... In this extremely passionate debate, we are convinced we will be able to do justice to both camps and therefore to accurately inform our readers' (1980: A9).

A more detailed explication of the balance doctrine and its application during the referendum debate was issued by the CBC, which is bound by broadcast legislation to observe balanced coverage. Two types of balance are mandated by this legislation: balance among different types of programming, and political balance within programming. According to Savage, Gilsdorf, and Hackett, the former is defined in section 2[g][i] of the 1968 Broadcasting Act, which states that the 'CBC should be a balanced service of information, enlightenment and entertainment for people of different ages, interests and tastes, covering the whole range of programming in fair proportion' (1992: 9). This rule of balance over the whole programming schedule is now extended to private broadcasters (see the 1991 Broadcasting Act). Balance within programming, which is described in section 2[d], requires programming to provide a 'reasonable, balanced opportunity for the expression of differing views on matters of public concern' (Cooke and Ruggles, 1993: 38–40).

In the referendum situation, the CBC's president at the time, A.W. Johnson, noted that the corporation's balance mandate might be misunderstood in relation to the its additional requirement to foster national unity through both its English- and its French-language services (Johnson, 1979b). Johnson, a high-ranking mandarin, was clearly concerned about the federal ministers' worries regarding how the 'national unity' mandate would be carried out in Radio-Canada. Clarification of the CBC's position came in the form of a series of public addresses given by Johnson as the referendum year approached. In a paper presented in November 1979 to the Parliamentary Committee on Broadcasting, Films, and Assistance to the Arts, Johnson declared that the CBC would not attempt in any way to influence the vote on the referendum (Johnson, 1979a). On the contrary, he said, the CBC saw it as its duty to provide equal coverage and show equal respect to both sides of the debate. Johnson also confirmed that Radio-Canada would pursue the same general policy as the corporation's English-language arm. The reasoning behind this position was both simple and clever. Johnson declared that he had been entrusted with 'a power,' which he described as 'the capacity to influence the agenda for discussion in Canada's leading public affairs forums.' With that power, he continued, there came a 'solemn public trust to use this power to enlarge the abilities and the capacities of the Canadian people to decide, to shape *their own* destinies ... free of manipulation, free of misleading or unfair influence' (1979a: 2–3; emphasis in original). Johnson argued that since the 'supreme value of our society and [national] identity [is] the exercise of freedom of speech,' any divergence from the path of a strict observance of the balance requirements would 'undermine the case for a nationhood of any kind' (1979b). In other words, the CBC formally opted for a balance of voices and of points of view, on *both* French and English radio and television networks – a position that made more than a few Canadian federalists unhappy.

As far as can be ascertained, the CBC did not wilfully compromise these publicly declared commitments to balanced coverage during the referendum debate. Prominent news-team personnel, including Elly Alboim, who was special editor of the CBC's Referendum Special Unit in Montréal, and Alan Handel, who was the field producer for Quebec Report,* agree that journalists and editors at the CBC and Radio-Canada trusted Johnson's commitment. Neither ever had any indication that balance and freedom of speech were anything less than the full policy of the CBC French and English news desks. On the contrary, there was an increased awareness of the need to remain even-handed because the stakes were so very high. As a result of this concern, broadcasters made sure that on a weekly basis programs were balanced in terms of the guests' political alignments and also in terms of the questions they were asked. This preoccupation highlights that Quebec journalists actively favoured balanced reporting – that the rule of balance was supported not only by the public and by spokespersons for media organizations, but by rank-and-file journalists. Gaye Tuchman (1972) explains that professional journalists support the doctrines of balance and neutrality because these help shield the journalistic community from outside criticism. She points out that the practice of quoting at least two sides of a story provides stylistic 'proof' that evenhandedness has been satisfied, even when the truthfulness of the two sides' claims have not been investigated.

Contradictions between Ethics and Practice

The doctrine of balance serves to protect journalists from outside criticism;

---

*Both Elly Alboim and Alan Handel of the News Department in Montreal were interviewed in 1984 by G.J. Robinson for this book. Other unrecorded testimonies by CBC or Radio-Canada personnel gathered by Armande Saint-Jean corroborate these professional interpretations.

but its application is not automatic, nor is it problem-free. This is because balance means different things to different people. During the referendum debate, balance for readers and viewers related to the adequacy of journalists' reporting practices. For journalists themselves, the balance doctrine raised another question: At what point do professional requirements inhibit private political behaviour? For media organizations, the doctrine of balance raised questions about the autonomy of editorial procedures as these related to pressures from advertisers and shareholders. During the referendum period, special interests and competing value structures clashed in all three of these domains.

Readers' and viewers' criticisms of 'unbalanced' reporting were of course inevitable, and were successfully pre-empted by the media's public announcements of their policies and positions regarding balance. Much more controversial was the political activism of a few Montreal journalists. François Demers contends that the activist role that journalists had fought to acquire during the 1970s resulted in a climate of confrontation vis-à-vis their employers, whom journalists generally perceived as politically biased as well as motivated by 'bottom line' issues (1989: 23). Journalists asserted that during the referendum campaign, media outlets interfered with their rights as citizens; not only that, but press concentration reduced the supply of objective, balanced, and varied accounts of referendum issues. Journalists believed that this concentration, and the 'bottom line' mentality, had convinced all Montreal newspapers to align themselves with the NO side.

The central issue in all of this was the enforcement of 'neutrality,' which enjoins journalists not to get involved in whatever it is they are covering. In MacFarlane and Martin's words, 'the political columnist may denounce the government of the day in the press of the employer's newspaper. [Yet] the same person may lose his job for taking an active role in the affairs of a political party' (1982: 35). Both English and French Quebec newspapers adhered to the rule of neutrality and either suspended or fired journalists who became politically involved in the referendum debate. Particularly contentious was the *Gazette*'s suspension of André Gagnon, who was forced to take a paid leave of absence from the paper when he refused to step down from chairing a YES committee meeting. The *Gazette* was widely criticized for this action because it supposedly amounted to persecuting an employee on the sole grounds of political affiliation. However, the same paper also suspended a NO supporter, Nick Auf der Maur, also with pay, and this undercut the argument that political bias was involved (Laprise, 1980a). Furthermore, a francophone paper, *Le Nouvelliste* in Trois-Rivières, also suspended two of its journalists, this time without pay, as stipulated in their collective agreement, for their involvement in the referendum campaign (Laprise, 1980b). In each of these cases, it was the combination of journalistic with political involvement that was frowned upon. When cases such as these occur, opinion often becomes split regarding which principle should be protected: the requirement of journalists to set themselves apart from the world they depict, or the right of those same journalists to carry out their political duties as citizens. While the doctrine of balance envisions these two ideals as compatible, provided that certain conditions are respected (namely, that journalists abstain from working in the field in which they are involved), these examples suggest that in a time of crisis, news organizations and the professionals working for them may be at odds as to which of the two ideals has priority.

It is now time to consider the impact that the balance rule had on the owners and managers of the media organizations. Journalistic concerns about editorial autonomy and news quality emerge primarily out of the 'business imperatives' of news enterprises, which are capitalist entities whose goal is not only to provide the best possible coverage of events, but also to remain financially solvent and bring in a profitable return for shareholders (Knight 1989; Dahlgren 1985a). Debra Clarke (1981) demonstrates that news production is constrained by a range of unofficial directives according to which professional considerations, such as the quality of the editorial product, are but one of many considerations. Other, more prominent concerns are advertisers' satisfaction, production efficiency, and market share. Florian Sauvageau offers examples of the impact of the business imperative on newspaper content in the francophone press; he notes that there is a lack of resources and encouragement for investigative reporting in Quebec's newspapers. By and large, he claims, most newsrooms provide no intellectual stimulus for quality reporting: journalists lack initiative and enthusiasm because leadership is nonexistent (Sauvageau, 1981: 47).

Debra Clarke (1981) documents a similar problem in many privately owned broadcast stations in Canada, which produce news reports only because they are required to do so by the CRTC. In such situations, most journalists follow routines and report what they are told by the dignitaries they meet, since they are preoccupied with 'getting the news out as fast as possible.' This explains how they gradually began to define themselves as 'news workers' producing a product like any other; in this sense they come to subscribe to what François Demers (1989) calls the 'good employees' model. This is the essence of the *embourgeoisement* process that has slowly taken place in the profession (Saint-Jean, 1993).

The impact of the business imperative on news content was particularly evident during the referendum period: all Quebec dailies came out against the Parti Québécois sovereignty-association option, even though it was known that a majority of francophones were for it. Predictably, manage-ments then tried hard to rein in those journalists whose personal political views were in conflict with the editorial stance of the paper. The use of staff suspensions on both francophone and anglophone newspapers corrobo-rates that during the referendum campaign, the corporate interpretation of the balance rule won out. The argument was that a journalist's political commitments might compromise a paper's *appearance* of neutrality in the eyes of both advertisers and shareholders and therefore had to be curtailed. *La Presse*, for example, refused to allow an editorialist, eighteen years on the paper's editorial staff, to pronounce himself in favour of the OUI side, in contradiction to the official editorial position established by editor and president Roger Lemelin (Francoeur 1980: 9). At *Le Soleil*, a similar situa-tion developed when the paper's editorial staff was refused the right to argue in favour of the OUI side (Leblanc, 1981: 123). These cases addition-ally illustrate that corporate control extends beyond political activity to editorial production. Editorials are supposed to reflect the position of the corporate owners and not that of the author. A singular exception to this rule was the policy adopted at *Le Devoir*, where the editorial board made a point of visibly supporting balance and freedom of opinion. Consequently, each editorialist was able to write her or his own editorial; this resulted in three articles supporting the OUI side and one the NON. This policy decision is recalled here precisely because it was at the time – and still would be today – a remarkable and extremely rare case of support for editorial independence.

This one exception notwithstanding, it is clear that the combination of business imperatives and journalistic ethics resulted in the balance rule being interpreted rather narrowly. In these circumstances, *balance* became associated with the representation of majority views, to the exclusion of contrasting opinions on the right and the left of the political spectrum. As a result, public dialogue was gradually narrowed throughout the referendum period, with the balance rule serving mainly to reflect the majority's defini-tion of the situation.

Balance Reconsidered

Within the context mentioned above, it is now possible to analyse some of the limitations of journalistic balance. What the doctrine of balance fails to account for is the role that all journalists play in constructing the reality they are presenting. The classical interpretation of the balance rule pre-sumes that information (news or events) exists independently, as 'facts out there' which are independent of the observer, and that it does not require the journalist's interpretive participation in order to come into being. From this premise, it follows that the journalist merely 'reads off' or presents the news, instead of reconstructing it. However, this interpretation ignores the personal, social, and cultural factors that come into play during the process of news construction and creation.

A simple illustration of reinterpretation through labelling is found in A.W. Johnson's speech (1979a) about the CBC's referendum coverage. While Johnson was careful to evoke the ethics of balance in calling for the coverage of different points of view, his selection of alternatives itself demonstrated a hidden bias. That is to say, in labelling the 'two sides' of the referendum debate as 'sovereignty-association' and 'renewed federalism,' Johnson was adopting a particular interpretive (ideological) position. According to sovereignists, the label 'renewed federalism' had been put forward strategically by the federalists to identify a nonexistent political position. For their part, the federalists argued that sovereignty-association was a label invented by the Parti Québécois in an effort to obscure its real goal, which was outright separation from Canada. Such labels – and by extension language in general – do not offer neutral descriptions. All namings are 'loaded' with the baggage of the political, social, and cultural references that they articulate in a given historical place and time, especially in a period of passionate debate such as the 1980 referendum campaign. The point here is that in the day-to-day practice of journalism, words and concepts are used without acknowledgement of their situational meanings or of the polysemic nature of language in general. Because the rules of balance usually fail to acknowledge levels of meaning, they replicate these initial distortions. Balance must therefore be viewed as an ideal, limiting position that is never reached in practice; in the same sense, all other journalistic principles, such as 'fairness' and 'objectivity,' are also ideals.

Labelling practices constitute only one aspect of the interpretive dimension of journalistic work. Another aspect is related to the need to arrive at a format and an angle for presenting events. Television news, as well as print (though to a lesser degree), must be engaging. This calls for rhetorical imagery that will capture and keep the audience's attention. The program analyses in Chapter 4 will indicate that the referendum leaders' personal characteristics were often highlighted to sustain and reinforce the theatrical dimensions of the referendum debate. This audiovisual imagery pitted the colourful and outspoken Pierre Elliott Trudeau against the expressive populist René Lévesque and contrasted both of these leaders with the 'humourless' Claude Ryan, who expressed himself in drier and more learned terms.

Yet another form of interpretative distortion grows out of language and cultural factors. As will be demonstrated in Chapter 5, during the referendum the underlying political points of view had to do with differing notions of 'nationalism,' the 'people,' and the 'state,' as outlined in the PQ's White Paper and the Liberals' Beige Paper. Because these concepts were interpreted as mirror images of each other, both the anglophone and the francophone referendum narrations achieved balance in *stylistically* similar ways, even while utilizing radically different narrative and rhetorical approaches. The two parallel discourses were also informed by sharply contrasting notions of Canadian society (Gagnon, 1980). Arthur Siegel (1978) documented differences among geographical regions in the CBC and Radio-Canada coverage, as well as differences in the types of national and provincial themes and values that the two news networks were reflecting in the run-up to the referendum. As Siegel put it: 'If English and French Canadians were on different planets, there could hardly be a greater contrast in the views and information the two audience groups were receiving and developing as a result of their linguistic division' (1978: 1).

While Siegel's concern is that these content differences may subtly undermine Canadian national unity, the point that needs emphasis here is that all events undergo a transformation as they are narratively reconstructed to address a particular audience group's political concerns. In these narrative reconstructions, journalistic practices, language use, entertainment, and cultural values are all in play. Consequently, balancing becomes extremely difficult if not impossible to achieve, except on the stylistic level. Disputes about referendum coverage must therefore move beyond unfounded accusations of bias and distortion, and toward an acknowledgment that balance is a journalistic ideal rather than an achievable practice. As Liora Salter explains (1993), balance is a contested concept and its definition remains ambiguous. The meanings of 'balance,' like the meanings of 'democracy,' reflect different groups' possibly conflicting analyses of social relations, social values, and media content. As a contested concept, balance is used to stake out claims regarding the proper content of the media and their role in society – claims that cannot be understood except as part of an ethical paradigm whose key concepts and categories are not universally accepted (Salter, 1993: 1332).

This analysis also indicates that the definitions of 'balance,' 'objectivity,' and 'fairness' are not fixed and unalterable for all times and places. These ethical frameworks have changed at least three times in Quebec since the 1960s. During the Quiet Revolution they meant the growth of journalistic autonomy and the extension of reportorial beats and themes. In the 1970s, union activism led to a journalistic militancy that interpreted the social responsibility ethic as antagonistic to management's business imperatives. At the time of the referendum campaign a process of *embourgeoisement* was already under way that favoured journalists disengaging themselves from the public debate. This process was accelerated by external factors, including the aftershocks of the 1970 War Measures Act, which fostered heightened self-censorship among many francophone journalists.

Our analysis demonstrates that during the referendum period, the call for balanced reporting was affirmed by both anglophone and francophone journalists. However, the *application* of the balance criterion had to be handled differently by the two station groups because they were addressing audiences that were politically and linguistically polarized. Anglophone professionals were writing for readers and viewers who were overwhelmingly committed to the NO side. For their part, French-language journalists had to address at least three different political audience positions: YES, NO, and uncommitted. Subsequent chapters will explain how these varying positions required different argumentation styles and different 'balance' strategies in Montreal's French and English news media.

PART II

CONSTRUCTING THE INTERPRETIVE GRID:
'FRAMING' THE REFERENDUM AS ELECTION

3
Television and Electoral Coverage: Changing Rules*

The Canadian Electoral Context

Until the mid-1970s, North American political scientists paid little attention to the role of the media in party politics. It was generally assumed that electoral politics and people's voting behaviour were determined by party identification and by socio-economic cleavages (Meisel, 1975). This focus was reinforced by American research, which had concluded that the media had a negligible effect on voting decisions (Klapper, 1960). According to Frederick Fletcher, these two traditions led the authors of a major work on Canadian voting to conclude as late as 1979 that there was no significant relationship between campaign coverage and party switching (1987: 341). Yet by 1984 there was evidence showing that citizens' voting practices in the previous decade had become more unpredictable and volatile. In the 1974 federal campaign the Liberals under Pierre Trudeau achieved a majority; in 1979 the Progressive Conservatives under Joe Clark were elected to form a minority government, which was defeated shortly after, in February 1980, in an election that returned Trudeau to Ottawa in time for Quebec's referendum campaign. In 1984, however, the Conservatives won a landslide federal victory under Brian Mulroney. Fletcher contends that this volatility can be explained partly by the increased role of television in electoral politics – a topic that Canadian political scientists have done little to study (1987: 342). As our introduction indicated, in this book we address this

---

* Because the referendum coverage was defined by journalists as electoral coverage, I have not referred to the small but significant literature on the role of the media in plebiscites. Among these are Colin Seymour-Ure and Betty Zisk's *Money, Media and the Grass Roots* (Thousand Oaks, Calif.: Sage, 1987), which examines the relationship between media coverage and voter attitudes in American state-ballot issues.

lacuna and explore exactly how television was used as a public opinion tool during the referendum campaign and how it constructed two very different public views of political issues for French- and English-speaking Montreal voters.

The Canadian electoral system grew out of the British system, in which local candidates compete for election in single-member districts, usually under the banner of a political party. Election is by a simple plurality. Also, in the Canadian party system the federal parties are organizationally distinct from their provincial counterparts – a situation which, as we shall see, complicated the organization of the federalist NO campaign in Quebec. In addition, there is no clear ladder from provincial to federal politics, as is the case in other federal systems, such as that of the United Sates. Senior provincial politicians rarely move to the national scene (Brodie and Jenson 1984, 252–70). Fletcher notes that the division between provincial and federal parties has remained intact, despite two 1970 reforms that have given federal parties more powers in the organization of elections. These reforms require that party labels be printed on federal ballots and that the national leader endorse local candidates (Fletcher, 1987: 344).

Thus, in Canada two factors seem to be most influential in predicting voter decisions: party affiliation, and regionalism. The impact of both these factors has, however, been eroded since the mid-1970s – that is, since television campaign coverage has increased. According to Harold Clarke and colleagues, 'hard core' party support, which involves voting for the same party without switching or abstaining, has been reduced to only 41 per cent of the electorate. The remainder of voters – nearly two-thirds of supposed party supporters today – are relatively uncommitted and react to campaign issues, images of party leaders, and the profiles of local candidates as rendered on the television screen (Clarke et al., 1984: 65, 130). All images, as we shall demonstrate in Chapters 3 to 7, are selected and constructed through media coverage, especially television. Regionally based political responses, which are fostered by Canada's bifurcated federal–provincial electoral system, have also been reinforced by television. Fletcher's analyses as well as our own referendum case studies confirm that far from homogenizing electoral agendas, television fractures them. Modern technologies such as satellite permit its message flow to be adapted virtually instantaneously to regional leaders' statements about national issues (Fletcher, 1987: 346–47).

Canada's campaign communication system comprises three types of campaign flows: unmediated messages (free-time broadcasts and spots); partially mediated information (broadcast interviews and leader debates); and mostly mediated news and commentary (Paletz and Entman, 1981: 41–5).

As we shall see, newspaper and magazine articles are the most heavily mediated, while television is more open to party influence through free-time broadcasts and spots. The balance between these three types of campaign message flows changed drastically between 1974 and 1984. Initially, parties were not permitted to buy time on television, and their free-time appearances were confined to preidentified speakers, which according to Dalton Camp rendered politicians as 'talking heads' (1981: xv). Since the mid-1970s, new rules have restricted paid advertising to the final half of the campaign, regulated the allocation of paid and free time, limited campaign spending, and provided for 50 per cent reimbursement of the costs of radio and television commercials purchased by the registered parties. The advertising reimbursement provision was dropped in 1983 on the grounds that it skewed party spending. All broadcasters, including the CBC radio services, are now required to make available prime-time spots at normal rates up to a total of six-and-one-half hours, divided among the parties according to a formula based on seats held in the House of Commons at the time of the election call, share of popular vote in the previous election, and number of seats contested in the current election (Fletcher, 1987: 348).

These rule changes affected campaign activities in three ways. First, free-time broadcasts permitted all parties to greatly increase their voter reach. A 1979 CBC research report noted that free-time broadcasts, which leaders used to promote key campaign themes, had an average audience of 620,000, and that party spots had been viewed by nearly 77 per cent of national respondents. Since then, free-time telecasts have been downplayed by the parties, which have switched their emphasis to advertising spots and regular news coverage in an effort to reach the more 'switchable' voters. Second, the new rules helped equalize access to the airwaves among the established parties. The new limits reduced spending by the Liberals and Progressive Conservatives, but increased spending for the NDP because tax credits for contributions were now possible. Third, the new rules promoted the use of television and radio spots. Expenditures on television advertising by the major parties jumped from 45 per cent of all advertising expenditures in 1974 to 76 per cent (roughly $4.6 million) in 1980, while print ads remained roughly stable (Fletcher, 1987: 349–51). Clearly, these changes affected the electoral information net during the referendum campaign.

The Canadian Electoral Information Net

The Canadian electoral information net, which is congruent with the country's 'news net,' organizes the dissemination of election information in such a manner that the national media set the tone. Because of the country's vast territory and small population of about 30 million, which is unevenly clustered in a narrow ribbon above the U.S. border, what Hackett calls the 'news net' is sustained through a division of labour between the electronic and print media (1991: 93). The electronic media gather and distribute potential news stories primarily from the national hubs; the press is most active on the regional and local levels. The notion of a news net is a useful metaphor in that it draws attention to the fact that news gathering is both 'selective' (i.e., it does not screen all regions and all kinds of events equally) and 'reconstructed.' Events in the large cities and in institutions at the population centres are more likely to be selected than those occurring closer to the periphery, where news bureaux have fewer correspondents and contacts. Canada's news net is made up of three types of media institutions – the national, the regional, and the local – all of which produce and transmit different kinds of news flows. 'Flow' refers to the movement of news from its generation (typically in interaction with journalists and officials within centralized bureaucratic institutions), through and between news organizations, to viewers/readers (Hackett, 1991: 93). Both nationally and internationally, news flow is quite skewed: it emanates outward from large cities or countries to hinterland areas. In Canada the national media are located in the country's densest population triangle, which is formed by Montreal, Ottawa, and Toronto. Regional centres cover smaller hinterlands; thus Moncton covers the Atlantic provinces, and Saskatoon covers the wheat and oil belts of Saskatchewan and Alberta. The third-tier local dailies and broadcast stations provide information in and about smaller cities and towns.

This geographical division of labour affects the content and flow of Canada's news net. Fletcher (1981: 8–10) notes that the national media not only attract larger audiences but are also read and viewed by the political, economic, and cultural élites that determine national public affairs. Thus, these media set the agenda for national discussion. In this context the national media include the CBC, whose English-language operations are headquartered in Toronto, and Radio-Canada (headquartered in Montreal), as well as two or three dailies: the *Globe and Mail*, *Le Devoir*, and possibly *La Presse*. Toronto is also the home of Canada's national news agency, Canadian Press (CP), which serves as a middleman in the production of information about Canada for the global network and in the distribution of international news within the country (Robinson, 1981, 155–6). This listing indicates that Montreal is the centre for the French-language media with national reach, both electronic and print, and that Toronto plays the same role for the English-language media outlets. The geographical stratification of Canada's news net is underscored by an additional factor: its linguistic bifurcation, which adds an interpretive dimension not found in unilingual news systems. This factor transforms the media outlets in Montreal and Toronto into national embodiments of seemingly homogeneous 'cultures' – Quebec's and English Canada's. Though these interpretive identifications are clearly inadequate and misplaced, the polarizations are sustained because there is little news exchange between the regional outlets themselves, because they in turn look to the centre for information about other parts of Canada. Such a system, as we shall see, has done little to strengthen the ties of Confederation (Fletcher, 1984: 202).

The parochial regionalism that the Canadian media system imposes on the communication flow is reinforced by divisions between the two major linguistic/cultural communities. French- and English-speaking Canadians virtually 'live in separate worlds' which are the outcome of several factors (Hackett, 1991: 100–1). At the level of ownership, few companies, even media empires, have extensive holdings of both French- and English-language media. At the level of editorial production and dissemination, few news organizations serve both francophone and anglophone audiences. At the level of content, variations are evident in the attention paid to local, national and international issues, and in the priorities assigned to Quebec versus Canadian government initiatives. My 1978 content comparison of French- and English-Canadian dailies demonstrated that Quebec papers devoted only 7 per cent of their news space to international reports, while English-Canadian papers devoted more than one-quarter (28 per cent) of their space to stories about other countries. The geographical focus of these reports also differed, with the Quebec press featuring stories about France (33 per cent) and the United States (34 per cent) about equally, and the English papers devoting nearly two-thirds (58 per cent) of their international stories to the United States (Robinson, 1981: 158). The prioritizing of Quebec over Canadian coverage is also demonstrated in a 1978 comparison of ten days of radio and television news programming. It shows that Radio-Canada divided its news attention almost equally between Canadian national issues (39 per cent); Quebec matters (32 per cent) and international events (29 per cent), whereas the CBC devoted 48 per cent of all its stories to Canadian national issues, 20 per cent to the English-speaking provinces, 8 per cent to Quebec, and the rest to international matters (Siegel, 1978: 13). These content differences suggest that in the period preceding the referendum, French- and English-speaking Montrealers were receiving very different news inputs from which to fashion a view of the country and of the world. This situation was exacerbated during the referendum period, when conflicting definitions of nationalism attracted highly segmented viewer groups.

In 1979–80 the Greater Montreal region, which includes all suburbs within a 35-kilometre radius of the city, had a population of 2.85 million. Linguistically, this population comprised three groups: francophones (61 per cent), anglophones (23 per cent), and allophones (13 per cent). The latter included Montrealers who spoke Italian, Greek, Portuguese, or other mother tongues (Caron, 1981: 16). All of these groups had access to broadcast programming, though only 48 per cent of households were cable subscribers at the time. Numerous studies since the 1970 Davey Committee have confirmed that francophone Quebecers prefer television over print and therefore spend more time than the other two groups with this medium. In 1979–80 they watched television an average 24.1 hours per week; English Canadians averaged 22.7 hours, that is, 1.4 hours less. This preference for television goes back to the 1960s, when high-profile newscasters, among them René Lévesque and Pierre Laporte, introduced investigative journalism and began to report the world beyond Quebec's borders. André Caron's comparative study provides a profile of the Montreal program schedule at the time of the referendum, and of Montrealers' viewing preferences. This profile demonstrates that there are no simple relationships between program availability and viewing practices and that the two language groups have different channel preferences and place different emphases on news as opposed to entertainment programs (Caron et al., 1983: 473). Also, the two language groups rarely view programs in the 'other' language. The interactions of these differing cultural, programming, and viewing practices will provide the larger demographic context through which the effectivity of media programs in referendum public opinion creation will have to be assessed.

Though our comparative study did not survey viewers directly, audience statistics provided by the Bureau of Broadcast Management indicate that in the autumn before the referendum, there were two public (CBFT, CBMT) and two private channels (CFTM, CFCF), which offered different program schedules. In general, the French- and English-language public stations offered more news/information programming, and a more extensive cultural and educational schedule, than the city's private stations. On the public stations, information programming constituted nearly one-third (32 per cent) of all programming, of which news was 18 per cent; while on the private channels information constituted 27 per cent of the schedule, of which news was 22 per cent (Caron, 1981: 129–30). Language also affected Montreal entertainment programming: English channels devoted 64 per cent of their schedules to entertainment, while the French devoted only 51 per cent to sitcoms and films and assigned the rest of the schedule (14 per cent) to cultural and educational shows. Both sets of channels placed information programming in second place, but the English offered almost double the amount of news (26 per cent of their schedule) as their French counterparts (15 per cent) – a finding that is corroborated by our own referendum investigations (Caron et al., 1983: 480).

While news programs were more available on English channels, francophones were more interested in this kind of programming, and watched it more consistently. In 1970, the Davey Committee found that nearly three quarters (72 per cent) of all francophone viewers watched a news program every day, whereas only two-thirds (66 per cent) of anglophones followed the same practice (1970: 85). In the lead-up to the referendum these predispositions translated into increased *actual* daily viewing of news programming on the part of francophones (31 per cent) over anglophones (22 per cent). Furthermore, BBM statistics document that among francophones, only soap operas were more popular than news programs, which were more popular than films (Caron et al., 1983b: 476). News, in sum, remains an important way of satisfying the information needs of postmodern existence. To satisfy these needs, francophones in 1980 preferred the public channel, while anglophones preferred the private one. The comparison of content categories by station indicate that these preferences may be related to the fact that the French public station CBFT 2 and the English-language private station CFCF 12 offered more information about Quebec than their competitors. On CBFT 2, Quebec news constituted over one-third (35 per cent) of the total program content; on CFCF 12 it constituted almost one quarter (24 per cent). The French private station, in contrast, devoted only 11 per cent of its programming to Quebec events, and the English public CBC channel an infinitesimal 5 per cent. These comparisons confirm the central-Canadian orientation of the CBC and the Quebec focus of Radio-Canada, which was noted earlier.

A final issue that has been well documented in Canada and on the European continent is the lack of viewer crossover *between* linguistic program offerings. This permits us to postulate that federalist francophones would not deal with their cognitive dissonance by viewing English-language news programs during the referendum period. In 1973, Sorecom Inc. of Montreal investigated French and English media use for the Gendron Commission and discovered that the 'two solitudes' were confirmed in media use patterns. Francophones used French-language media, and anglophones listened to English stations and bought the two English dailies (Sorecom, 1973). According to André Caron, these patterns were holding steady in 1979, when only a small minority (12 per cent) of French-speakers were watching English television stations. Of these, 8 per cent chose Canadian stations and 4 per cent the American signals. On the English side, only an infinitesimal 4 per cent tuned in to French stations (Caron et al., 1983a: 476–7). Caron surmised in 1981 that these data could be partially explained by the greater availability of English stations via cable, as well as by viewer age. A growing group of young viewers is turning to English cartoon programs when French ones are not available, and their changing youth culture also assigns different values to the use of English among bilingual Montrealers (Caron et al., 1983b: 9–10, 61–3). In addition, our own study demonstrates that political affiliation is also an important predictor of viewer preferences, and that this interrelated with language in complex ways. Though these figures seem startling, they are similar to the 11 per cent crossover that the European Broadcasting Union has recorded for European viewers whose choice of foreign-language programming is not as burdened by language politicization as that of Quebecers (Robinson and Hildebrandt, 1983: 70).

One can thus conclude that Canada's news production net, with its French and English hubs, provides not only a *systematically* structured reception context for French, English, and allophone Montreal viewers, but also a *linguistically* and politically skewed meaning context through which the three language groups 'made sense' of referendum events. In this public sense-making process, the media select the issues for debate and predispose viewers to 'see' the world from particular vantagepoints. These 'frames' or 'maps' help viewers construct understandings about the body politic; about what is good and valuable, and bad and threatening; and about what is related to what on a given day in the 'public' realm of citizen interest.

To understand the processes of mapping and transforming events into news stories, we decided to scrutinize the news product itself and then relate it to its conditions of reception. These conditions of reception included not only the language of the news channel that households chose to watch, but the ways in which messages were visually packaged. David Altheide calls this audiovisual packaging 'formatting' and defines formats as 'rules and procedures for defining, selecting, organizing, and presenting information and other experiences (in visual form)' (Altheide, 1985: 9).

Inquiries into the visual characteristics of news programming have been scarce and have tended to focus on the verbal component of the program flow; yet the audio and visual components of news discourse are intricately related. Canadian news formats consist of visually illustrated stories that utilize a dramatic language of the sort familiar to North American viewers through realist fiction. Examples are the informal verbal greeting and the visual lead-in, which are designed to draw the audience into the discourse. Visually, news programs are composed of highly stylized filmed reports from correspondents in the field and of graphic devices that are easy to recognize for the viewer and that therefore serve as building blocks for connecting and making sense of the audio and visual elements of the discourse.

To analyse how audiovisual teletexts are constructed and 'make sense,' we developed a dramaturgical theory based on Goffman (1959). For Goffman, all public behaviour, whether it is a chance encounter in a coffee shop or the presentation of a news program, is part of a dramaturgical situation in which people respond to social rules. Seeing society as a collection of rule-governed games means drawing attention to the conventions and strategies that are accepted in a given social setting. The drama analogy goes back to Kenneth Burke (1973) and others, who note that dramatism starts in a theory of action rather than a theory of knowledge and assumes that life does not just happen, but rather is constructed out of aspects of reality as well as people's interpretations. This invites one to consider the matter of motives in a perspective that treats language and thought primarily as modes of action. Such a theory is able to relate the behavioural features of everyday life to journalistic reconstruction practices as well as to the ways in which viewers create meaning in relation to a given text.

Goffman's work suggests to us that the performance dimensions of Canadian news programs are constituted through actor roles, through the settings in which these roles are performed, and through the ways in which the viewer/audience is addressed. In a news program, the stage is the high-tech newsroom with its monitors and its desk, at which the anchor sits. In the news drama, journalists perform four types of 'in studio' roles: anchor, commentator, reporter, and interviewer. All of these 'constitute' the news show through their retelling of the news events of the day. In addition, there are three 'outside' or 'interviewee' roles: news maker, expert, and person-in-the-street. Like a Greek chorus, they are part of the supporting cast in the sense that they comment on or help illustrate the actions of the primary actors. Each role has a voice, the importance of which is determined by its function in the dramatization of the news event and by the ways in which it is visually rendered. 'In studio' roles usually take up more visual space on the television screen and are rendered 'face to camera'; 'outside' roles are often pictured in middle distance and are usually photographed in profile.

To further clarify the relationships between roles, voices, and visual renditions in a news program, we drew on the work of Ian Connell, who studied news programs in Britain and discovered that 'visual modes' are limited and can be described in terms of locations, the type of journalistic report being rendered (interview, 'piece to camera,' voice-over), and the role the person is enacting (1980: 141). By combining his visual schema with our dramaturgical theory, we are able to elucidate two 'stylistic' issues, which Altheide began to consider in *Media Power* (1985). These might be called a station's 'visual grammar,' which has remained unclarified up to now, and the combinatory rules through which the unique visual presentation modes are constructed. Visual grammars and combinatory rules help us to locate stylistic differences in news programs based on language, and to explain how these affect the ways in which French and English viewer groups acquired the meaning frames through which they then make sense of referendum issues.

Previous research asserted that visual presentation styles are similar on news channels in England and the United States (Glasgow University Media Group, 1980 and 1982; Connell, 1980); our own comparison suggests the opposite. To our surprise, we found that audiovisual packaging of television news programs on Montreal's French and English stations utilized *different* visual paradigms. Consequently, we are able to argue that the two linguistic audiences were not only presented with different event selections during the 1980s referendum campaign – a fact that previous research had already suggested – but, more importantly, that language determined both audiovisual styles and the modes of address that the stations employed to communicate with their diversified viewer groups. We shall demonstrate in our comparison of French- and English-news programming that the cultural specificity of visual packaging is most obvious in the varied utilization and rendition of the anchor and reporter roles and in the ways that journalistic products such as interviews and reports are presented. Theoretically, these stylistic characteristics are important to studies of the 1980 referndum because they demonstrate that viewer groups were *actively involved* in the co-construction (with journalists) of stations' program styles, and of the types of meaning frames through which referendum events were explained.

Three types of comparisons were used to arrive at the audiovisual profile of the French- and English-news programs. First we subjected *all* of the station material from the five key referendum events to an audiovisual analysis in order to determine visual modes and presenter roles. The five events were the PQ's White Paper platform announcement; the referendum question presentation; the tabling of the Liberals' Beige Paper platform; the Quebec Assembly debate explaining the advantages of sovereignty-association; and the last week of the referendum campaign. Visual mode analysis (see Appendix B) determines whether a report came directly from the studio, was shot on location, and/or included 'actuality' film or video-taped reports. Presenter role analysis determines how the news presenter (anchor, commentator, reporter, interviewer) and interviewee (expert, news maker, person in the street) roles were utilized in the French- and English-news programs.

A second type of comparison *combined* the visual modes and presenter role analyses with their visual renditions, to arrive at a set of standard *visual paradigms*. The visual paradigm analysis utilized twenty-three possible combinations of roles, modes of presentation, and backgrounds, and compared their frequency in the French and English news programs. We applied these more detailed, second-stage comparisons to a 'composite week' of seven days of news programming (seventy programs in all) selected from each period in the referendum campaign. Such an analysis eliminates news variations grounded in economic decisions (such as scarce weekend coverage and lack of news teams) as well as those resulting from the unpredictability of news events themselves. It also establishes how the hierarchy of news voices is created in a news program and how the 'importance' of such voices is visually established. The Monday plus weekend coverage came from the Parti Québécois White Paper presentation in November 1979. Thursday was selected from the Liberals' tabling of the Beige Paper at the beginning of January 1980; Friday came from the National Assembly debate of March 1980, and Tuesday and Wednesday were chosen from the final week of the referendum campaign in May 1980. This gave us an extensive corpus of seventy news programs for the second-stage *stylistic* analysis; twenty-eight of the programs were in French and forty-two in English. From this corpus we additionally compared selected news programs to begin to illustrate the *content* and *meaning* implications of the French and English program renditions. Together, these extensive, layered, and increasingly focused analyses will provide evidence of what van Dijk (1988) calls systematic 'ideological overdeterminations,' which resulted from stylistic differences in audiovisual news program presentations by the French and English stations.

'Visualization,' as Stephen Kline points out, is initially identified with the concrete, but itself provides the means for a narrative style that merges the concrete and the interpretative within a well-defined set of 'realist' story structures. Journalists are materialized, locations and events are depicted directly and immediately, and sources are seen to be speaking for themselves; at the same time, the information presented in a news story is organized within a narrative argument that conveys of itself the qualities of impartiality. These are expressed rhetorically through four basic principles of journalistic presentation: neutrality, expertise, objectivity, and balance (Kline, 1982: 24).

Our subsequent stylistic analysis will consider these journalistic values in terms of the ways in which the news *discourse* is constituted by its roles and voices, and the ways in which the different voices are visually rendered. It will be shown that neutrality, expertise, objectivity, and balance are constructed by the frequency and the length of time that a voice is heard/seen on the screen, and by the ways in which the arguments of these voices are validated both rhetorically and visually. To undertake these comparative analyses, we categorized the French and English stations' news discourses into five different components that could be timed and counted. In our analysis, a 'newscast' refers to a particular news program such as *Ce Soir* or *City at Six*. A 'news story' is a class of reports on a particular occurrence in the world. Example: a referendum rally, for which different types of reports would be offered. A 'news item' designates an angle or subplot of a complex news story. Example: a vox-pop interview with a citizen leaving a rally. Finally, a 'segment' refers to the smallest audiovisual component of an item. Example: the reporter's question that is heard and the citizen's response that is filmed from a single visual angle.

The Visual Style of Francophone and Anglophone News Channels: Program Characteristics

Though francophone audiences showed greater interest in the news (Caron and Couture 1976), both our overall comparisons and our 'composite week' comparisons indicate that in 1979–80, Montreal's French channels carried fewer news programs and devoted about half as much time to the news as the English channels. Table 3.1 reveals that the French channels CBFT and CFTM aired only four news programs daily, which lasted a total of 78 minutes. The English channels CBMT 6 and CFCF 12, in contrast, broadcast six news programs, for a daily total of 138 minutes. However, these substantial differences in total news time do not imply that the francophone stations covered substantially fewer stories: Table 3.1 also docu-

TABLE 3.1
Average number of daily stories by station and newscast (composite week:
total 70 programs)

Language	Station	Program	Stories	Total
French	CBFT 2	Ce Soir	14	30
		Le Téléjournal	16	
	CFTM 10	Le 10 vous informe	10	
		Nouvelles TVA	6	16
English	CBMT 6	City at Six	14	
		National	12	
		City Tonight	4	30
	CFCF 12	Pulse	13	
		CTV National	12	
		Late Pulse	7	32

ments that the average number of stories covered daily (in the composite week) was almost equal, with the two French stations airing thirty on the public channel and sixteen on the private channel. The comparable figures for the English stations were thirty and thirty-two stories respectively.

If the average number of stories in Montreal's anglophone stations was considerably higher (62:46), and if those stories consumed double the time, one must assume that they were structured differently – that is, that they had more items and segments. Yet the relationship of items and segments to time was not straightforward. Our overall and composite week comparisons show that the average item length was virtually the same for both types of newscasts (66 seconds), but that the duration of segments was not: segments on francophone stations lasted about four seconds longer (27 seconds) than those on anglophone ones (23 seconds). What made English-language stories longer, therefore, was the greater *average* number of items per story (1:3 as opposed to 1:2), combined with a greater *average* number of segments per item (1:4 as opposed to 1:3). These length differences made the English-language coverage more variegated, as well as more difficult for viewers to decipher. From the point of view of intelligibility, the French-language newscasts seemed to be visually more simply structured – and thus, some researchers argue, more easily comprehensible (Sturm and Grewe-Partsch 1987).

To explore the impact of visual styles on meaning construction in francophone and anglophone news programs, we undertook a more focused, third-level comparison of how different news presenter roles and visual modes were used. This helped us ascertain whether differences in visualization techniques are also related to language, and if so, how. The 15th of May, 1980, the day on which we compared ten news programs, was a Tuesday at the beginning of the final week of the Quebec referendum campaign. All four Montreal stations – two French (CBFT/CFTM) and two English (CBMT/CFCF) – consequently carried a plethora of information about the referendum. Even though the six-month-long coverage was coming to a climax, the ten newscasts paid some attention to other international, Canadian, and Quebec issues. On the international scene, there were reports about the Afghanistan situation after the Soviet invasion, Ted Kennedy's Democratic candidacy, and the welfare of Cuban refugees in Florida. On the national scene, the top story was a welcome drop in the Bank of Canada rate, although a possible postal strike, a hike in telephone rates, and a Trudeau/Davis meeting in Toronto also garnered some interest. In Montreal there was less good news: various school boards were facing strikes, fires were reported, and a telethon was announced; in yet another story, Montreal was described as the drug capital of Canada. But altogether, referendum coverage dominated the news agendas of both the French and the English stations.

Though a one-day content comparison cannot provide accurate information on the usual news priorities of a station or station group, the 15 May 1980 coverage reflects previously documented French-station preoccupations with Quebec stories. However, the Canadian and international content differences that scholars like Caron had noted in 1976 did not materialize, because the 1980 referendum campaign overshadowed international news on the Canadian political agenda. Five days before the referendum vote, francophone stations were devoting an average of 51 per cent of the total news time to this issue, and anglophone stations 61 per cent. These figures, however, obscure each station's *unique* referendum coverage, which was designed to reinforce station identity and thus viewer loyalty. The main event of 15 May 1980 was a speech by Prime Minister Trudeau indicating that a NO vote would mean YES for constitutional renewal and for special status for Quebec; coupled with this was a response to Trudeau's declaration by both provincial party leaders. All stations, both French and English, agreed that this was one of the most important stories of the day. Three out of four stations covered the Trudeau speech in toto, and all four focused on the responses to it by Mr Lévesque and Mr Ryan. Another important event that merited coverage by all four channels was the Pinard-Hamilton opinion survey, which predicted a possible defeat for the YES side.

Beyond that, however, each station selected its own referendum items, which meant that each developed its own news angles to differentiate itself from the others. Radio-Canada surveyed French responses in Paris, while TVA continued its regional focus and covered responses from the Saguenay, the Laurentians, and Abitibi. On the English side, CBC sampled reactions in Washington to the sovereignty-association option, and CFCF situated the referendum in the context of Quebec history.

With this general sketch of the different amounts and kinds of news stories available to French and English Montreal viewers on 15 May 1980, we can now assess the interplay between the audiovisual styles, as well as the ways that news roles were made visible in the two station groups. Such a comparison is useful, because it opens the way for a preliminary discussion about how visual packaging affects the ways in which a news text makes sense, and about which roles/voices have the greatest authority to propose an interpretation.

Constituents of Visual Style in Francophone and Anglophone Newscasts

When the public is asked to differentiate between television and newspaper reporting, the usual response is that TV permits us to see for ourselves what goes on in the world, while newspapers mediate and report the day's events. In Canada, as elsewhere, television is the most believed and the most important medium for both international news and Canadian news of national importance (Davey, 1970: 6). Broadcast journalists around the world are aware of these audience expectations and conceive 'the first priority of a TV news program [as] presenting the viewer with the plain unvarnished account of happenings' (Glasgow University Media Group, 1980: 193). For audiences and producers alike, television news discourse is believed to be opaque – to convey the 'truth' about an event rather than a *version* of the truth. Where does this belief in television's lack of mediation come from, considering that both media follow the same journalistic reporting conventions?

One suggestion is that the visual construction of the journalistic canons of neutrality, expertise, objectivity, and balance is less obvious, because viewers have learned about them from photography. The Glasgow study suggested that neutrality is indicated by depersonalizing the newsroom and by seating the anchor before a blank wall. Expertise is demonstrated through the scheduling of reporter voices, which 'let us in' on what is *really* happening. Objectivity is conveyed by the seamless interweaving of in-studio commentary and on-location film footage. Balance seems to be inherent in the ways that news stories are hierarchized, with the most important stories coming first and the anchor introducing topics or wrapping up the program with a few well-chosen words.

Visual Modes

These very sketchy remarks indicate that visual presentation styles consist of at least three components – visual inputs, locations, and roles – which taken together enable the viewer to discover a speaker's relationship to the camera and to the visual unfolding of a story. According to Stephen Kline (1982), the interrelationship of these three variables reflects a station's orientation to outside sources. It also confers legitimacy on certain speakers, and on certain ways of portraying events. In considering the component parts of the visual discourse, our study divides the relationships between location and speech into five location variables. Four of these are 'live studio' (piece to camera, reporter speaking, interview, and debate), and the fifth is live outside-studio. All of these are derived from journalistic work practices. The visual inputs consist of seven types of 'actuality film': film without commentary, film/voice-over, film/captions, stock footage, film/piece-to-camera, filmed report, and filmed interview. Many of these are combined with stills and graphics. The five location variables and seven input variables together provide twelve possible combinations of *visual modes*.

The first discovery that our comparison of francophone and anglophone stations made is that the use of visual modes in the telling of news stories was severely restricted. Table 3.2 indicates that only five of twelve modes were widely used, and that together they accounted for over 93 per cent of the ways in which news items (which constitute a story's subplots) were presented. The five preferred visual presentation modes for both language groups were (in decreasing order of importance) film and voice-over, piece to camera, filmed interview, filmed piece to camera, and film. The two piece-to-camera formats indicate that in-studio personnel were not only in control of the verbal agenda, but also dominated the visual presentation through their direct relationship to the camera. Their 'framing' of a story, through the selection of story angles and visual staging, also demonstrates that journalists heighten the believability dimension of their story versions. The three outside roles – news maker, expert, and vox-pop – could enter this media sanctum through only one mode, the filmed interview. Furthermore, the fact that four of the five modes included film or video indicates

TABLE 3.2
Visual modes on francophone and anglophone stations (by number of items;
total 10 programs / 108 stories)

	Francophone Number	%	Anglophone Number	%
Film & voice-over	45	26	127	34
Piece to camera	78	45	102	27
Filmed interview	6	4	67	18
Filmed piece to camera	19	11	34	9
Film	18	10	18	5
Voice-over & captions	0	—	12	3
Stock footage	0	—	7	2
Live report	3	2	2	0.5
Live location	1	0.6	2	0.5
Film & captions	2	1	2	0.5
Interview & captions	0	—	2	0.5
Filmed report	1	0.5	0	—

that the station had virtually total visual control, because film, in contrast to live inputs, can be and is edited for news programs.

As Table 3.2 shows, other presentation modes, such as voice-over and captions, stock footage, reporter live, and location live, all of which represent 'immediate visual presence,' were scarcely used. Only 2.6 per cent of all French and 6 per cent of all English items were presented in these formats during the referendum coverage. Comparing francophone and anglophone stations provides three additional insights into the visual-format differences between the two language groups. First, the piece-to-camera mode was used much more often by francophone stations (45 to 27 per cent), which according to Knight (1989) seemed to give them their more 'populist' visual quality. Second, there was the francophone stations' greater use of film, which accounted for 10 per cent of all item presentations compared to only about 5 per cent on anglophone stations. Third and most important was the English stations' almost five times greater use of filmed interviews (18 to 4 per cent) which made their visual style more varied and open to voices located outside the studio. We will return to the interpretive implications of these visual packaging differences after discussing the different ways the two station groups used their news presenter roles.

David Menaker suggests that a news show's appeal lies in its presentation of daily events as 'excitement governed by order.' He notes: 'News shows [try] to inject excitement into merely routine symbolic events – signings, arrivals, departures, press conferences, which masquerade as the drama that in the real world lies behind a resignation' (1979: 235). A station's news personnel are the stars who 'enact' this order creation every night for their particular viewer groups. It is the anchor who embodies this order by directing the flow, offering previews, and creating summaries and linkages. Furthermore, when the anchor is presented as a *sign* of himself or herself, the narration becomes more realistic and lifelike. Theresa de Lauretis points out that the choice of the sign-vehicle (casting) becomes a choice of the content conveyed *in addition to* that of the language used (1979: 111). All anchors perform as consummate actors, even if they are simply being themselves. Futhermore, in 1980 Montreal they dressed in expensive and conservative upper-middle-class attire, were all physically attractive, and produced what Goffman calls 'fresh talk,' which sounds spontaneous and helps link disparate items (1983: 208). Montreal at the time had no station like Toronto's CITY-TV, which is pitched to a younger urban viewership, and whose anchors wear more 'hip' attire. All news personnel must be assumed to be equally well versed in the skills of their craft; even so, how they 'come across' and are responded to by the viewers differs markedly. In Montreal during the referendum period, TVA's 'urbane' Pierre Bruneau contrasted with the more 'tweedy' Bill Haughland of 'Pulse' news; thus visually embodying francophone and anglophone viewers' preferred dress codes.

Table 3.3 demonstrates that francophone and anglophone stations choreographed their news personnel very differently. The English penchant for filmed interviews correlated with a much greater use of the interviewer role. As shown in Table 3.3, anglophone channels had seventy-three instances of this role, in contrast to the francophones' two instances. This heavy use of the interviewer role, combined with a greater use of filmed interviews, visually conveyed and reinforced the audience's sense of access – of being part of the news process – which was a second aspect of English programming's 'openness.' Strangely enough, even though six different news events probed public opinion, francophone stations used interviews as subplots or discussion angles only twice. Neither the Pinard/Hamilton poll predicting the NO win, nor the Paris and Washington reactions, nor the polls in Ontario or Abitibi or among the Inuit merited interviewer involvement. Since our comparison combines public with private station results, the economic argument (i.e., a lack of news teams) is ruled out as an explanation. Instead, we must conclude that the overwhelming use of the anchor role to retell news events has something to do with journalistic practices introduced in the mid-1960s, and with the 'star' quality of

TABLE 3.3
Roles on francophone and anglophone stations (by number of items;
total 10 programs / 108 stories)

Roles	Francophone Number	%	Anglophone Number	%
Anchor	89	56	108	30
Reporter	63	40	173	47
Interviewer	2	1	73	20
Commentator	3	2	5	1.5
Anchor and reporter	1	1	5	1.5
Total	158	100	364	100

Quebec columnists mentioned by Armande Saint-Jean in Chapter 2. Table
3.3 furthermore indicates that although the anchor and reporter roles were
the mainstays of news programming, the two language groups emphasized
them differently. For the francophone stations, the anchor was far and
away the dominant role, appearing in more than half (56 per cent) of all
items. Anglophone stations, on the other hand, favoured the reporter role,
which appears in 47 per cent of all items. This difference, as we have seen,
privileged the francophone piece-to-camera visual mode, as noted in Table
3.2. It also shows that in-station news presenter roles were visually much
more highly legitimated than outsider roles. Politicians, experts, and people
in the street, whose images stand for themselves, were never rendered in the
piece-to-camera visual mode, and their oblique relationship to the camera
demoted their voices and statements to an inferior supportive role in the
visual packaging of the news discourse.

Visual Paradigms

Theoretically, the seven news roles can be associated with twelve visual
modes to provide a hypothetical seventy-two possible combinations, or
audiovisual paradigms (Connell, 1980: 145). Yet as we have already seen in
Table 3.3, seven of the visual modes are rarely used. Furthermore, because
the anchor and reporter roles are the major 'stars' in constituting the news
discourse, only twenty-four audiovisual combinations actually appear in
Montreal's news programming. Of the top ten possibilities, francophone
stations utilized four most frequently in their referendum coverage; all
told, these accounted for almost four-fifths (72.5 per cent) of all item pre-

TABLE 3.4
Top ten visual paradigms by language (in number of items;
total 10 programs / 108 stories)

Visual paradigms	Francophone Number	%	Anglophone Number	%
PC&A&GB*	47	27	40	11
FV&R	38	22	104	28
PC&A&SB	23	13	21	6
FLMPC&R	18	10.5	33	9
FN	15	9	17	5
PC&A	8	5	25	7
FV&A	6	3.5	19	5
GVO&A	4	2	0	—
INTNMAKR	4	2	21	6
INTEXPR	2	1	23	6
Other	9	5	63	17
Total	174	100	366	100

*See Appendix B for list of abbreviations.

sentations. In contrast, English stations utilized all ten visual paradigms. This reconfirms that the greater image variety on English-language stations resulted from the fact that their news discourses were constructed around two news presenter roles instead of just one.

Table 3.4 indicates that the characteristic visualization strategies of the two station groups was remarkably different. Among the French stations, two anchor-based visual paradigms – piece-to-camera/anchor/graphics background (27 per cent) and piece-to-camera/anchor/stills background (13 per cent) together accounted for nearly half (40 per cent) of all item renditions. This anchor predominance affected French program renditions in general, considering that voice-overs were done by anchors as well as by reporters. Altogether, the anchor role thus appeared in half (50.5 per cent) of all news items.

Table 3.4 furthermore indicates that English stations privileged the two reporter-based audiovisual combinations – film/voice-over/*reporter*, and film/piece-to-camera/*reporter* – which together accounted for 37 per cent of all items. These two reporter-based visual styles were supplemented by two much less important anchor-based paradigms: piece-to-camera/*anchor*/graphics, and piece-to-camera/*anchor*, which were used in only 17 per cent of all English-station item presentations. The less frequent use of anchor-based subplots left more room for outside voices, like the news-maker/politician and the expert, to become part of the English news discourse. These two roles appeared in about 16 per cent of all items – almost double the francophone number. The fact that the top five anglophone audiovisual paradigms accounted for only 61 per cent rather than 80 per cent of all item renditions helps substantiate the conclusion that the English-language audiovisual news discourses were constructed out of a greater number of roles and voices, and thus appeared more variegated.

Visual Grammar

It now remains to be seen whether the two visual styles resulted in unique audiovisual narrative formats for the French and English station discourses. To get at this question, we must move to a more complex analysis in which the basic constituents of our news presentation grammar (modes, roles, paradigms) are compared in terms of time (which will provide insights into the *tempo* of the presentations), and in terms of the numbers of *image changes* that viewers were confronted with. This will help us discover which image/shot changes were associated with which narrative components.

For this analysis, we subdivided the total number of news stories in our composite week, into their constituent news items, and then counted the number of visual or role changes (segments) that occurred within items. Table 3.5 indicates that francophone news items that reported story subplots consisted of shorter, less complex units. Fully 43 per cent of all francophone items had only *one* visual rendition (segment); another 40 per cent had two to four visual changes. Also, in the francophone discourse there were no news items with more than seven different camera settings. Since item complexity is directly correlated with image/shot changes, it is clear that fewer visual changes occurred. The francophone visual style was thus slower and more straightforward, presenting most news angles from one *fixed* camera perspective. In contrast, the anglophone news discourse featured stories with more items and subplots. On average, there were two items to the francophones' 1.25. The visual rendition of these subplots was also more complex. Less than one-third (30 per cent) of all anglophone items had a single camera setting; about two-fifths (39 per cent) had two to four camera changes; and the remainder (31 per cent) had five or more visual cuts. These differences in visual complexity were related to the greater number of roles and voices used to constitute the anglophone news discourse; they made its visual style much more 'alive,' with many more visual and camera changes occurring at more frequent intervals.

TABLE 3.5
Comparison of French and English news item structure (by number of
segments; composite week: total 70 programs)

No. of segments	Francophone Number	%	Anglophone Number	%
1	30	43	28	30
2	12	17	13	14
3	6	9	11	12
4	10	14	12	13
5	5	7	5	5
6	5	7	5	5
7	2	3	6	7
8	—	—	4	4
9	—	—	3	3
10	—	—	2	2
11+	—	—	5	5
Total	70	100	94	100

Many researchers, including Teun van Dijk (1988), have indicated that in addition to story complexity, narrative beginnings and endings also play an important role in how story arguments are visually constructed. Table 3.6 compares the 'visualization' of story beginnings in the francophone and anglophone news discourses and finds that the anchor dominated 60 per cent of the French but only 39 per cent of the English beginnings. Visually, the frontal rendition reinforced the anchor's authority; also, the anchor had from one-and-a-half to over three minutes to introduce the story. Both groups of stations resorted to reporters in the second segment, with the preferred visual mode being the film/voice-over, though francophone stations retained the anchor/piece-to-camera as an important alternative. The point to be made here is that item beginnings (segments 1 and 2) were dominated by in-station news personnel who, because they made the introductory remarks, set the context for how the story was to be interpreted by their respective viewer groups.

In segment 3, French and English news discourses followed quite different patterns, with the news-maker role dominating the former and the reporter or interviewer roles the latter. The absence of a dominant visual mode suggests that the third segment determined the *orientation* of the item: it set the stage for the way the argument was going to be validated. This could be done either by in-studio personnel or by outside experts. In

TABLE 3.6
Comparison of French and English item structure by preferred visual paradigms
(as % of segment totals; composite week: total 70 programs)

Segments	Visual paradigm	Francophone %	Anglophone %
1	PC&A&GB	60	39
	PC&A	10	23
	PC&A&SB	24	18
2	FV&R	41	40
	FV&A	11	19
	FLMPC&R	14	8
3	FV&R	24	18
	INTEXPRT	4	14
	FN	40	8
4	FV&R	57	53
	FLMPC&R	14	13
	INTNMAKR	5	8
5	FLMPC&R	36	29
	FV&R	9	21
	FN	9	14
6	FLMPC&R	57	52
	FV&R	29	9
	FN	0	9
7	PC&A&SB	50	0
	FV&R	0	37
	FLMPC&R	0	16
Last segment	FV&R	28	22
	FLMPC&R	25	32
	FV&A	8	18

segment four, there was again agreement between the two groups of stations, with the reporter taking the dominant role and the film/voice-over the preferred visual format. In segments five and six reporters continued in the dominant role, but once again the visual formats of the two types of stations differed widely: francophones used the piece-to-camera (36 per cent), in or outside the studio; anglophones had three almost equally distributed visual modes: film/voice-over, piece-to-camera, and interview. Most final segments ended with the reporter in either piece-to-camera or voice-over mode. For francophone stations, shorter items ended with the anchor/piece-to-camera wrapping up the account.

Concerning the visualization strategies of the two station groups' news arguments, we may conclude that the anglophone stations used a greater variety of visual paradigms, and also told their stories in more detail, using more items of greater complexity. Nearly half of anglophone items had four or more subplots, compared to less than 17 per cent in the francophone discourse. Though both station groups featured news personnel in their story beginnings, a look at third segments indicates that their verification styles were quite different. Francophone stations use visuals, stills, and graphics to validate their argumentation, while the anglophones favoured film/news-maker visual modes, which permitted a politician to speak in her or his own voice.

Our stylistic comparison indicates that the news story flow was mainly between news personnel roles. Such a textual construction corroborates Menaker's point that a news program's appeal lies in its presenting daily events as 'governed by order.' The order, it appears, is created by the news personnel themselves, who appear on the screen nightly and whose order creation is therefore trusted by the viewers. Also, the flow of argumentation is overwhelmingly unidirectional, moving from the anchor to the reporter but rarely back to the anchor. The reporter role thus emerges as pivotal in linking the studio to the event 'as it happens out there.' Menaker is, however, mistaken in claiming that the argumentation style follows the pyramidal structure of the press. If one divides the newscast into three equal parts, francophone stations follow a U-shaped visual argumentation style and anglophones the reverse. Anglophone stations use an ascending/descending pattern in their newscasts. How this affects text intelligibility for viewers is not yet known.

Visual News 'Grammars'

Our comparative study of the visual packaging of audiovisual news programming made two important discoveries. First, that the *constituents* or inputs of what we have called the visual news 'grammar' are uniform across the globe; yet, the ways these audiovisual constituents are *combined* are language- and therefore potentially culture-specific. The Glasgow Group (1980, 1982) identified these inputs as news personnel, film, tape, interviews, and still photographs/graphics. Such a classification, we have discovered, though accurate, is static and misleading. It fails to address the issue of how audio and visual components are interrelated. Our discovery of characteristic 'visual modes,' which combine presenter roles with a small number of visual paradigms, has enabled us to demonstrate that the visual combinatorics of the grammar are much more complex than expected. Such a grammar clarifies how methods of visualization (film, video, live), journalistic products (report, interview), and locations (in or outside the studio) are connected to what we have called 'presenter roles.' The ways in which presenter roles are visually rendered provides important information about a role's relationship to the camera. The visual rendition signals a role's hierarchical importance in reconstructing the news story and thus the voice's rhetorical power. News personnel are not only visually privileged by remaining on screen for longer periods of time, but also take verbal precedence over outside roles. They can speak for and about others, while outside roles such as politicians, experts, and people-in-the-street are frequently seen but not permitted to speak in their own voices. The news footage 'shows' their images, but their messages are usually 'voiced over' by reporters or anchors.

One must conclude that the universality of news presenter roles around the world is largely determined by professional production practices and by economic criteria. Together these dictate the number of news personnel a station can afford to employ and the most cost-effective audiovisual renditions. Among the professional practices that encouraged uniformity before the use of video was the need for visual substitutability, which led to standardized ways for recording location interviews (Tuchman, 1978: 105). Visual product uniformity is further reinforced when reporters give their camera people precise instructions about the visual coverage they want (Clarke, 1981: 27). Audience expectations, acquired through the process of becoming visually 'literate,' encourage the use of only a small number of the possible visual combinations. These audience expectations privilege a 'transparent' visual syntax that responds to the desire of viewers to 'see for themselves' when watching the news (Hall, 1980: 6). Since visuals shown without sound are quite ambiguous, intelligibility and narrative flow must be achieved through stock footage of comings and goings, and through formal greeting situations that make the 'visual syntax' easy to decipher. As Table 3.4 demonstrated, the symbolic (nondescriptive) use of most visual material aids in this task.

The second important finding of our comparison of audiovisual grammars in news programs is that these visual grammars are culture-specific. This discovery suggests that though the professional news ideology of impartiality is generally accepted in Western democracies, the ways in which this impartiality is visually *expressed* in the news discourse varies from country to country and from language group to language group. A particularly clear example of this is found in German-language news discourse, where the North American anchor role is subdivided into three: the news reader, the news commentator, and the news producer/commentator.

TABLE 3.7
Francophone and anglophone visual styles (composite week: total 70 programs)

Style components	Francophone	Anglophone
Structure		
Story length	2 items	2.6 items
Item length	2 seg.	3.7 seg.
Item duration	66 sec.	36 sec.
Segment duration	27 sec.	23 sec.
Visual mode (location plus input)		
Studio/Piece-to-camera	45%	27%
Location/Film/Voice-over	26%	34%
Studio/Film/Piece-to-camera	11%	9%
Location/Film/Interview	3%	18%
Role utilization		
Number of roles	2	3
Anchor	56%	29%
Reporter	40%	47%
Interviewer	1%	20%
Visual paradigm (role plus visual mode)		
Piece-to-camera/Anchor/Graphics	40%	17%
Film/Voice-over/Reporter	22%	28%
Film/Piece-to-camera/Reporter	10%	9%
Interview/Expert or news-maker	3%	12%
Visual grammar	*U-shaped*	*^-shaped*
Segments	Shorter	Longer
		More complex
Visual paradigms	Few, less varied	More
		More varied

Each of these roles is rendered in a unique manner and utilizes a different validation strategy. Only the news reader claims to present the 'facts'; the other two roles, like editorialists in the press, comment on or elucidate these facts (Robinson, 1987: 58–78). Table 3.7 provides a summary of the main stylistic differences in the visualization strategies of Montreal's French and English station groups.

Table 3.7 demonstrates that anglophone newscasts during the referendum were more numerous (six daily, rather than four) and about twice as long as francophone ones. Also, they presented more items of greater complexity, which is why the average total number of stories covered by the two groups of stations differed markedly (62:46). In addition, anglophone visualization strategies were richer, incorporating more visual modes and visual paradigms. Three visual modes (piece to camera, film, interview) were about equally prevalent on the English stations, whereas on the French stations, piece to camera (in studio or filmed) predominated. More than half (56 per cent) of all items were presented in this manner.

The greater number of visual paradigms utilized in the anglophone news discourse was a result of how roles are correlated with visual modes. Our comparison demonstrates that three roles figured prominently in the anglophone news discourse, in contrast to only two roles in the francophone. On the English stations the roles of reporter (47 per cent of all items), anchor (30 per cent of all items), and interviewer (20 per cent of all items) maintained a descending order of audiovisual presence. On the French stations the anchor was clearly the star performer (56 per cent of all items), and the reporter was subordinate (40 per cent of all items). The visual effects of these differences in role utilization were reflected in and reinforced by the number and kinds of visual paradigms that the two news discourses incorporated.

An examination of how these roles were made 'visible' also helps us pinpoint how 'objectivity,' 'neutrality,' and 'balance' are signified in different ways in the two news discourses. In the visually more static French news discourse, objectivity was guaranteed primarily through the frequent visual presence of the anchor on the screen and the utilization of the piece-to-camera visual mode (40 per cent of all items). The anchor's role included three responsibilities: to present and/or read unillustrated items; to introduce reporters or commentators, and films and tapes; and, very occasionally, to appear fleetingly between two different items to punctuate a change in subject matter. However, the unvarying visual rendition of this role erased the anchor's interpretive interventions in the French discourse. Objectivity was also signalled by the French anchor's appearance in 56 per cent of all story subplots. The anchor's veracity was attested to by the fact that this role was the most important in the news discourse.

In the anglophone visualization strategy objectivity was signalled by the variety of audiovisual textual components and by the reporter's linking function. Stylistically, reporters were rendered in three different visual modes. Of these, the long, uninterrupted piece-to-camera shots were most important, because they conveyed the same rhetorical importance as was accorded to the anchor's voice. Objectivity was conveyed through the reporter's linking function to the outside world. This was accomplished both visually and orally by pieces interrupted visually by news-makers or by people-in-the-street whose opinions were solicited. Both of these devices suggested a participatory and interactive audience link, which seemed 'real' because it modelled face-to-face interpersonal conversation. Through these visual paradigms, reporters and interviewers became stand-ins for the home viewer, who was symbolically included in a seemingly two-way interpersonal communication circuit. The English news personnel asked the questions we at home would have asked; thus, they 'told it like it is.' Objectivity in this case was signalled and reinforced stylistically by the implied interactivity of the English news discourse. Neither the French nor the English news discourses however, utilized visual segments 'iconically' (descriptively) to validate the 'you are there' feeling that viewers crave. Our comparison shows that only one visual mode (location/film/interview) and one visual paradigm (interview/expert) provided an opportunity for *unmediated speech renditions* of any kind. In the English discourse, only 18 per cent and 12 per cent respectively of all visual segments were rendered in this fashion. The French discourse was almost hermetically sealed to outsiders; in only 3 per cent of all segments were outside voices able to speak to the viewer directly.

This bare description of news presenter roles and visual paradigms does not address the question. *Why* did Montreal's French and English station groups develop such divergent visualization strategies? Armande Saint-Jean, in Chapter 2, suggested three possible historical events that might have fostered such differences in journalists' professional practices and values. All of these together might have resulted in the privileging of the anchor role so that it dominated French-language news discourse during the 1980s. There was, first of all, the belated introduction of the columnist role in the mid-1960s and the 'stardom' that Judith Jasmin and René Lévesque achieved on television through their investigative reporting. The anchor role may have been further enhanced as a result of the censorship that francophone professionals were subjected to at the time of the War Measures Act in 1970, when their reports were censored by the CBC's English headquarters in Toronto. My own investigation of station logs, and my interviews with English broadcast personnel, show that the War Measures Act led to greater involvement of middle management in public affairs programming and to the elimination of vox-pop interviews; also, on the French side *all* Radio-Canada programming had to be pretaped. These interventions led not only to more homogenized retellings of past events, but also to extensive self-censorship and to the development of a 'factual' narrative style to defuse the shocking nature of the events recounted (Robinson, 1975: 52–3). Furthermore, it was noted that French-language professionals subscribed to what David Weaver and Cleveland Wilhoit call a more 'engaged' or adversarial role during the 1970s, while their union struggled for greater autonomy in the news production process (Clift, 1980; Godin, 1981; Raboy, 1983). Anglophone professionals at the time were not as heavily involved in such union activities, possibly because they subscribed to a more 'neutral' professional role, one that emphasized the interpretive and disseminating aspects of news work and was similar to that of their American colleagues (Weaver and Wilhoit, 1991: 113–16). These professional and historical differences in the journalistic experiences of the two news corps provide the broad context out of which stylistic differences in the French- and English-language news discourses might have arisen; however, other factors may also have been at play. Since we lack careful comparative analyses of news discourse from the 1960s and 1970s, the explanations offered here are nothing more than informed conjecture; we hope that others will one day perform these analyses.

Our bare description of news presenter roles and visual paradigms also misses what Menaker calls the 'aesthetic dimensions' of the television personae, which help sustain the 'excitement governed by order' and guarantee the 'believability' of newscasts. This excitement is created not only through personal mannerisms of tone, demeanour, and attire, but also by the ways language is used and arguments are made. To show how the rhetorical political context for the referendum coverage was determined, we must now consider in detail the journalistic 'news values' (Gans, 1979) that were adopted with respect to that coverage. Such professional news values specify how events will be selected and classified, how news angles will be developed, and how, in the case of the referendum coverage, the news narratives for Montreal's varied citizens/viewers were built up over time.

4

The Referendum on Quebec Television: Broadcast Rules and Content Frames

The Media and Public Opinion Formation

Traditional public opinion scholarship has assumed that the media are 'neutral' distribution networks funnelling assorted types of information to diversified mass publics. In Charles Wright's terminology, these publics are viewed as anonymous and as undifferentiated by message producers (Wright, 1959). Such a model fails, however, to account for the substantial ideological role the media play in helping politicians develop public consensus. It also neglects the role of listeners/viewers and their 'stocks of knowledge' in the construction of journalistic messages. A new group of reception theorists have begun to address these issues. They argue that meaning does not reside 'out there' in the words on a page or the pixels on a television screen; rather, it arises out of an interpretive interaction between viewer and image, reader and text. These interactions, which take place so frequently that we hardly notice them, are embedded in particular institutional, historical, and cultural settings that inevitably condition the production of public meaning (Allen 1987: 5). Stuart Hall and others have argued that in democratic societies the media constitute the public discussion stage on which the major issues of the day are debated and different points of view are aired. By fashioning this consensus, the media provide the essential preconditions for democratic public-opinion formation, which is based on the opportunity to reconcile disputes through discussion rather than through confrontation or violence (Hall, 1979: 341–2).

Thus, the media's most important political role is to make the consensus view of society *visible* as a feature of everyday life and to convince viewers, as citizens, that they are part of a 'public' that shares a common stock of knowledge. The development of such a consensual point of view has two important political implications for Western democratic societies. It suggests that the multiplicity of subgroups share roughly the same interests and have roughly the same power in political life. The ideological labour of public-opinion creation is thus reflexive. It helps both to *constitute* the notion of 'society' as an ordered public stage on which legitimate teams of protagonists and antagonists play out their political roles, and it *demonstrates* this order symbolically to its audience through the structure of the news narrative. It is not yet well understood how media narratives 'reframe' descriptions of political events and thus create public consensus on divisive political issues. Nor is it clear what role viewers play in this complex process of creating public meaning.

In Canadian political life, the victory of the Parti Québécois in the 1976 provincial election marked a watershed: for the first time, a sovereignty movement had been legitimated. The PQ, which had previously been politically unimportant, had been propelled onto the national stage, where it began to challenge the country's existing federal arrangements. In this situation the media had a vital interpretive role to play. They had to 'naturalize' the Quebec independence movement and interpret its political program in such a way that both its supporters and its opponents would continue to feel part of the Canadian political system. This chapter explores how this process of public-meaning creation was undertaken by one English station – Montreal's CFCF, which at the time of the 1980 referendum had the most English-language viewers. Our detailed semiotic analysis will shed light on the types of meaning frameworks that were used to mesh audience and journalistic understandings as to what the referendum was *really* about.

At least three cognitive frameworks seem to have been operating. On the pragmatic level, they included a series of assumptions about the unfolding political process and about who the relevant political actors were who were participating in the debate. Though the vote would ultimately affect all Canadians, these actors were provincial politicians and the Quebec public, and only indirectly the federal government. But this neat division was in fact untenable, because Prime Minister Pierre Trudeau, who headed the federal Liberal Party at the time, was himself a Quebecer and took part in the campaign. A second set of frameworks emerged from the ongoing historical debate about Quebec's special role in the Canadian federation. This debate was grounded in a notion of 'nationalism,' which was codified for the YES side in the Parti Québécois's White Paper and for the NO side in the Liberal Party's Beige Paper. These will be explored in greater detail in subsequent chapters. Here, we want to inquire into the journalistic frameworks that defined the 'proper' television rendition of the referendum.

The Referendum as 'Election' Frame

Our Goffmanian approach assumes, in contrast to formalist semiotics, that journalists' work practices leave visible traces on the news programs they produce. We therefore looked at the professional values that structure campaign reporting. For television personnel, campaign reporting is framed by 'knowledge in use' about routines, interview techniques, and professional ideologies such as 'balance.' Political reporting is also informed by meaning frames relating to what a given political event is 'about,' which journalists share with their viewers. Both 'knowledge in use' and 'frames' determine the selection of events for reportage, as well as the treatment of different classes of events.

In the electoral realm as in others, frames must harmonize with the 'definitions of the situation' provided by the different audiences that make up society. The society in which the 1980 referendum was being contested was socially and ethnically diverse. According to Goffman (1974), frames are built up by the members of a given group out of attitudes toward everyday life. It follows that news frames delineate not only what events news producers consider pertinent, but also what viewers/readers judge to be relevant in the political realm. The attitude toward everyday life is what enables the competent citizen to reduce the complexities of the daily environment; it is what directs him or her to *what* to notice in direct experience. These attitudes are socially constructed; even so, they remain relatively stable over time. The political assumptions underlying the news producers' as well as the Montreal viewer groups' interpretations of the Quebec referendum were of this nature.

In the case of the referendum, this 'framing' reciprocity was created in part through the political and legal rules that defined the event. More importantly, however, it was sustained through 'naming' and the use of familiar campaign reporting formats. Although the referendum was strictly speaking a provincial undertaking, an initiative by the Liberal government in Ottawa affected how the French and English Montreal stations were going to cover the story. In the fall of 1979, before the referendum debate commenced, a Cabinet directive instructed the CRTC to require all broadcasters to store referendum-related program tapes for possible future evaluation. In response to this, the CBC played it safe and contextualized the extraordinary plebiscite about Quebec independence, as an ordinary election campaign. Chapter 3 demonstrated that a number of equal-time and fair-opportunity rules contextualize election coverage in Canada. Moreover, since elections take place in a predictable manner, there are well-established and standardized journalistic procedures and practices for electoral campaigns. These include equal time for party coverage and daily mention of provincial parties' campaign activities. Also important are the conventions of seeking responses from Canada's nine other provincial capitals and from the federal prime minister. All electronic and print media in Quebec accepted these conventions and utilized the 'electoral' frame to cover referendum activities.

Election reporting, however, implies not only routinized work procedures but also 'conventions of narration' and story 'angles' that are more difficult to discern (Schudson, 1982: 98). In North American and European democracies, news workers have various alternatives for framing electoral activities. Three of these were possibly applicable to the referendum situation. They included the idea that elections may be viewed as a competition between different political interests and values, so that the merits of these values are the primary focus of reporters' attention. Elections may also be viewed as a discussion between citizens engaged in collective deliberations about their common future; this approach places the focus on a dialogue between the equally empowered people and their duly elected representatives. Another way of thinking about elections is to view them as a partisan game played for personal advantage or power (Mendelsohn, 1993: 150). Canadian research into electoral campaigns demonstrates that both print and television journalists have usually framed elections as a partisan game – a precedent that also coloured the referendum coverage.

Earlier we investigated Goffman's 'theatre of public life' by exploring the ways in which the French and English stations *visualized* their news programming; in this chapter we focus on how the legitimated teams of news personnel and politicians *enacted* democratic politics on Montreal's news programs. The audiovisual treatment of the news team personnel and its voices will be scrutinized here through what van Dijk (1988) calls semantic and pragmatic analysis. Semantic analysis uncovers how meaning is constructed in a discourse, while pragmatic analysis considers which 'speech acts' (Searle, 1969) are appropriate in particular social situations. According to van Dijk, news discourses consist primarily of assertions that are strung together into particular schemata or narrative patterns with recognizable openings, closings, and metaphors (1988: 27). The fact that they have syntactic, semantic, and pragmatic regularities indicates that news discourses are not only texts, but also forms of interaction. Engaging in discourse creation, as journalists do, involves participating in the *interpretive* processes of public meaning creation, as well as in the staging of social interaction.

Semantic and pragmatic analysis enables us to scrutinize the narratives of the referendum campaign by considering both the language used and the types of dramas enacted. Rhetoric *conveys* authority through the styles and modes of persuasion used by the actors, whereas drama *enacts* authority through the speaking order of roles and voices. It appears that the journalistic decision to treat the referendum as an election invoked a pre-existing sports style of narration based on adversarialism. This involved the use of concepts such as 'team,' 'fight,' and 'score' (Soderlund et al., 1984; Wagenberg et al., 1988). It also legitimated confrontation in order to simplify the narrative and thus make it more exciting. This suggests that journalists do not invent, but rather appropriate pre-existing narrative styles, which then function as *scripts*. This has two interpretive consequences. Scripts help journalists select newsworthy events; but for viewers/readers, they narrow the interpretive alternatives by invoking sets of preferred topics (Goffman, 1974: 9). In 'adversarial' election reporting, there are only four major narrative contexts. Matthew Mendelsohn notes three of these:

- Polls, standing, momentum, and the prediction of winners.
- Strategy, insider information, backroom disputes, and hidden tactical motives on the part of the participants.
- Campaign events (i.e., 'show' itself), as well as judgments about whether these events and performances were successful (1993: 152).

Frederick Fletcher (1987) discovered a fourth narrative context: the highlighting of leaders' activities over those of other party candidates. (This tends to work against the coverage of women incumbents.) While election coverage may employ different foci at different times, the stress on leaders' personalities has been a campaign staple since the late 1970s. Frizzell, Pammett, and Westell's study of the 1993 election found that in spite of this preoccupation, 'issues' and 'process' were also important, with the emphasis on these varying from election to election. In the 1984 coverage, process dominated; in 1988, issues dominated; in 1993 the two were about equal (1994: 94). Television reporting in particular has strengthened the focus on leaders and thereby encouraged voter choices based on the personal qualities of party heads, rather than on party platforms. Richard Carty (1986), who undertook a historical survey of Canadian election coverage, concluded a decade ago that television has accelerated the interpretive trend to personal politics – a trend the implications of which for democratic practice we will explore in Chapter 8.

The main purpose of the following case study of CFCF's *Pulse* news program of Friday, 7 March 1980 (which was part of the composite-week selection on which Chapter 3's audiovisual comparison was based) is to demonstrate the existence of referendum scripting as a 'game,' and to explore the narrative conventions arising out of this kind of journalistic scripting. We also wish to demonstrate that narrative and visual scripts enhance each other and create lines of argumentation that are ideologically *overdetermined.* Following Goffman, such narrative overdeterminations arise from a set of political outlooks that are shared by news personnel and the viewers who choose their particular channel. These interpretive over-determinations, which were particularly visible in the handling of the PQ booklet news story, were reinforced by a set of narrative devices that have been called 'binary oppositions.' As we shall see, binary oppositions can be constructed out of any aspect of a given situation. In the referendum situation they included the colours associated with different parties, the emotional tones struck with respect to leadership styles and the visual framing of different political personalities, and the language used in interviewing those personalities or reporting their actions. In illustrating such sign over-determination we cannot prove that our reading of the text was 'intended' by those who created it, or shared by all listeners/viewers. It does, however, enable us to posit that these systematic textual configurations were supported by anglophone television producers and their viewers in making sense of the referendum platforms presented by the Parti Québécois and the provincial Liberals.

The Referendum as Adversarial 'Electoral Game'

The referendum as 'election' and the 'game' frame are clearly evident in the *Pulse News* program of 7 March 1980, which covered (among other things) aspects of the March 1980 debate in the National Assembly. The PQ had orchestrated this debate carefully, by having different ministers address different benefits of sovereignty-association for Quebec. Claude Ryan's Liberals were unprepared for this concerted action, and public opinion polls noted substantial increases in voter support for the YES side after the debate had ended. We have chosen this particular broadcast for more detailed semiotic analysis because it was part of our composite week analysis (see Chapter 3), and because it included a wide range of program formats. Among these were leader interviews, opinion polls, and a discussion of a PQ document arguing for independence. This document was couched in a political rhetoric that was diametrically opposed to the political values of anglophone and allophone viewers; for this reason, news personnel had to ideologically reinterpret it so that it would fit into both their own and their viewers' 'definitions' of the referendum situation. In the following analysis we do not try to prove the 'correctness' of our particular reading; rather, we try to demonstrate how rhetorical and visual reconstructions of newsworthy events create a unique and overdetermined set of meaning frames through which a station's particular viewer groups are encouraged to make sense of selected political events.

The Montreal portion of the private station's news program lasted eleven minutes, but we will consider mainly those items specifically related to the referendum. The newscast opened with the last few seconds of *The Price Is Right*, a game show that preceded the evening news in the 1980s. As the game show's credit sequence rolled, a station announcer provided the evening's television line-up in voice-over. After the game show's credit sequence ended, a card appeared promoting yet another program, to be aired later in the week. Then the station's musical logo, the 'CFCF 12 Montreal' theme song, was played, and then the news began. Visually, the show opened with white lettering on a black background giving the day and date: FRIDAY, 7 MARCH 1980. It immediately cut to a shot of a car struggling up a slippery hill. Dramatic theme music had by then begun. In the upper right-hand corner of this image of the car was a computer-graphic headline relating this shot to Montreal's long-standing strike of blue-collar workers. It was reported that snow had still not been cleared from Montreal streets. The next shot was of people walking on a sidewalk. The headline linked this image to the results of a referendum poll that had been released that day. There followed a brief shot of a referendum statistics chart, and the newscast's visual logo – a revolving globe with the word PULSE written on it. The newscast then cut to the main newsreader, who introduced himself, the headlines, and his two colleagues: the sports and weather announcers, who gave five-second introductions to their topics. The first story dealt with the blue-collar strike. This lengthy report contained different items highlighting the effects of the Montreal city workers' strike on snow removal and administration.

Then followed four news stories related to the referendum. The anchor was seated in front of a graphic representation of a ballot box with a red Maple Leaf printed on its left side and a blue Fleur-de-Lis on its right side. Above it, a hand emerging from the left was depositing a ballot. The anchor then announced that a new poll had been released; its results were presented in tabular form by an off-screen reporter and then merged into an interview with provincial Liberal leader Claude Ryan about the poll results. The anchor, still seated in front of the same graphics, then introduced a story on premier Lévesque's reaction to the poll. This story began with his response; subsequent items filled us in on the premier's campaign and his appearance on an open-line radio show. Still before the same graphics, the anchor then read a short item about the PQ house leader, Claude Charron, who 'admitted' that his party members had been coached to present a disciplined front before the National Assembly cameras. This was followed by the anchor, now seated before the PQ party logo, introducing another story about a newly published PQ booklet, which was described as a 'simplified version of the PQ platform [designed to] sell' sovereignty-association.

Visual semiotics argues that television news makes sense to us as viewers because the verbal dominates the visual. Herbert Gans has aptly called television news 'visual radio' (1979: 147). What he means by this is that the verbal element of the discourse usually allows for the semantic fixing of the images by the spoken text – though in exceptional circumstances, such as the student facing the tank in Tiananmen Square, the opposite could be true. This verbal dominance is represented in the continuous flow of commentaries, reports, and interviews emanating from anchors', reporters', and commentators' voice-overs. This flow, which Raymond Williams (1974: 86) considers the unique characteristic of the television medium, is linear in time and thus quite different from the meaning creation of newspapers, which is partially fixed by the visual matrix, which McLuhan called a 'mosaic.' In the few seconds between the end of *The Price Is Right* and the beginning of *Pulse*, the evening's television line-up was made known, either by the use of graphics or through the voice of an off-screen announcer.

This is the first instance of flow: voice-overs drown out credit sequences, promos fill in the time between shows, and so on. The function of this unending flow of words and pictures is to arouse the curiosity of viewers and persuade them to stay tuned to the same station. Since programs and commercials form a whole, it would be a mistake to speak of commercials as interruptions. Rather, it is the absence of a commercial or of some other material – indeed, the presence of a gap – that constitutes an interruption. Programmers work to avoid 'dead air.' One need only think of the effect produced when a news clip fails to roll on cue or when the screen goes blank for a few seconds. The absence of material is an interruption; the presence of material, whether visual or verbal, creates the desired flow. Commercials, promos, and music are ways of filling up space, of suturing potential gaps.

The flow elements that exist in the spaces between programs – commercials, graphics, and voice-over promos (i.e., promises of more to come) – are also present within the news program proper, where flow has an additional role to play in meaning creation. Here, it represents the distillation of the twenty-four-hour day into reportable happenings, which are 'told' by the three news personnel roles. The roles and their recountings of the day's occurrences achieve added believability because the role incumbents are familiar to the audience. We demonstrated in Chapter 3 that a station strengthens this familiarity visually, by rendering the anchor at eye level, as though he or she were sitting in the viewer's living room. The visual link between the studio and home is further validated through the direct address and 'folksy' modes of speaking to Montreal's varied language communities. The varied modes of address signify not only familiarity with common usage, but acceptance into a particular language group. As the previous chapter demonstrated, the audiovisual syntax also orders and hierarchizes the news personnel roles themselves through the manner and the frequency of their visual appearance. Differing amounts of screen time and audiovisual renditions signal to the viewer how important the anchor, reporter, interviewer, and weather voices are in recounting daily events. The visualization techniques employed in news programs demonstrate that professional status and signification levels are systematically and complexly intertwined; at the same time, reader studies confirm that viewers 'learn' to interpret these texts.

The television news discourse creates a narrative that is intrinsically different from other narrative forms. Some of its formal characteristics are obvious, others much less so. Stories are recounted in the past tense, headlines in the present. Items are short and are presented in a linear manner, like beads on a chain. The threads that hold this narrative tapestry together are the conventions of realism, which North American viewers/readers have learned from realist novels. The language of news prose has a special relationship to the everyday world: it both frames and accomplishes discourse. In television news, this discourse creates an aura of 'actuality' rather than 'fantasy' and in that sense represents the claim of being factual. Our program segments indicate that this aura of being factual is achieved in a variety of ways. The use of the past tense for retelling stories indicates to the viewer that real time and studio time are one and the same. It establishes the present-tense retelling as an authoritative and objective statement about something that has happened and passed into the realm of the immutable. It links the anchor to the viewer, who then is encouraged to feel that he or she is participating in a public event. What is not emphasized is that this participation is more like that of a theatre audience than that of a conversation partner (Scannell, 1992: 322). It involves listening to and interpreting the retelling of the day's news stories and thus participating in a form of public life not accessible before broadcasting was introduced.

'Facticity' is further enhanced in television news programs by the station's not showing how it rearranges time and space in the interviews it presents. The viewer is thus led to believe that his or her own space, the political space, and the studio space are on one and the same continuum. Finally, photographic images respect a visual perspective that seems to put viewers behind a camera, giving them the impression that they are seeing for themselves (Tuchman, 1978: 111–13). Together, these presentational devices create the illusion that television is a neutral transduction – that it presents a 'window on the world.' The medium's continued believability is supported by the fact that viewers are usually unaware of editorial restructurings, of the visual patching of archival with other kinds of filmed material, and of the ways that anchors and reporters affect the meanings of public events through editorial lead-ins and story summaries.

The Verbal Construction of Overdetermination

Much of the early scholarship on the news failed to make clear that the creation of meaning and construction of consent require intensive ideological labour on the part of the media. Organizational research tended to subsume this labour under the rubric of 'editorial work,' because journalists themselves view it as such. Content analytical studies also failed to consider the ideological labour involved in persuasion, because the categories used in textual analysis were static and externally imposed. They failed to pick up the interactive relationships that link meaning producers with the points of view of their publics. News personnel, as we have seen, gain their persuasive capacities by speaking 'the same language' as their viewers, on both the linguistic and the ideological levels. This is possible because they and their viewers share the same 'definitions' of political situations.

The creation of overall meaning proceeds on at least three narrative levels: typification, story construction, and the assignment of roles. In the reporting of the ongoing referendum battle, the 'election as horse race' framing of the retellings selected out four topics: party standings, tactical motivations, leader characteristics, and performance criteria (Mendelsohn, 1993). Adversarial reporting heightens polarization by focusing on *oppositions* between party leaders, functions, and goals, rather than on their communalities. During the referendum debate these recurrent polarizations, as we shall see, included both visual and verbal signifying schemes, among them the following: the reds and the blues; federal versus provincial players; the YES and NO sides in the battle; and the activities of the party leaders, René Lévesque and Claude Ryan.

An examination of the news items that made up the referendum segment of the *Pulse News* program permits us to explore in greater detail how visual restructuring and editorial commentary created a context for interpreting specific political events in a 'preferred' yet seemingly 'neutral' and 'common sense' way for *Pulse* viewers. We have already mentioned that in the television news discourse, the verbal dominates the visual and is used as a meta-discourse in a variety of ways. In the four stories, the verbal meta-discourse incorporated four voices with different functions – the unseen station announcer, the anchor, the reporter, and the interviewer – as well as extra-station people such as politicians and experts, who appeared as the subjects of the reports. An anonymous off-screen voice announced the different segments and in this way functioned as the station's 'emblem,' giving it its specific tone and colour. Within the news program, the anchor's voice not only *connected* the flow of particular news items, but on the meta-level provided interpretations by commenting on the events themselves even while introducing them. This is well illustrated by the treatment of the opinion poll: The anchor first gave the main result of the poll – a small increase for the NO side, which had lost support as a result of the National Assembly debate. He then commented: '*Pulse* news managed to reach Quebec Liberal leader Claude Ryan this afternoon, and he said that the job of painting sovereignty-association as independence is having some good results, but some work still needs to be done.' The anchor stated not only what the item was, but also the effort involved in reporting it, and then went on to paraphrase its content. The reporter's voice in turn added *specific details* about the poll, which the audience recognized as a device for summarizing party standing and voter intentions. Here the reporting voice read specific poll results and noted: 'There is still great ignorance among the electorate about the referendum.' He ended: 'The recent Liberal convention and the debate in the National Assembly have probably changed all that.'

The sequencing of the four referendum stories shows that all three journalistic voices participated in constructing the meaning grid; and that the process was self-consciously reflexive, in that it melded visual interviews with the poll results, linked the place of the news program to the overall schedule of the television station, and generally worked to produce a feeling of normalcy and authoritative commentary. The news narrative thus became a tale within a tale. Everything that had happened was presented as though it were a story of that day's television programming. Within the newscast, each subevent (e.g., the poll, the leader interviews) acquired its meaning from the state of the referendum 'game' as a whole; the NO side was described as 'behind,' as documented by the poll results. Individual reporters doing interviews were framed within the flow of the newscast and did not draw attention to themselves as individuals. Since everything took place at the level of 'telling,' the 'tellers' and their story versions were in command. They not only chose the items to be reported, but also provided viewers with the election-as-'game' perspective, through which the political events they reported on became narratively fixed.

The Visual Construction of Overdetermination

Meaning creation on the visual level is secondary to the interpretive grid created by the voices of the anchor and reporters. Here, the visual element functioned in a support capacity, reinforcing the initial decision that the four disparate referendum items were to be treated as part of an ongoing story in which there would be future installments. To achieve visual coherence, the same graphics (a blue ballot box decorated with a red Maple Leaf on the left, a blue Fleur-de-Lis on the right, and a hand depositing a ballot) were used as a backdrop for all but the fourth news story – the discussion of the PQ booklet. This story was accompanied by another graphic, the PQ party symbol, which had striking similarities to the *Pulse* logo and was displayed in the same space. Both of these graphics functioned as *distillations* of political events and as party platforms. Discourse theory suggests that within both the verbal and the visual 'frames of reference' established by the voices and graphics, three levels of signification were operating here (Barthes, 1977: 19–27). On the first level, a sign stands for itself; on the second and third levels, signs and signifiers come in contact with cultural meanings. Through the graphics, the discourse (i.e., what is shown and said) and the meta-discourse (i.e., what is said about what is shown and said) converge. Graphics must be simple – that is, they contain all the important oppositions, which are validated by a given point of view. In a sense, then, they are the distillation of the news producers' and viewers' imaginary political universe.

Closer analysis of the Maple Leaf and Fleur-de-Lis graphics indicates that the red/blue colour codings were not innocent. In fact, they established a series of oppositions arising from second- and third-order significations. The blue ballot box with a red Maple Leaf on the left and a Fleur-de-Lis on the right, and with a hand depositing a ballot, signified a great variety of things. On the denotative level, the sign was self-contained, and viewers could read the graphic as a particular ballot box with decorations. In Canada, however, the Maple Leaf and Fleur-de-Lis also have second-order cultural meanings: they stand for Canada and Quebec, as symbolized by their flags. Furthermore, depending on which political world view or ideology the viewer accepted, the ballot box graphic had an additional, third-order meaning: it symbolized the NO and the YES forces, the Liberals and the Péquistes, the federalists and sovereigntists, and the English and French positions in the referendum campaign. Our analysis shows that the 'web of facticity' introduced on the news discourse's verbal level was thus reinforced by the visual signifying frameworks, which were themselves constructed in terms of recurrent isotopic oppositions. They too operated at three levels, though levels two and three of the visual signification process were generally unnoticed by viewers, because they depended for their impact on how both the signifier and the signified were valued. Obviously, these evaluations were going to differ for federalist and péquiste viewers: they were thus 'latent.' On the CFCF news program, the federalist political values were assumed to be shared by both the English-language station personnel and the viewer groups for whom it was offering programs.

It is only when these latent grids of intelligibility are ambiguous, or challenged for one reason or another, that they rise to the level of consciousness and inspire comment. This was the case with the fourth item: the coverage of the PQ booklet's publication. Here the reporter was visibly upset that the booklet was utilizing the same colour symbolism as the *Pulse* ballot box graphic, that is, red figurines to represent the federalist position and blue ones to illustrate the PQ stance. The reporter flipped open the PQ booklet so that the camera could scan the pages to show the large red stick figures representing federalist initiatives which seemed to be menacing the smaller blue ones. The reporter then made such comments as: 'TV coverage has a great impact on how the PQ is planning its campaign ... Of course, the booklet over-simplifies the federal case ... According to this, the "reds" are exploiting the "blues" ... The duplication of federal and provincial services is displayed as waste ... The apparent solution to all of these problems is equal representation.'

This sequence indicates clearly that the PQ booklet's illustrations, which also opposed red to blue as Canada to Quebec, threatened the station's implicit validation of the 'red' side as 'good.' The task of the *Pulse* reporter's meta-discourse was therefore to take hold of this other signification schema and to point out that it lacked the calm and reason of the *Pulse* web of signification. By explicitly pointing out that the PQ booklet bore values different from those of the TV station, the reporter was containing and discrediting the booklet's message. This was a very rare instance of *Pulse*'s meta-discourse alerting viewers to the PQ's alternative meaning grid (ideology). At the same time, CFCF was assuming that its viewers were in accord with its own federalist meaning framework. Thus, a latent web of signification – the colour symbolism – was used to construct a conscious signification. In this process of meaning stabilization, ideologically overdetermined interests were made to look natural and universal. They were linked to the 'common sense' ways of doing and seeing things, which were assumed to be shared by CFCF reporters and viewers. Dorothy Smith notes that such linking has the effect of making the political power features of our own society mysterious, by preventing us from recognizing them as problematic (Smith, 1974: 12). 'Ideology as contrasted with knowledge identifies ... the interested procedures which people use as a means not to know' (ibid.: 3).

The 'Leader' Focus in the 'Game' Account

The coverage of the referendum campaign and the development of patterns of intelligibility (isotopes) basically involved the semantization of the sociopolitical values of the NO and YES sides. If, after Roland Barthes (1977), we define a narrative character as a proper name or other signifier to which various units of meaning are attached, then we may view the NO and YES camps in the referendum 'battle' as primary signifiers. Additional units of meaning develop out of the various contexts in which leaders and followers are covered. Throughout the 1980 campaign these configurations of attributes, such as party standings, tactical motivations, and the 'salient' characteristics of leadership associated with the Liberal NO and PQ YES forces, developed diachronically as well as synchronically in opposition to each other. To elaborate on this, individual segments, and the programming of various channels as a whole, must be analysed. Our chapter introduction suggested that the ballot box graphic used colour and image contrasts to signify and reinforce this opposition. But the oppositional narrative went even deeper; it is also manifested in the ways in which the activities of the two leaders were recounted by the English station. The phrasing of the anchor's introduction to the NO leader's activities ('*Pulse* news managed to reach ...') suggests both a difficult accomplishment and one probably achieved by *Pulse* alone. The anchor's final phrase – 'Some work still needs to be done' – underscored that the NO side was catching up in the polls. This remark was immediately followed by the image of Liberal leader Claude Ryan, who began by saying: 'But I'm quite optimistic we'll achieve that.' The conclusion of the anchor's introduction and Ryan's opening words were thus presented as parts of a single phrase. This is a common method for establishing flow; here, it was also a means of validating the anchor's editorial introduction as factual, by presenting it in juxtaposition with Ryan's unedited statement – and by splicing the two together to form one news clip. The reporter interviewing Ryan spoke only midway through the interview and was not clearly visible until the interview was well underway. Thus, Ryan's remarks at first seemed to be directed at, or in response to, the anchor's introduction; not until part of the way through the item did the reporter replace the anchor as the newscast's representative. Such structuring heightened the ideological continuity between the station's meta-discourse and Ryan's own voice; this continuity would have been less marked if the anchor's introduction had been followed by a reporter-originated question.

Following the interview with Ryan, less significant poll results (i.e., those not related to the referendum itself) were presented by a commentator other than the previous anchor. This sequence itself was clearly bracketed: the change in voices signalled a change from actuality to 'expert,' almost academic commentary, which in this case took on a public-service air. This segment was followed immediately by coverage of Lévesque's response to the poll results. There was a nearly perfect A–B–A symmetry in this, in the sense that partisan statements were divided by a neutral analysis, 'event' stories by commentary, and the anchorperson's discourse by that of the commentator.

The coverage of Lévesque's response was introduced as follows: 'Premier René Lévesque says he hasn't had time to study the Radio-Canada poll. He refused to make any specific comment when shown the results by *Pulse*'s Bob Benedetti today in a Sherbrooke radio station ...' Lévesque then began: 'Well, the only thing I'll tell you is this ...' At one level, the introductions to the coverage of Claude Ryan and René Lévesque were similar: a reporter was dispatched and 'managed to reach' the leader. The impression given was that Ryan was tracked down and proceeded to deliver a reasoned response; whereas Lévesque was confronted with the results and did not know how to respond. In the latter case, the *confrontation* became the event covered rather than (as for Ryan) the *content* of the response.

The visual presentation reconstructed and heightened the oppositional aspects of the two interviews. It featured the Liberal leader alone, shot at eye level, in front of the *Caisse d'économie des policiers de Montréal*. The interview was thus isolated from any meaningful context, in that there was no indication provided of his reason for being there. René Lévesque, in contrast, was shot from above, surrounded by a chaotic crowd of reporters inside an unidentified radio station. Clearly he was not participating in a prearranged press conference or interview but rather in a meleé. This manner of shooting evoked the reason-emotion opposition that was recurrent throughout the referendum campaign in the coverage of Ryan and Lévesque. Here, this opposition translated into a meta-communicational juxtaposition of approval and rejection. Thus, Claude Ryan was permitted to *enact* his leader role in a *rational and collected* manner, answering questions while wearing a formal coat and hat. His adversary, meanwhile, was pictured as wild-haired and smoke-surrounded in his scrum with reporters – a situation that made him look and sound *confused and irritable*.

The station's interpretive overdetermination and implicit approval of the NO side was narratively supported by the manner in which the interviews themselves functioned as events in the construction of the news program. Ryan's interview was of interest for its content: it could easily have been presented in written form without losing any of its intelligibility. In the case of Lévesque, the 'event' did not lie in what he said (a series of challenges, quips, and refusals to speak), which resulted from a confrontation over the poll results (which he had not yet heard about), but in the situation itself. There was a subnarrative in Lévesque's confrontation with English reporters, in his attempts to escape them, and in his defensive questions as to the source of *Pulse*'s early information about the poll results. Because the intelligibility of this sequence depended on the combination of verbal and visual discourses, there were no phrases that could be isolated and meaningfully paraphrased or transcribed from the event of the interview itself. Lévesque had interpretive control wrested from him, in the sense that his responses were submerged within an audiovisual situation of confrontation – a situation that was reinterpreted as newsworthy in itself. In this case, two phenomena with radically different status as events were presented in a linear and logical sequence – that of the two leaders' responses to the opinion poll – which suggested that they were on the same level of intelligibility. In fact, as we have shown, they were not. The oppositional leader characteristics that were constructed through these interview renditions were positive for Ryan, who stood for the federal side, which anglophone and allophone Montrealers were known to support; while those of Lévesque came out negative. In the eyes of CFCF reporters and viewers/listeners, an irritable and confused man could not possibly put forward a viable political alternative.

The two interviews appeared after the poll, an event that had to be retold and interpreted within the larger opposition established between the NO and YES sides. More important, however, is that the poll was immediately reinserted into the political lives of the party leaders. Here, the TV news discourse was merely following a narrative paradigm that personalizes important events. This has been referred to as the Americanization of political discourse in Canada and Quebec. Such Americanization, however, seems not to result from Canada's geographical proximity to the United States, but rather from utilizing sport reporting conventions for electoral coverage. In sport reporting 'captains' stand for their 'teams' just as politicians stand for their parties or nations. Such a personal focus makes otherwise abstract events like party politics more intelligible, while at the same time effacing historical comprehension and replacing it with opposition. According to Bernard Roshco, such a news rendition conveys 'acquaintance with' rather than 'knowledge about' political occurrences (Roshco, 1977). Patterson's 1980 study supports the contention that the move toward the 'game' frame in election coverage is of recent origin in North America. He reports that in 1940 Paul Lazarsfeld, Bernard Berelson, and Hazel Gaudet found that about 35 per cent of American election news dealt with the fight to gain the presidency, while a substantial 50 per cent treated the subjects of policy and leadership. By 1976 these proportions had been reversed and the majority of reports were focusing on the strategic manoeuvres of the contenders (Patterson, 1980: 26). The same study also found that television news reporting, because of its shorter stories, utilized this narrative frame much more extensively than print.

Journalistic Values and Storytelling Modes

Robert Darnton notes (1975: 176) that we must know four things in order to understand how journalists function as communicators. These are the structure of their milieu, the city room; their relationship to editors, other reporters, and sources; the way they are 'broken in' as reporters; and how standardized 'storytelling' techniques influence their writing of news. As previously mentioned, North American news 'selection' theories have concerned themselves extensively with the first three but have failed to deal with the fourth. This is because 'storytelling' modes fall into the 'ritualistic' domain of communication, which deals with the creation of cultural meaning. According to Darnton, the journalist learns about this narrative domain in covering the *faits divers* (filler items): 'To turn a squeal sheet into an article requires training in perception and in manipulation of standardized images, clichés, angles, slants, and scenarios, which will call forth a conventional response in the minds of editors and readers. A clever writer imposes an old form on new matter in a way that creates some tension –

will the subject fit the predicate? – and then resolves it by falling back on the familiar ... The trick will not work if the writer deviates too far from the conceptual repertory that he shares with his public and from the techniques of tapping it that he has learned from his predecessors' (1975: 189–90). Since this ability is based on narrative modes (such as those of fairy tales and penny novels) that are usually taken for granted in a particular cultural milieu, it is understandable that most journalists are unable to describe this talent – they simply say they have a 'news sense.'

According to Herbert Gans, news values are made up of three different kinds of value judgments, which he calls journalistic importance judgments, editorial reality judgments, and reportorial views about the nature of society and leadership (or enduring values) (Gans, 1979: 280). Together, these judgments produce the interpretive framework in which journalists do their work. They specify the angles, slants, and scenarios that Darnton refers to above. Our comparisons indicate that these value clusters are useful in understanding the referendum coverage in the French and English Montreal media. Journalistic 'importance judgments' encompass four sets of considerations, which together determine what *type* of coverage an event will merit. Event classifications are grounded in four considerations: where the event fits into the governmental hierarchy; what its political impact on the nation is thought to be; how many people may be affected; and whether the event has relevance to the past or to the future of the country (1979: 153). Our comparisons suggest that the referendum was considered an important event in Canadian political history that had the potential to affect large numbers of people. It was therefore given top billing throughout the eight months leading up to the May 1980 vote, garnering hundreds of hours of coverage from a large and (as Chapter 2 indicated) often specially constituted journalism corps in the city. Furthermore, much of this coverage appeared on the front pages of Montreal newspapers (as Chapter 5 will demonstrate) and was 'bracketed' and made manifest on Montreal's television news programs. One of these stations, the privately owned CFCF, accomplished this highlighting and bracketing through recurring visual symbolism (a ballot box with flags) and through colour coding. Other stations used other symbols and imagery in order to set themselves apart in Montreal's competitive news program schedule, which encompassed ten different programs. All of these symbols were colour coded and signified the 'special' status being given to the referendum coverage.

According to Gans, 'editorial reality' judgments involve assumptions about the nation, the society, and its institutions, which constitute the environment in which news-making takes place. Many reality judgments are stereotypes, accurate or inaccurate; journalists borrow these from else-where because they are available, as well as familiar to themselves and to their viewers (1979: 201). In the case of the referendum, we have already demonstrated that early on, the CBC made the 'reality judgment' that the referendum was going to be covered as an election rather than a constitutional crisis or a struggle between federal and provincial governments. Elections and their particular coverage signify Canada's status as a democracy; also, elections are held regularly, and thus permit citizens to participate in political life in an orderly manner. We suggest here that the journalistic reality judgment that the referendum was to be covered like an election tended to underplay the 'revolutionary' and disruptive potential of a majority vote for Quebec sovereignty. This judgment implied that the outcome of the referendum would be like any other regional no-confidence vote, in which an orderly exchange of parties would occur and the incumbent party would implement its campaign promises.

Our CFCF case study corroborates that electoral coverage tends to highlight party leaders and tends to describe campaigns in sport metaphors. In a 'game' narrative, the story line and an oppositional style are more important than substance. The electoral 'game' frame, which reports gains, losses, and strategies rather than the issues on which leaders disagree, tends also to dampen audience polarization, by obscuring fundamental power and status differences in the political arena. As such, it recreates and supports a specific notion of North American politics that is based on consensus. This differs from the adversarial type of politics that in Europe grows out of the proportional-representation model of democracy. Furthermore, the narrative use of binary oppositions – for example, the 'rational' Claude Ryan and the 'emotional' René Lévesque, and the 'reds' and the 'blues' – simplifies and accentuates the electoral story line and makes the accounts of routine speeches and travel stops more interesting. It also provides a simple interpretative value grid into which all kinds of events can easily be integrated. Our referendum study additionally suggests that Gans's news judgments functioned as 'construction rules' for the referendum narrative. They helped journalists accomplish their 'interpretive labour' in a manner that was easily intelligible to their designated publics. Their narrative work helped them 'screen' what would be selected for presentation, and 'frame' how the selected events would be played. Single news stories, as we have seen, were not reconstructed in terms of any *intrinsic* merit, but in terms of how they advanced and sustained the overall referendum 'game' frame.

Gans's third and final set of 'enduring' value judgments relates to reportorial views about the nature of politics that are shared by news personnel and their particular viewer groups. In the referendum situation these amounted to a distillation of Montrealers' common-sense understandings of the major players in the referendum contest, and what this contest was *about*. Enduring values are those which are found in many news stories which endure over time. Gans points out that in the United States they include a belief in enthnocentrism, altruistic democracy, responsible capitalism, small-town pastoralism, individualism, moderation, social order, and national leadership (1979: 42). Undoubtedly, many of these values are also found among francophone and anglophone journalists in Canada. In the Canadian context, notions of politics include views about such things as the 'good' nation, the 'good' society, and 'good' leadership. Of course, these depended during the referendum on the news channel's and the audience's attachment to the 'federalist' or the 'sovereignty' cause. *Pulse's* rendition of the PQ booklet sequence was particularly eloquent in pointing out how latent political assumptions created different meaning hierarchies for anglophone and francophone news personnel. At *Pulse* the underlying judgment was that Canada represented the 'good' nation and the 'good' society. Its 'goodness' was measured by such things as its presumed tolerance for individual rights, in contrast to a sovereign Quebec's anticipated intolerance. Claude Ryan spoke Italian on more than one occasion precisely to underline Canada's tolerance of ethnic diversity; he also suggested frequently that a sovereign Quebec would not preserve civil liberties. Enduring values are included unconsciously in news judgments and therefore do not conflict with objectivity (Gans, 1979: 197). In fact, Gans argues, such values make objectivity possible. Consequently, news values can change over time, as Schudson (1978) has demonstrated. Yet for a particular historical period, as our next chapter will show, news values remain relatively stable; one result of this is to make journalists feel detached, and comfortable in the knowledge that they need not import personal values into their work.

What we have demonstrated here is that attention to the way that news 'makes sense' contributes to our understanding of the news production process in a variety of ways. To begin with, it shows that news is a discourse rather than an event. It is made up of news personnel roles, voices, and visual representation styles. During the referendum campaign all of its discourses were constructed from a point of view, because they had to make sense for Montreal's distinct viewer groups, whose political attitudes toward sovereignty-association were codified by language. The journalistic work context that shaped the referendum coverage consequently included not only peer influences and journalists' own images of their publics, but also inherited narrative techniques that had been learned in particular cultural settings. Narratives utilizing binary oppositions simplified complex political issues into two easily understandable camps: the federalists and the *indépendantistes*. These oppositions, in turn, encouraged the audience to 'see' and interpret political events from a particular point of view.

Our analysis has clarified some aspects of the tripartite sense-making processes that television news programming accomplishes through rhetorical and visualization strategies, all of which incorporate implicit value stances. Taken together, the initial importance and editorial reality judgments, and the enduring values to which Montreal's news organizations subscribed, formed a consistent view of Quebec's political world, or an ideological stance. Questions of bias must consequently be reconsidered, since they exist in the very act of narrating *any* event. Kenneth Burke (1973) argues that ideological preconceptions are the *sine qua non* of human existence. Human beings have no way of apprehending social reality except through the meanings they attach to their surroundings. These meanings are influenced by actors' status and power, by the actions they are attempting, and by the goals they are trying to achieve. Complete objectivity remains a reportorial and analytical ideal. Chapter 2 demonstrated the historical contingency of one's own discourse and the acknowledgment that stories can be narated in different ways. Together these interpretive processes sensitize the analyst to the overdetermination of mediated discourses, as well as to the interactive nature of public meaning creation. A constructivist point of view explains both the complexity and the impermanence of news discourses and thus highlights the fact that media accounts remain a 'symbolic battleground' in ethnically and socially diverse postmodern societies such as Canada.

Our analysis has also demonstrated that journalistic and audience roles must both be rethought. Journalistic roles are not passive or opaque; rather, they are powerful roles that occupy what Marshall Sahlins (1976) calls the 'synaptic' creative space shared by artists, advertisers, and market researchers. The success of news producers and personnel depends on their ability to read their audiences' perceptions accurately, through the everyday political 'knowledge' that they share with their viewers. As we have demonstrated, this shared political meaning grid defines how leaders, followers, causes, strategies, and goals of campaigns are interpreted, precisely because they are *socially* determined. During the referendum, social determinacy arose from the fact that the NO and YES viewers knew their side's party platforms, party roles, and the Canadian electoral process in which the campaign was unfolding.

The viewers' role in the signification process is also an active one. Viewers do not respond to programs like a 'tabula rasa'; rather, they are active co-constructors of public meaning creation, bringing their own pre-existing political knowledge grids into play. Processes of 'audiencing' and viewing are thus reflexive and circular. They depend both on the complex meaning potentials inherent in a text, and on the interpretive competencies of the readers/viewers who are paying attention. Reader response theorists consequently argue that audiencing behaviour cannot be 'read off' from social categories such as class, race, and gender, though these do contribute to the assessment of interpretive 'competencies' (Fiske, 1987). Rather, audiencing behaviour is a more inclusive process that takes place in many settings where textual contacts activate meanings and pleasures. Our case study suggests that during the referendum, the different interpretive competencies that viewers brought to television programs were based not on differences in individual psychology, but rather on the social relations or interpretive communities to which Montreal's linguistically diverse viewers belonged.

This chapter also corroborates reader response theorists' claims that narrative styles affect the symbolic universe through which political events and processes are explained. If the referendum had been narrated as a citizen consultation rather than as a 'game,' the boundaries of this discourse and of viewers' interpretive options would have been enlarged. Kathleen Jamieson argues that the games approach empties campaign rhetoric of substance by making it impossible to critically investigate the veracity of leader statements or to raise questions about leaders' competence to govern (1992: 166). The CFCF news program provided one illustration that though the referendum 'game' frame enabled reporters to select and unify unrelated happenings – such as poll results, PQ party publications, and leader interviews – into a coherent narrative, it failed to provide a context for discussing alternative strategies for satisfying Quebec's search for uniqueness in the Canadian federation. The implications of this for democratic political practice will be discussed further in Chapter 8.

Reception theorists have furthermore corroborated that television framings *do* affect viewer interpretations. Shanto Iyengar's controlled experiments found that television's 'episodic' narrative approach – which he defines as 'the portrayal of recurrent issues as unrelated events which just "happen"' (1991: 143) – tended to lead viewers to attribute responsibility for political outcomes to an individual's *character*, rather than to the social conditions or socio-political forces that are constantly reconstructing the realm of politics. When a *thematic* approach was used – which he defines as a focus on collective outcomes of public policy debates – viewers avoided personalizing complex issues and were better able to grasp and imagine alternative political solutions (1991: 18). If television news representations are not the actions of living persons, but *reports about their actions*, the evaluation of a leader's role and importance must be established through more than a head count that merely records mentions in news stories. To use a theatrical metaphor, it suggests that a campaign and a leader's role in it are built up and constructed through many different scenes, all of which are validated differently by viewers on different sides of the political fence. In this validation process, the concepts of 'nation' and 'people' become crucial components in contextualizing the political debate and in orienting political interpretations. It follows that we must investigate the changing rhetoric of Quebec nationalism in greater detail – a task we undertake in the next two chapters.

PART III

SITUATING THE NARRATIVE:
FRENCH/ENGLISH UNDERSTANDINGS OF
QUEBEC NATIONALISM

5

Press Interpretations: Distilling the White Paper and Beige Paper Versions of 'Nationalism'*

The previous two chapters explored how journalistic practices of visualization and the decision by media personnel to cover the referendum plebiscite as though it were a Quebec election provided Montreal viewers with a set of political frameworks which assumed that Canadian politics would continue to be played by the rules developed after the Second World War. This chapter begins to explore how these conventional assumptions came to be challenged by new notions of Quebec nationalism, which had their origins in Lesage's election victory of 1960 and the commencement of what has since become known as the Quiet Revolution (Lapalme, 1988). For the next twenty years, successive governments of different political persuasions modernized Quebec's economic and educational institutions, using the state as the motor for modernization. The *Societé général de finance-ment* (SGF) and the nationalization of key industries like electricity were to guarantee the financial resources for Quebec's economic and social development, which was spearheaded by the provincial ministries of education and cultural affairs (Desrosiers, 1993: 134–7). In the process, Gilles Gougeon asserts, the three previous versions of Quebec nationalism were transformed yet again, into what has become known as *nationalisme québécois*, which constituted the backdrop against which Claude Ryan's Liberals constructed their proposal for renewed federalism (1993: 132–9).

This chapter explores how two different versions of Quebec nationalism were conceptualized by the Parti Québécois and its Liberal rivals, and what future shapes they envisaged for the Canadian federation. We will focus on

---

* The research assistance of Daniel Downes in collecting and analysing the newspaper data for this chapter is gratefully acknowledged.

two issues: first, how the Parti Québécois White Paper and the Liberal Beige Paper conceptualized sovereignty-association and renewed federalism; and second, how journalists on Montreal's French and English newspapers covered these alternatives, and the types of rhetorical strategies they employed to convince Quebecers to choose one or the other option.

The White Paper and Beige Paper and Their Rhetorics of Nationalism

Graham Fraser, who was the Quebec correspondent for the *Globe and Mail* during the Lévesque era, observed that Quebec is a society in which language, in every sense of the word, is of enormous importance. It is no accident, therefore, that the political leaders who dominated the referendum all showed a superb command of language and generated a public discourse of exceptional quality (1984: 215). This public discourse was anchored in the two parties' platform documents. In scrutinizing these two documents, we will not only focus on how they conceptualized the province's political future, but also on the rhetorical strategies they employed to convince Montreal's varied publics to believe in one or the other option. The White Paper and Beige Paper provided a new political map for the Canadian federation. The Parti Québécois began developing its option soon after it came to power in 1976; this task was entrusted to Claude Morin, who was placed in charge of referendum strategy as a whole. This does not mean, however, that the White Paper emerged without heated debate between the more temperate and more radical factions of the party. Both wings had had varying degrees of influence in defining PQ goals during the preceding twelve years (Morin, 1991; Pinard and Hamilton, 1981). The Parti Québécois had spent the first six of these years legitimating itself and seeking representation in the National Assembly. In the 1970 election it won seven seats, in 1973 only six; then, in 1976, it won a stunning majority of 71 out of 102 seats with 40 per cent of the popular vote. Political observers attributed this victory to the party's rejection of outright secession in favour of *étapisme*, or gradualism, and to its promise to consult the electorate about independence through a referendum. Calling such a referendum in the first portion of the mandate was a calculated risk, but one worth taking, considering the enormous personal popularity of René Lévesque (Fraser, 1984: 195–8).

While the Quebec government was articulating its view of sovereignty-association, the province's Liberal Party was also at work formulating its own position on constitutional reform. The Liberals began this task by setting up a constitutional committee in April 1978, immediately after Claude Ryan was elected the new leader. The committee consisted of lawyers Louis Label and André Tremblay, with Lina Allard as co-ordinator and deputy Reed Scowan responsible for translation issues. This committee began to formulate its own platform in the fall of 1979 after engaging in twelve months of discussion and analysis with Liberal organizations across the country. The resulting Beige Paper followed a different rhetorical strategy from that of the White Paper. Instead of simply countering the Parti Québécois's White Paper arguments, it articulated a stance on constitutional reform that would become the blueprint for a federal initiative on 'reconstituted federalism.' Ryan at first took little part in the work of the committee; but the November 1979 tabling of the White Paper galvanized the one-time editor of *Le Devoir* into action. Over Christmas, he took control and wrote the opening and closing chapters, including the important statement of principles at the beginning of the document. Ryan and committee chairman Raynald Langlois jointly introduced the Beige Paper at a news conference in the new year (Fraser, 1984: 216–17).

The Parti Québécois's White Paper, titled 'D'égal à égal,' and the Liberal Party's Beige Paper, titled 'A New Canadian Federation,' were published within about two months of each other, on 2 November 1979 and 10 January 1980 respectively. Originating from opposing parties, the two documents constructed very different accounts of Quebec's political past as well as its political future. The Quebec electorate was being asked to choose between a sovereign Quebec that would be associated economically with Canada, and a reconstituted federalism in which Quebec would be given 'special status' in language and culture, as well as some powers at the time held by the federal government.

How were the two documents rhetorically constructed, and how did they generate their persuasive power? According to Teun van Dijk, rhetoric explores *how* things are said rather than *what* the messages are that are being published and distributed (1988: 78–82). The rhetorical dimensions of discourse, as strategies of persuasion, depend on a communicative partnership between those who encode and produce the message stream and those who decode it. Through persuasive strategies the speech partner is not only encouraged to *understand* what has been said, but also to *accept* the assertions as the 'truth' or at least as a possible version of the truth (van Dijk, 1988: 83). Key terms in the persuasive narratives of the White Paper and Beige Paper documents were 'the state,' 'the nation,' and 'the people.' Such terms objectify social relations and turn them into what Richard

Handler (1988: 6) calls 'bounded objects,' which like things take on properties. Nations thus come to have individual 'cultures,' 'roots,' and 'destinies,' all of which the documents and the media renditions looked at in an effort to describe and gain assent for the two versions of Quebec's political future. Part of the answer to complex questions about the media's persuasive power lies in how key terms such as 'nation' and 'people' are constructed and then inserted into particular types of persuasive discourse. Broadly speaking, the discourses of the two documents were polar opposites of each other, and used the concepts of 'boundedness' and 'autonomy' mentioned by Mary Douglas (1966) to arrive at oppositional framings. These framings were constructed around six assertions, which we have called 'canonical formulas' (see Table 5.4). This chapter's final section will demonstrate that these formulas affected the referendum agenda in a systematic manner.

Because the White Paper generated much more public attention and media coverage, we will begin with an analysis of its rhetorical thrust, and then turn to the Beige Paper for subsequent comparison. The first thing to notice is that the White Paper created a new type of national subject, the 'peuple québécois,' who were now grown up and ready to face their destiny (Charland, 1987: 134–5). These 'renamed' French Canadians, and others living in the province, had received their new designation only about a decade earlier, when the term first appeared in the founding document of the Mouvement Souveraineté-Association (MSA), which René Lévesque had organized in 1967 after leaving the Liberal Party. The designation 'Québécois' had by 1980 acquired wide currency and was being used even by Quebec federalists. With the coining of this term, the new political subjects also acquired a new national identity, the Quebec 'nation.' This nation's history was going to be presented in the White Paper as the justification for secession and for creating a new state.

To tell the story of the 'Québécois,' as the document does, is implicitly to assert the existence of a collective subject; this permits the nationalist rhetorician to impute the 'nation' as the protagonist in a historical drama, as experiencing, suffering, and controlling its own destiny. The White Paper (1979) reconceptualized the province's history as having eight periods and argued that it was during the period of Lesage that the 'nation' decided to become 'maîtres chez-nous.' The document's title, 'D'égal à égal' ('Equal to Equal'), imputes that by 1980 the 'nation' had 'come of age' and like an individual was ready to 'choose to live independently.' 'Sovereignty' in this rhetorical construction was equated with 'making a choice' and was presented as a normal stage in human and national development.

The PQ account of the early French in North America began: 'Our ances-tors put down their roots in American soil at the beginning of the seven-teenth century ... North American by geography, French by language ... this Society had a soul, a way of life, traditions that were its very own' (1979: 12). The White Paper went on to remind its readers that to be *Cana-dien français* was to be a member of an impotent minority without a proper homeland or state apparatus. Consequently, this *peuple québécois* remained subject to Canada's federal government in Ottawa – a state that was ulti-mately foreign and 'other.'

Precisely because such metaphors draw the boundaries of national exist-ence so sharply, they invite speculation about what is *not* included in national life, as well as about what is. Mary Douglas contends that a posi-tive vision of national affirmation is invariably accompanied by negative visions of 'pollution,' 'assimilation,' and 'death' (1966: 113). The rhetoric of *nationalisme québécois*, which is grounded in an ideology of individuated being, equates this being with ownership of property and choice-making. Through 'choice' the individuated being imposes itself on the external world. A nation does the same thing by choosing and acquiring a unique culture, the existence of which both follows from and proves the existence of the nation itself. To define existence in terms of boundedness and auton-omy is to structure everything outside the Québécois as the 'other.' Con-ceived in these terms, the federal government and English Canada became the 'other' because they interfered with Quebecers' choice-making.

To enter the White Paper's rhetoric is to identify with a second persona, a set of fictional beings that exist only in the realm of words. As McGee observes, a *peuple* is a fiction that comes into being when individuals agree to live within a political myth (1975: 238). The explicit explanatory strate-gies contained in the White Paper utilized what Kenneth Burke (1954) called a 'binary opposition' and a 'sacrificial principle' to develop a dra-matic theme for creating narrative order. The binary opposition classified the *peuple québécois* as the victims and the 'Canadian federal regime' as the villains, who (in the document's own words) 'favoured the legitimacy of a Canada become English.' 'It is quite natural,' the document continued, 'that in such a regime the interests and aspirations of the Québécois should take second place' (1979: 23). The document then called on the *peuple* to rise up and 'destroy' the 'dependency' under which they were living.

According to Maurice Charland, this ideological rhetoric is effective for two reasons: it exists beyond an individual person's body and life span, and it is oriented toward action (1987: 143). The text of the White Paper con-jured up dangerous memories of British conquest and rule that went beyond individual readers' historical experiences but were, by analogy, transferred to the known, Canadian federal institutions. The rhetoric of the White Paper suggested that the hold of the Canadian federal institutions had to be broken if the Québécois were to become free. The action called for in the White Paper was to vote YES for sovereignty and the creation of a new nation-state. Such action would result in narrative closure around both the notion of the 'destruction of dependence' and the realignment of the reader with the textual persona, the *peuple québécois*.

The Beige Paper (1980) developed an explanatory rhetoric oriented around a very different dramatic theme. It rejected the notion that the *Canadiens français* are defined by their subjugation by a hegemonic English majority. Instead, it pointed out that Quebec had always been a 'distinct and unique society, with all of the attributes of a national community' (1980: 10). The Beige Paper rhetoric presented the history of Quebec as one in which Canadian federalism was a positive resource. It argued that as a result of Canada, Quebec not only had the chance to develop freely, 'in accordance with its own nature,' but was also able to participate in the life of a larger social and economic system 'without renouncing its own identity.' Responding to the rhetoric of cultural nationalism, the document additionally argued that the Quebec people had not been subjugated but were in fact one of two 'founding peoples' of modern Canada. As such, they were members of a distinct cultural and (especially) linguistic community. To be a Quebecer was to be a member of a cultural group whose continued existence was best served by political participation in a larger federation. The Beige Paper's explanatory rhetoric highlighted that the White Paper's promise of 'destruction of dependence' had a cost – namely, the destruction of a country whose larger community had been an asset. It then concluded that the Québécois should 'choose Quebec AND Canada because one needs the other to fulfil itself. We [the Quebec Liberal Party] are convinced that one can, at the same time, be an authentic Quebecer and a true Canadian' (1980: 140).

French and English Press Coverage of the White Paper and Beige Paper Tablings

We have already noted that journalists play an active role in the political process, by not only transmitting but also selecting, condensing, and retelling major news events on a daily basis. It was therefore to be expected that the persuasive strategies utilized by Montreal newspapers in covering the White Paper and Beige Paper tablings would be different from those found in the documents themselves. The White Paper devoted its first three chapters (about half of its pages) to reconstructing the historical subjugation of the Quebec people since 1760; yet the journalistic recounting of the document focused on the present. Gaëtan Tremblay and Claude-Yves Charron's text-linguistic comparison of the document and its coverage discovered that Chapters 4 and 5, 'A New Deal' and 'The Referendum,' were the two major foci in the press coverage (1981: 8–10). These chapters described the proposed new 'community' institutions, such as the commission of experts, the court of justice, and the monetary union, through which equality and economic interdependence were to be guaranteed in the future. The newspapers also focused on the referendum process, and on the negotiation and implementation phases that were to follow a YES victory. Teun van Dijk explains these differences in rhetorical strategies by pointing out that the news discourse is an instance of a speech act of assertion. Such speech acts express propositions that are not yet known to the listener/reader and in so doing focus on the novel, the short-term, and the here-and-now (1988: 83).

The journalistic persuasion process in the news reports differed from the rhetorical thrust in the PQ and Liberal documents. Because of their short-term emphasis, news discourses stress the factual; they also anchor events in a larger network of other facts, which are selected for their attitudinal and emotional impact (van Dijk, 1988: 84–5). The factual nature of the journalistic discourse is enhanced through the 5W format of news writing (who, what, where, when, why), by the use of numbers to signal precision, and by direct-source quotes in situations where opinions are polarized. As Chapter 4 indicated, all of these stylistic and rhetorical features are present when events are inserted into well-known situation models and use familiar narrative scripts. The back-to-back Lévesque and Ryan interviews, with their contrasting visual renditions, illustrated this point. Regarding these encounters on the campaign trail, the interest lay not in the *facts* of their meeting, but rather in the contrasting rhetorical *manner* in which the two leaders were covered by the media. Lévesque was 'grilled' by reporter questions, while Ryan was able to respond 'rationally' to a single reporter. This demonstrates that rhetorically, the 'politics as game' metaphor not only called for antagonistic framings, but also used them to simplify the complex political challenges that both referendum alternatives were posing for Canadian federalism. Antagonistic framings add colour to otherwise routine meetings, discussions, and compromises, which are what politics is usually all about.

We undertook four types of rhetorical macroanalyses of the press reports about the White Paper and Beige Paper tablings to compare how francophone and anglophone Montreal newspapers constructed their narrative re-creations and their 'facticity' claims. Because there was only one English newspaper in the city, we chose to compare the *Gazette* with its French counterpart, *La Presse*, which has a similar broad, middle-class readership. Our analyses compared the numbers and types of reports offered by the two papers, as well as their major foci; we also considered their speaking voices and their political alignments. Van Dijk (1988) identified all of these as crucial components in pinpointing the rhetorical thrust of a news discourse. Sample periods were *all* of the six days in which there was coverage – namely, 2–4 November 1979 for the White Paper and 10–12 January 1980 for the Beige Paper. The evidence will show that though both the French- and English-language papers' editorial stances supported the NO side, their coverage and balance strategies were markedly different.

Since the White Paper and Beige Paper contained the platforms for the PQ and the Liberals in the referendum debate, they received substantial coverage. Both newspapers dealt with these documents as ongoing stories and provided coverage for three consecutive days after each was tabled. *La Presse* provided a total of eighteen articles about the two tablings, including ten on the first day. *The Gazette* had a total of twenty-eight stories, including sixteen on the first day. Three textually different types of coverage can be distinguished: regular articles, including reactions; document reprints, which we have called 'excerpts'; and articles about unrelated topics. In earlier chapters we demonstrated that various reporting techniques affect how claims to 'truth' and 'veracity' are stylistically indicated. In television discourse, eyewitness reports are most effective in signalling veracity, because they convey the 'you are there' feeling to the viewer. Newspapers can achieve a similar effect through document reprints, which constitute a unique type of 'quoting.' Regular articles in the two newspapers included descriptions of the two documents, with reactions from other political players, and document reprints, which provided selected text portions. Stories not related to the tabling events used these events to broaden the relevance of the newspaper's coverage.

Table 5.1 indicates that both papers covered the White Paper tabling slightly more extensively than the Beige Paper tabling. Out of *La Presse*'s eighteen articles, ten covered the White Paper event and eight the Beige Paper event. The *Gazette*'s twenty-eight articles divided into sixteen devoted to the White Paper and twelve to the Beige Paper. In both newspapers there were related articles that expanded the narrative context in which the tabling events were discussed. Because *La Presse* addressed a francophone readership with varying political leanings, it offered only one

TABLE 5.1
Stories devoted to the White Paper and Beige Paper tablings in the *Gazette* and
La Presse, 2–4 November 1979 and 10–12 January 1980 (number of stories and space
percentage)

Story type	No. of stories		Space (col/in)		% Total	
	White Paper	Beige Paper	White Paper	Beige Paper	White Paper	Beige Paper
The *Gazette*						
Article	6	6	81	93	14	15
Excerpts	6	5	202	172	33	28
Related	4	1	60	12	9	2
Totals	16	12	343	277	56	44
Overall	28		620		100	
La Presse						
Article	3	6	43	81	3	5
Excerpts	6	2	794	730	47	44
Related	1		25		1	
Totals	10	8	862	811	51	49
Overall	18		1673		100	

unrelated article: an account of the death of Pierre Maheu, who would have been the White Paper's principal author, had he not died earlier in the year. One can surmise that the focus of the coverage was kept narrow to reduce the chances of offending any of the reader groups, whose political leanings varied. The *Gazette*, in contrast, expanded its narrative context by offering five related articles. These included a report on the civil service strike that disrupted the White Paper tabling, a short item about Prime Minister Pierre Trudeau's pique at being distracted by a sound technician during his press conference, and a set of proposals presented to the Quebec government by an anglophone rights group that discussed the civil rights implications of the document. The English-language paper could risk topic expansion because it knew that its readership was politically homogeneous and overwhelmingly against the sovereignty-association option.

Table 5.1 additionally indicates that both papers devoted a considerable amount of their total coverage space to document excerpts and summaries (as opposed to interpretive articles). *La Presse*'s six document excerpts took up 47 per cent of the total editorial space devoted to the White Paper tabling. Furthermore, these excerpts were highlighted by being provided as a tabloid insert that completely reprinted sections 4 and 5 of the document. For the Beige Paper tabling, a similar strategy was used: two excerpts took up 44 per cent of the paper's total coverage. The *Gazette* also used text excerpts to legitimate the 'neutrality' of its reporting practices; however, it gave itself more interpretive freedom. The paper produced six text excerpts from the White Paper and five from the Beige Paper; together, these took up 34 per cent and 26 per cent respectively of the total coverage space. This indicates that while both papers constructed balance stylistically in terms of two criteria – a *mix* of articles, and *document reprints* – La Presse utilized the latter almost exclusively so that only 9 per cent of its total editorial space was available for reports about the tabling events. In contrast, the *Gazette* retained about 40 per cent of its editorial space for such reporting. This substantial difference suggests that reprints were a 'safe' way for the francophone paper to provide its politically differentiated reader groups with relevant information. Because different article *types* convey different attitudes of the writer to the subject matter, it can be argued that document reprints are *read* differently, since they stand outside the journalistic signification system. They call on citizens/readers to bring their own political interpretations to bear on the material and to make up their own minds without journalistic mediation.

A second way of comparing the two papers' differing coverage strategies is to compare the story sources or voices selected to speak for the respective documents. These voices confirmed the veracity of the texts, and also suggested the political leanings of the two newspapers in the referendum debate. We assumed that YES and NO spokespersons would be speaking in favour of their own documents, in order to ensure the most sympathetic renditions of their respective platforms. For this reason we grouped stories into three classifications: First, stories with a YES camp focus, which included all those in which the views of the YES campaign were expressed and their spokespersons featured. These included YES campaign reactions to the tabling of the documents, stories featuring YES campaign issues, and news analyses of the White Paper's contents. Second, stories focusing on the NO camp. These included reactions to the Beige Paper tabling, comments by NO campaign members, and analyses of the Beige Paper's contents. Third, stories that were neutral in the sense that either no sources were quoted, or these sources were balanced between the YES and NO camps.

Table 5.2 indicates, surprisingly, that both newspapers selected Liberal (NO) sources to speak about the White Paper tabling. It must be assumed

TABLE 5.2
Story sources for the White Paper and Beige Paper coverage in the *Gazette* and
La Presse, 2–4 November 1979 and 10–12 January 1980 (number of stories)

Story Type	*Gazette* Story sources				*La Presse* Story sources			
	No.	YES	NO	Neut	No.	YES	NO	Neut
White Paper								
Stories	6	1	5	—	3	—	3	—
Excerpts	6	—	—	6	6	—	—	6
Related	4	1	2	1	1	—	1	—
Totals	16	2	7	7	10	—	4	6
Beige Paper								
Stories	6	1	5	—	6	1	5	—
Excerpts	5	—	—	5	2	—	—	2
Related	1	—	1	—	—	—	—	—
Totals	12	1	6	5	8	1	5	2

that these spokespersons were ideologically against the document. In *La Presse* all three stories, plus the related story about the civil service strike, were told from the NO side's point of view, while the six excerpts, as we have seen, were reprinted without comment. Regarding the *Gazette*'s six stories and four related accounts, only two sources were from the YES side. The two YES voices featured were those of René Lévesque and Claude Morin. The remaining six reports all featured NO sources. Only one report was neutrally balanced with a spokesperson from each camp featured. As expected, both newspapers' Beige Paper reconstructions called on NO side spokespersons to explain the 'renewed federalism' option. These persons included Claude Ryan, Joe Clark (whose party fell from federal power in February 1980), premiers from English Canada, prominent federal Liberals including Jean Chrétien, and business leaders in Montreal, Toronto, and New York. In the *Gazette*, furthermore, the one related story featured a PQ point of view – Claude Morin's criticism of the Beige Paper document. *La Presse* provided no related stories on the topic of the Beige Paper tabling.

Such double-contextualization, with the NO voices clearly in command of both document reconstructions, smacked of ideological one-sidedness on the part of both newspapers. They had *stylistically* observed interpretative balance by featuring documents without commentary; yet their ideo-

TABLE 5.3
Tone of the White Paper and Beige Paper coverage in the *Gazette* and
La Presse, 2–4 November 1979 and 10–12 January 1980 (number of stories)

Story type	Gazette Story tone				La Presse Story tone			
	No.	Pos	Neg	Neut	No.	Pos	Neg	Neut
White Paper								
Stories	6	—	5	1	3	—	3	—
Excerpts	6	—	2	4	6	—	—	6
Related	4	—	4	—	1	—	—	1
Totals	16	—	11	5	10	—	3	7
Beige Paper								
Stories	6	5	1	—	6	5	1	—
Excerpts	5	1	—	4	2	—	—	2
Related	1	—	1	—	—	—	—	—
Totals	12	7	2	4	8	5	1	2

logical predispositions were obvious in two ways. The first related to the organizational level: both newspapers declared their support for the NO side at the beginning of the campaign and thereby signalled their scepticism for the PQ project. The second related to the journalistic level: both papers chose more Liberal than PQ voices to speak for *both* of the contending documents. Together, these practices did much to foster a more negative tone in the White Paper coverage, even while satisfying the balance and neutrality criteria of responsible journalism. Gaye Tuchman (1972) may well be incorrect in describing 'objectivity' as *merely* a 'strategic' ritual. Depending on the types of quoting practices followed, objectivity can also function as an interpretive device that *conveys* negativity.

This will become evident in our comparative analysis of the two newspapers' coverage in terms of their evaluative 'tone.' This tone could be positive or negative – that is, favourable or unfavourable to the document in question. Alternatively, it could be neutrally balanced between the two documents. Table 5.3 demonstrates that both the *Gazette* and *La Presse* utilized an overwhelmingly negative tone in their White Paper coverage. Of *La Presse*'s four stories, three utilized a negative tone and only one was neutral. Since the paper selected its spokespersons mostly from the Liberal camp, it was these sources who predisposed the paper to its mainly negative coverage. Of the *Gazette*'s ten news stories, nine were written from a point of view against the document; even the six document excerpts included two negative renditions. The negative tone was achieved mainly through headlines such as FIRST REACTION: PQ'S 'NEW DEAL' MEANS OUTRIGHT INDEPENDENCE, and through statements made in the document summaries. The paper declared, among other things, that the White Paper represented no dramatic changes from PQ policy and expanded little on Lévesque's 'vague outline' for change (the *Gazette*, 2 November 1979: 1). Nova Scotia's premier John Buchanan, was quoted as saying that the White Paper was simply 'a rehash of Parti Québécois statements over the past number of years' (the *Gazette*, 2 November 1979).

In contrast, the two papers' Beige Paper coverage overwhelmingly used a positive tone. Five of the eight stories in *La Presse* and seven of the twelve stories in the *Gazette* were supportive of the document. The language used in reports was that the Beige Paper provided 'reform English Canada can grasp.' There were references to the 'reasonableness' of the document's proposals, and to its 'positive' outlook. When introducing the Liberal proposals, the *Gazette* identified the text with its architect, Liberal leader Claude Ryan, both in the headlines and in the narrative reconstructions. Peter Cowan of Southam News commented: 'Claude Ryan's eminently reasonable constitutional reform proposals are a firm reminder to English Canada that it has a choice between negotiating with Quebec, or breaking up the country ... Just as the White Paper supplies the ammunition to supporters of the Yes vote, so Ryan's document will provide the philosophical underpinning for the federalist cause ... (the *Gazette*, 10 January 1980: 1, 6). In general, the *Gazette* supported the Beige Paper proposals on the grounds that its ideas were 'attractive and workable' (the *Gazette*, 10 January 1980: 6). Set against Premier Lévesque, Ryan was presented as a leader in contact with the rest of the country. 'He and his followers,' wrote the *Gazette*, 'have consulted political leaders across the country' (the *Gazette*, 10 January 1980: 6). Only two of the *Gazette's* stories employed a negative tone, chastising the Liberals for not being as articulate as the NO side and criticizing Prime Minister Trudeau's distrustful attitude toward Claude Ryan.

What conclusions can be drawn about the *Gazette's* and *La Presse's* different coverage strategies and about the divergent ways in which their coverage was legitimated as 'authoritative' and 'neutral'? Barbie Zelizer provides some important clues to answering this question by noting that all journalistic writing is based on quoting practices. Through quotes, 'the journalist is able to separate ideas from their contexts of utterance and reincorporate them within new ideologically specified contexts without having to take an overt stance' (1989: 384). Furthermore, quoting practices are not uniform, but rather constitute a mode of address that can be tailored to different reader groups (1989: 382). In the 1980 Quebec referendum the *Gazette* was addressing a relatively politically homogeneous anglophone and allophone audience that was against the sovereignty-association option, whereas *La Presse* had to satisfy a readership with divided political loyalties that spanned the YES, the NO, and the uncommitted sides. The *Gazette*, as we have demonstrated, utilized three rhetorical strategies, some of which differed markedly from those in the French newspaper. To begin with, it made extensive use of news-maker statements to argue the NO side position. Sources referenced were other provincial premiers as well as the federal prime minister, Joe Clark. The paper furthermore selected the same English-Canadian spokespersons to comment on the PQ's White Paper as it did for the Liberals' Beige Paper. In addition, the *Gazette* placed the two tabling events in an expanded relevance structure, interviewing local, national, and international business communities about the economic implications of the sovereignty-association option. A legitimation strategy that overwhelmingly employs the statements of spokespersons is called by Zelizer an 'oral' strategy because it converts the basically written convention of a text's publication (the tabling events) into an act of retelling that is primarily oral (1989: 381). This focus on individual voices to legitimate its coverage differed sharply from the one employed by *La Presse*.

To negotiate its readers' multiple political affiliations, *La Presse* followed a different rhetorical strategy. Recall that this newspaper devoted an amazing 94 per cent of its total coverage space to document excerpts and only 6 per cent to interpretive articles. Such a quoting practice placed the White Paper and Beige Paper statements outside the journalistic narrative and denied them generalizability beyond the specific instances in which they were uttered. In such a stylistic setting, journalistic voices can remain mute behind the document texts and signify their neutrality by *not* commenting. Yet in the few reports that were published about the two tabling events, *La Presse* followed the same legitimation practices as the *Gazette*. It used sympathetic spokespersons to comment on the two tablings and because of their political leanings, these spokespersons introduced a negative slant on the White Paper and a positive one on the Beige Paper. According to Zelizer (1989), reproducing extensive document portions without comment constitutes a rhetorical strategy that legitimates the neutrality of coverage by the very act of publication. Yves Gagnon (1980: 175) chastised *La Presse* for its document reproduction strategy, arguing that it resulted in a situation of 'anti-communication' for the francophone readership, because it would have taken five hours daily for readers to wend their way through the proffered material. We agree with Gagnon that the strategy of 'relaying' the two documents offered extensive interpretive freedom to the paper's various reader groups, but made this freedom contingent on a great deal of reader involvement. Gagnon, however, failed to note that such a quoting strategy is perfectly legitimate *stylistically*, because it maintains journalistic norms. By limiting their interpretive articles to ten out of eighteen for both events, *La Presse* journalists were able to assert their interpretive authority by covering the important tabling events, even while detaching themselves from the *content* of the documents themselves.

The above comparison indicates that quoting practices are rhetorical devices, and are important to journalists because they are among the few presentational devices that directly reflect a vital news-gathering task – that of 'sourcing.' It is no surprise, then, that journalists use quotes to lend authority to the stories they tell. For journalists, quoting practices become the framing devices which determine what is relevant to the reconstruction of news events. Articulation of these boundaries is intricately and reflexively related to reader understandings. We have shown that in regard to the tabling events, journalists relied strongly on speaker referencing to make their news stories intelligible to Montreal's various reader groups. In the reporting of both document tablings, the speaker references in both *La Presse* and *The Gazette* were to the same group of provincial Liberal and English-Canadian politicians, all of whom favoured the NO side in the referendum battle. Through their framings and their quoting practices, the newspapers set up what Tuchman (1978) calls a 'web of self-validating facts' that guaranteed the 'truthfulness' of the journalistic reconstructions by creating the illusion of a signifying whole. In Zelizer's view, quoting thus has as much to do with legitimating journalistic practice, as it does with relaying information to audiences (1989: 374). The different quoting practices of *La Presse* and *The Gazette* suggest that quoting is a form of 'saying' – that is, part of the rhetorical arsenal through which readers are persuaded. Through quoting practices, the material is recontextualized and reinserted into ideologically specific contexts. Quotes, whether they are paraphrased, incorporated in the text, or presented in an indirect voice, provide journalists with a way of addressing simultaneously what they perceive to be different reader groups (1989: 384). In the next chapter we will explore how this persuasion process is accomplished in the television medium.

The Rhetorical Structure of the White Paper and Beige Paper Coverage

The struggle between the PQ and the Liberals over the meaning of Quebec's future was evident not only in the unique ways in which *La Presse* and the *Gazette* selected and reinterpreted the two platform documents for their respective francophone and anglophone audiences, but also in the manner in which the rhetorical thrust was articulated. According to Kenneth Burke (1954), 'sacrificial principles' create narrative order and develop a dramatic theme. For the PQ White Paper, this narrative principle could be summarized as 'the destruction of dependence,' while for the Liberal Beige Paper it was 'the destruction of the country.' Table 5.4 indicates that these narrative frames were argued through a very restricted repertoire of only six propositions, or 'canonical formulas.' The same table also demonstrates that these canonical formulas were constructed as mirror images of each other, thereby conforming to the Manichean oppositional approach, which previous chapters have isolated as an important stylistic aspect of campaign reporting. It shows as well that the canonical formulas sharply curtailed *how* the PQ and Liberal visions of the province's future could be talked about. We will use the front-page coverage of the White Paper and Beige Paper tabling events in *La Presse* and the *Gazette* to demonstrate how canonical formulas were used as a *rhetorical frame* by both newspapers.

We will also explore in greater detail how the negative tone that was generated by selecting mainly NO voices to speak about both document tablings, was reinforced stylistically through journalistic quoting practices. According to Barbie Zelizer (1989) there are five types of quoting practices in journalistic writing, each of which conveys a different level of authority or believability to the voice making the claims. Among these are accounts that (a) use the direct voice of quotees, (b) place the direct voice of quotees into the reporter's text, (c) permit the reporter to talk in the quotee's words, (d) use quotes from other sources (media) to legitimate the account, and (e) use no quotes of political actors at all to reconstruct an event (1989: 375). In this hierarchy the reporter's power to influence meaning creation is in inverse order to the above listing; thus, the reporter has the most interpretive freedom in case (e), where no actor quotes at all are used to retell an event. Our front-page story comparisons of the *La Presse* and *Gazette* accounts of the two tabling events indicate that most of these accounts were rendered in the (c) and (e) modes, in which reporter voices have the greatest interpretive freedom. This ascendancy of the journalistic voices is reinforced by three further narrative implications of quotes: first, quotes blur who the *real* speaker is; second, the voices of quotees are usually not allowed to stand by themselves; and third, the voices of quotees are additionally contextualized through print-specific practices such as blocks,

TABLE 5.4

The canonical formulas underlying the White Paper and Beige Paper argumentation strategies

White Paper arguments	Beige Paper arguments
1. Quebec is more than a province: Quebecers are culturally distinct and should be recognized as a nation equal to the English Canadians.	1. Quebecers do not constitute a national group: Quebec is a province among others, Quebecers an ethnic group among others.
2. Historically, the Québécois are an oppressed people whose aspirations can best be met by (political) sovereignty and (economic) association.	2. The view of Quebecers as oppressed is based on a distorted view of history. Quebec's aspirations can best be met within a renewed Canadian federalism.
3. Since no federation can, by definition, allow a sovereign nation with its accompanying privileges to exist within its borders, renewed federalism simply maintains the status quo.	3. The combination of sovereignty and association amounts to a form of federalism. The rejection of federalism consequently means separation.
4. Sovereignty and association are inseparable; one can and should have both.	4. Sovereignty and association are mutually exclusive attributes; one cannot have both.
5. A NO vote will take away Quebec's leverage in its struggle for change; a YES vote will give it leverage in this struggle.	5. A YES vote will alienate the rest of Canada and lead to an uncertain future depending on the outcome of sovereignty-association negotiations: a NO will guarantee positive change within renewed federalism.
6. The NO side is deliberately trying to present an (as yet uncertain) renewed federalism as a qualitative change.	6. The YES side is deliberately trying to play down the real impact of sovereignty by emphasizing an (as yet uncertain) association with Canada.

boxes, and headlines. We will now illustrate each of these narrative implications.

The first set of propositions in Table 5.4 illustrates the construction of the 'Québécois' as a new rhetorical subject who, because of their cultural distinctiveness, have 'nation' status (White Paper, 1979: 23). In discussing this new nation, reporters from both *La Presse* and the *Gazette* used their own voices to frame the documents, thereby keeping control over how meaning was created. The belief that Quebec is a nation was most explicitly expressed in Louis Falardeau's article, headlined LE LIVRE BLANC SUR LA SOU-VERAINETÉ. Speaking in his own voice (e), Falardeau described the White Paper's notion of the Quebec of the future: 'Un pays pleinement souverain, mais très étroitement lié au Canada dans le but de préserver un espace économique commun: voilà le Québec que le gouvernement Lévesque propose aux Québécois dans le Livre blanc' (*La Presse*, 2 November 1979: 1). Graham Fraser used the same narrative strategy in his article, headlined PQ SPELLS OUT ITS 'NEW DEAL'. He commented: 'Some of the difficulties in combining political sovereignty and economic association became clearer yesterday, as Premier René Lévesque presented his goals for Quebec's future to the National Assembly ... According to the PQ White paper, the province would become a country with a seat at the United Nations, but would not have its own currency (the *Gazette*, 2 November 1979: 1).

The oppositional canonical formula countering the PQ's claim that Quebec is a 'nation' was offered in the Beige Paper, which argued that while Quebec was a distinct society whose rights must be protected, the guarantee of such rights 'must not contradict the fundamental principle that all the cultural partners within the federation are fundamentally equal' (Beige Paper, 1980: 22). Ryan, speaking in his own voice, was quoted (b) as follows: 'Quebec sees itself and expresses itself as a society which is French in language and in spirit ... Within the Canadian political family, Quebec society has all the characteristics of a distinct national community' (the *Gazette*, 10 January 1980: 6). While Lévesque's White Paper was described through the reporters' voices in both the francophone and the anglophone newspapers, Ryan was allowed to render the Beige Paper meaning in his own words, which were directly quoted in the *Gazette*. This signified that the Liberal leader had the authority to interpret his own platform, and also conferred a more positive tone on the coverage.

The second set of canonical formulas hinges on the particular interpretation of the relationship between the terms 'nation' and 'people.' In this rare case a YES voice was quoted directly (b), but the headline negated its authority: MORIN BRANDS IT ALL 'TANGLED FEDERALISM'. In the article that followed, Michel Auger then wrote: 'Morin said: "the Liberal proposals would make permanent the fundamental inequality the present regime imposes upon the Quebec people"' (the *Gazette*, 10 January 1980: 1). The PQ's solution to the oppression of the Quebec people was to establish a separate homeland. Ignoring the subject of the PQ narrative, the *Gazette*'s Hubert Bauch let Ryan contest these assertions directly by quoting him (b). His article, A HOUSE OF CARDS – RYAN was introduced in the following manner:

'Opposition leader Claude Ryan yesterday said "the entire sovereignty-association premise is based on a biased and distorted view of Canadian history"' (the *Gazette*, 2 November 1979: 1). *La Presse*'s bureau chief followed a slightly different quoting strategy, using Ryan's words without directly quoting him (c). This gave Ryan's interpretation less authority than if he had been quoted directly. 'Selon le chef du Parti libéral, M. Claude Ryan, le Livre blanc confirme ses appréhensions quant aux intentions véritables du gouvernement qui veut avant tout réaliser l'indépendance ... Il déplore de plus que le document soit basé sur une analyse faussée et biaisé du fédéralisme canadien' (*La Presse*, 2 November 1979: A19).

The third and fourth pairs of canonical formulas addressed the perceived contradiction between the rights of a Quebec government and the powers of a central Canadian government. The White Paper argued that 'the Quebec government has always faced a dilemma: either give in to the trend towards centralization inherent in the Canadian federal system, or uphold at any cost the exercise of its constitutional rights, despite federal intrusions' (1979: 24). The White Paper concluded that 'no version of federalism' will be adequate for Quebec. *La Presse*'s Lysiane Gagnon paraphrased (e) Lévesque's conclusion in the following way: 'Affirmant qu'il s'agissait là d'un véritable "cadeau du ciel", le premier ministre Lévesque s'est livré à une virulente critique des positions constitutionnelles du chef libéral Claude Ryan, l'accusant de faire passer les intérêts du Canada avant ceux du Québec et de vouloir faire du Québec une province comme les autres' (*La Presse*, 12 January 1980: C11). Peter Cowan's article, headlined FEDERAL COUNCIL KEY TO SUCCESS OF PLAN: RYAN, permitted Ryan to explain his plan in his own words (b): '"The success of the Quebec Liberal party's proposals for a new Canada hinges on Canada-wide acceptance of the proposed Federal Council," Party Leader Claude Ryan said yesterday ... The Liberals want to abolish the Senate and replace it with a council comprised of provincial representatives having the power to ratify or veto certain House of Commons measures' (the *Gazette*, 11 January 1980: 4).

The fifth set of canonical formulas was found mainly in the White Paper coverage and interpreted the effects that a YES or a NO vote would have on Quebec's future. Peter Cowan's article, PQ DOCUMENT ATTACKS DEADLOCK IN FEDERATION, narrated (e) the document's implications from the writer's own point of view: 'A major objective of the Quebec government's White paper is to convince Quebecers no substantial reform to the federal system is possible. The 120-page document, entitled "Quebec-Canada: New Deal" builds a case for a "yes" vote in next spring's referendum on sovereignty-association – meaning an independent Quebec in a common market and monetary union with Canada' (the *Gazette*, 2 November 1979: A1). Lysiane Gagnon used the same commentary (e) style in her REPRISE DES THÈMES DE LA CAMPAGNE DU 'OUI', noting: 'Le Livre blanc reprend méthodiquement les principaux thèmes qui se dégagent déjà de la campagne réferendaire du "oui" – et qu'on retrouve notamment dans les discours du premier ministre Lévesque: la continuité par rapport aux revendications des gouvernements antérieurs, le danger que représenterait un "non" majoritaire au réferendum, la fierté, la compétence, la scolarisation acquises ces dernières années, les richesses objectives dont dispose le Québec ...' (*La Presse*, 2 November 1979: A18). While the argument in the *Gazette* placed the White Paper in the context of past constitutional debates and thus tinged its arguments negatively for its readers, the coverage in *La Presse* utilized Quebec's accomplishments during the Quiet Revolution as its context. It thus offered its polarized readers a variety of ways to evaluate the document, both positively and negatively.

The last set of canonical formulas summarized the essence of the rhetorical attacks that both sides hurled at each other throughout the campaign. In them, each side accused the other of ideological manoeuvring. In its summary arguments, the *Gazette*'s unique quoting practices, which permitted Ryan but not Lévesque to speak in his own voice, were particularly obvious. Hubert Bauch noted that Ryan called the White Paper 'thinly disguised separatism on a shaky foundation' (the *Gazette*, 2 November 1979: 1). Ian Anderson dismissed the White Paper by asking an aide to Joe Clark, 'What's new in the report?' and then quoting his answer: 'It's more or less what we've been hearing for the past couple of years.' Both of these examples indicate that the thrust of the NO attack was to argue that the White Paper was ideological and poorly thought out, and that its intent was to sell separation under the less threatening guise of sovereignty-association. Lévesque himself was presented as a weak leader. An ironic tone prevailed when Joel Ruimy used Levesque's own words against him while reporting on the National Assembly's reaction to the White Paper tabling: '"Opposition parties in the National Assembly should read the government's White paper on sovereignty-association before attacking it," Premier Levesque said yesterday' (the *Gazette*, 2 November 1979: 12).

The YES side's attacks were no less vehement and personal. In Michel Auger's report, Claude Morin's own voice was used to deride the Beige Paper as 'tangled federalism [which] serves only to mask the status quo' (the *Gazette*, 10 January 1980: 1). Yet in the *Gazette*'s coverage as a whole, the *indépendantiste* voices of the YES campaign were vastly outnumbered by the combined voices of the NO side; not only that, but the authority of their voices was subverted through journalistic quoting practices. *La Presse* quoted Pierre Trudeau approving of the Ryan project: 'Les propositions constitutionelles formulées par son homologue québécois M. Claude Ryan constituent "une base de discussion extrêmement sérieuse"' (*La Presse*, 10 January 1980: A9). Overall, the coverage praised the Liberals for their 'non-revolutionary' and 'comprehensive' agenda for constitutional change. The Beige Paper was, for both the NO campaign and for the Montreal press, 'a useful basis for a sober, statesmanlike discussion' (the *Gazette*, 10 January 1980: 7). These interpretive polarizations echoed and reinforced the visual polarizations established in the CFCF interviews with the stolid Ryan and the dishevelled Lévesque (see Chapter 4). The reportorial reconstructions of the two newspapers show that overall, the eight front-page articles covering the White Paper tabling were more highly mediated than the six Beige Paper reports. Four of the former were rendered as pure reporter narration, two made use of quotees (c) without acknowledgement, and one each used other sources or a direct actor quote to establish veracity. In contrast, the six Beige Paper reports paraphrased (e) only Morin's critique, and quoted only one outside source (d). Generally, in most of the reports on the two tablings, Ryan was permitted to set the interpretive agenda himself (b).

Legitimation Strategies

Zelizer's (1989) characterization of journalistic discourse as one that incorporates a variety of quoting practices enables us to explain two previously unexplained rhetorical phenomena. The first addresses how newspapers construct the stylistic balance that audiences read as 'objective' coverage of a political event. The second deals with how two discourses with the same content can be made to appeal to audiences with very different political points of view. The foregoing comparisons indicate that *La Presse* used a 'documentary' and the *Gazette* an 'oral' approach to constructing balance. The *Gazette*'s oral approach reconstructed the White Paper and Beige Paper tablings as orchestrated choruses in what Yves Gagnon called 'a very aggressive and polarizing debate against Québécois nationalism' (1980: 180). This news chorus, with voices selected predominantly from the NO side, informed anglophone and allophone readers that the referendum was not an election like all others, but rather an event of crucial importance to Canada's federal survival. To legitimate its rhetorical thrust, the *Gazette* quoted provincial and federal politicians individually, as well as representatives of American financial markets. Because these voices were presented as *quotes* taken from other legitimate news sources, the fact that they favoured the NO over the YES side in no way invalidated the paper's stylistic claims to neutral coverage.

Gagnon's comparative study also found that in making its pitch, the *Gazette*'s narrative repertoire was much more variegated than that of *La Presse* and other French papers. It featured interviews, polls, and unrelated news stories, all of which served to enlarge the 'relevance structures' and thus the political discussion agendas in terms of which English-speaking readers were able to assess the referendum debate. Most of these stories were of the human interest variety, such as James Quig's series, 'The Anglophones.' According to Gagnon, the *Gazette* attempted to recreate the texture of everyday life and to address people's concerns in colourful and easy-to-comprehend language – an approach not attempted by any of the French-language papers (1980: 176).

La Presse, as we have seen, faced a much more difficult task in constructing its stylistically balanced accounts, because these had to satisfy the neutrality expectations of a politically trisected readership. How could the paper satisfy the information needs of francophone readers who were in favour of the YES platform, while at the same time speaking to those who were politically neutral or on the NO side? To reduce political discord, *La Presse* opted for redefining the extraordinary referendum as an ordinary election, and focused mainly on recording the official views of the parties and party leaders as presented in the National Assembly. Such a framing, as we have demonstrated, led *La Presse* to legitimate its journalistic discourse by quoting published documents with a minimum of commentary. This strategy offered the various reader groups an opportunity to come to their own interpretative conclusions about the evidence. The rhetorical strategies, consequently, seemed distant and cerebral and seemed to be addressed mainly to the intellectual élite rather than to the general public (Gagnon, 1980: 180). Gagnon's comparison of all French-language Montreal dailies found that none of the papers addressed the daily concerns of their mass readership or followed up on the political implications of a vote for secession or for federalism. Furthermore, their focus on the francophone majority led them to overlook the interests of anglophones and immigrants, and this added credence to the accusations of ethnocentrism that were levelled against them, as well against the Parti Québécois campaign (1980: 177–8).

Zelizer's (1989) analysis of journalistic quoting practices sheds light on a second issue: how discourses with the same content features are able to appeal to audiences with different political points of view. We have demonstrated that quoting practices facilitate multiple sense-making strategies by blurring distinctions between speakers and readers. These blurrings affect time and place, as well as the status of the voices that are given interpretive authority in the text. Zelizer observes that in the news discourse, 'quotes bring together discourses of "now" with discourses of "before." They blur the distinction between present and prior speakers and present and prior authorities. They merge distinctions about the dialogue which functions as authority and the authority which functions as dialogue. Quotations thereby provide metaphorical resting places for speaker voices, primarily those of journalists, who can choose which kinds of spatial and temporal junctures to bring to the discourse' (1989: 371).

La Presse's 'documentary' strategy offers a excellent example of how quoting strategies provide a 'metaphorical resting place' for the journalistic speakers. It demonstrates how the active meaning-making power of journalistic voices is hidden by having the White Paper and Beige Paper seemingly speak for themselves. Thus, even though *La Presse*'s coverage, like that of the *Gazette*, overwhelmingly featured NO-side speakers, this was not immediately evident to readers, because the three polarized francophone reader groups were able to *personally choose* to pay attention only to those text portions that were congruent with their political beliefs. *La Presse*'s strategy of publication *without overt commentaries* on the documents' contents thus hid the paper's editorial commitment to the NO side in such a way that the 'neutrality' taboo was not seen to be broken.

A number of important conclusions about text/reader relationships emerge from Zelizer's discovery that quoting practices are hierarchically nested, giving journalistic voices control over the news discourse. The different quoting practices in the two papers demonstrated that journalists played an active role in the narrative struggle for public-meaning creation about the referendum. They co-constructed their political discourses with the provincial political parties not as equal partners, but as dominant rhetorical leaders. Our comparative analysis furthermore shows that different types of quoting practices attract and construct different types of reader predispositions. This was particularly evident in *La Presse*'s 'documentary' quoting strategy, which permitted all three types of francophone audiences to select their own mix of White Paper and Beige Paper material for interpretive work.

In the process of publication, the much richer PQ and Liberal documents with their complex argumentation strategies thus underwent a 'reduction' in meaning. There has been continued debate about this process in the literature on democracy. We will join this debate in Chapter 8. For the moment, it is important to note that the canonical formulas demonstrate that Montreal's press prepared two very different political maps for francophone and anglophone readers to understand the referendum options. Yet because these meta-meanings were grounded in the pre-existing political discourses of *nationalisme québécois* and *federal reconstruction* respectively, it was possible for the proffered interpretive maps to take on *opposite* political meanings without explicit acknowledgment. All Montreal readers could use these maps to construct their own positions on the political continuum between the YES and NO sides. The canonical formulas, as the political distillations of the YES and NO side arguments, began to structure the referendum debate as a whole – a process that began with the tabling of the docments and continued right up to the referendum vote on 20 May 1980. In this process the binary and oppositional 'election as game' narrative, which we documented in Chapter 4, was provided with two different political meta-framings into which future occurrences like the 'Yvettes' event could easily be incorporated without any change in the rhetorical thrust. More generally, this chapter has demonstrated that news discourses are structured ways of speaking about public issues that have developed different persuasive traditions in print and in broadcasting. We will explore these traditions in greater detail in the next chapter, which compares how the White Paper tabling was narrated by Montreal's French and English television stations.

6
Interpreting the White Paper on Television

Previous chapters showed that journalists and the media organizations for which they work are active rather than passive participants in the political process. They not only 'record' public events, but also select them and shape the ways in which they will be talked about. Journalists create the very categories in terms of which public events are made known. According to Herbert Gans (1979), they achieve this through editorial selection and through narrative practices that determine the angles, slant, and scenarios through which political events are recounted. In newspaper reporting these narrative strategies include unique quoting practices that permit reporters' voices to remain 'outside' the news discourse they create.

In this chapter we will consider whether Montreal's electronic media used narrative strategies similar to those of the city's newspapers in covering the PQ's White Paper tabling. Three different kinds of narrative practices contributed to the varied White Paper accounts in *La Presse* and the *Gazette*. These related to differences in event selections, differences in the choice of voices permitted to comment on the events, and differences in the 'tone' or validation these voices lent to the events they were commenting on. Chapter 5 demonstrated that the newspapers' reporting practices were framed by the differing ideological positions of their Montreal readers – positions that ranged on a continuum between the YES and NO political platforms. In the press, as we have seen, these platforms were simplified into a binary opposition between *nationalisme québécois* and renewed federalism, and were argued through a very small number of canonical formulas. Denis Monière notes that the political promises of the referendum contestants were equally oversimplified, with the YES side *propagande* promising 'the destruction of dependence' and the NO side urging a vote against 'the destruction of the country' (1980: 108). Our comparative analysis of the television coverage of the White Paper tabling is based on five days of coverage (1–5 November 1979) on all local and national newscasts aired in Montreal. This was ten newscasts a day for a total of fifty. Each day, four of these newscasts were presented in French (*Ce Soir, Le Téléjournal, Le Dix*, and *Nouvelles TVA*), and six in English (CBC's *City at Six, The National, City Tonight, Pulse, CTV National* and *Late Pulse*). Three of the days included in the sub-analysis (3–5 November 1979) were also part of the composite week sample on which this book's general analysis of the referendum campaign has been based.

Television News Stories: Speakers and Cast of Characters

We have already demonstrated that all attempts at treating public opinion formation by the media as a process that can be directly 'read off' from the content, overlook the fact that television programming is more than content. It is also a complex sign system, created collectively by producers and viewers, through which the public world is experienced and made known. David Menaker notes that the television news story is visually illustrated and uses the dramatic form and language of realism (1979: 235). News programs therefore select and condense reality according to conventions such as these: newsworthiness (extraordinariness, paradox, conflict, deviance); empiricism (the natural existence and preponderance of facts); narrativity (providing accounts in a dramatic story format); and objectivity (allowing contesting points of view to have a voice) (Knight and Taylor, 1986: 234). These conventions restrict the power of metaphoric association and produce a language that is largely referential. This means that the 'realistic' narrative functions as a signifier of objects and stresses knowledge of things. Northrop Frye calls the realistic narrative mode 'an art of extended or implied simile' (Frye, 1957: 136). It draws attention to the similarity between what is written and what is known. The iconic quality of the visual imagery of 'action shots' and the realistic mode of narration are two powerful strategies for capturing an audience and leading it to interpret events from the point of view of the storyteller. In contrast to the print media – which, as Chapter 5 demonstrated, use various forms of quotes to signify realism – television news discourses employ action imagery to recreate the medium's authenticity. This footage seems so 'natural' and so 'windowlike' that the viewer forgets that the narrative itself is restructuring reality in what Peter Dahlgren has aptly called the 'dynamics of telling' (Dahlgren, 1985a: 357). News stories, as we know, have a beginning, a middle, and an end, as well as rising and falling flow, as conflict and denouement unfold.

To unravel how news programs, as reconstructions of the 'theatre of public life,' signify, we drew on discourse analysis. This level of analysis helped pinpoint stylistic forms and journalistic modes of address, and ideological idioms and rhetorical figures of speech, as well as the particular forms of knowledge that were validated in Montreal's French and English news programs. Following Stephen Kline (1982), we developed four main analytical categories to 'deconstruct' the news discourses: speaker roles, casts of characters, events, and 'components of argumentation.' The seven speaker roles were divided into two groups: four news presenter roles (anchorperson, reporter, commentator, interviewer) and three outside sources (news maker, expert, person-in-the-street). Each of these was known to be situated in a particular relationship to the camera, recreating visually the social hierarchy of the station as well as the station's relationship to the political voices being covered. The *characters* or sources of referendum news stories were divided between the YES and NO forces, and represented the two identifiable political positions in the referendum campaign. The YES forces included Premier Lévesque and PQ spokespersons; the NO forces included Prime Minister Trudeau and other federal politicians, Claude Ryan, and provincial Liberal Party spokespersons. Other characters, not readily identifiable with either side in the 1980 debate, were not included in the analysis. They appeared in just over one-third of francophone (38 per cent) and anglophone (36 per cent) news segments studied. Characters and *events*, although intimately related, were handled separately in our analysis. 'Events' refers to the kinds of happenings that were covered as referendum items/stories on a given news program. The variable was conceptually related to what was considered 'newsworthy' and was thus based on journalistic practices. Eleven different types of events could be distinguished, including meetings, tablings, speeches, document unveilings, polls, and press conferences.

Our dramaturgical approach enabled us to do two things at the same time. First, it enabled us to compare and clarify the processes through which the textual meanings of the referendum news dramas were *co-created* by Montreal's television stations and their audiences. These audience-based news discourses manifested both narrative commonalities and ideological differences, which were based in pre-existing viewer knowledges concerning referendum issues. Second, the dramaturgical approach permitted us to show that significance arises from both textual and narrative configurations. The 'enactment' of democratic politics in news programming provides politicians, news gatherers, and the public with stylized roles to play. According to Joseph Gusfield, the visualization of these roles *creates* the order and consistency that together constitute the notion of 'society' on which public opinion rests. Consensus gets built up about heroes and villains; and because the moral and rational grounds of authority are assumed to be discoverable, it becomes possible to make policy (1981: 22). In this way, public opinion creation and sense making are constructions, albeit fragile and elusive at times. During the referendum these constructions were dependent on pre-existing viewer knowledges concerning referendum issues – knowledges which (as we showed in Chapter 5) differed markedly for Montreal's French- and English-speaking viewers.

Chapter 3 indicated that there were a number of cognitive frameworks that helped co-ordinate audience and journalistic understandings of what the referendum was *about*. Among these were notions of Quebec's unique role in the Canadian federation, concepts of democratic practice, and equity rules concerning how party information was to be disseminated during electoral campaigns. The media play a crucial dissemination function in the political process, and have themselves devised campaign-reporting routines that have translated these public-information responsibilities into practice. As we have seen, these routines include journalistic conventions about what classes of people are considered legitimate players with recognizable voices in campaign reporting. According to these conventions there are four groups of political players: politicians, journalists, experts, and the public. These roles and their speaking voices, it will be demonstrated, are systematically related to the types of topics they address and to the manner in which they are permitted to advance their arguments in the television news narrative (see Appendix C).

Many researchers have noted that television news and documentary film create meaning in very different ways. The Glasgow University Media Group, one of the first to explore these differences, pointed out that in the news, shots are used to illustrate the audio text (1976: 29). Consequently, the rules governing their juxtaposition come not from the visual but from the audio track. Television newscasts are cut according to a *journalistic* logic, which Herbert Gans has called 'visual radio' (1979). This logic is much more complex than filmic logic, because on news film, things referred to in the commentary are often abstractions that cannot easily be rendered on the screen. As a result, a snowy street scene with sliding cars is not merely what it shows – it is also a *symbol* for the 1980 Montreal maintenance workers' strike. Local viewers interpret it as such, because of the juxtaposition of the audio track with the visual shot. The rules governing the juxtaposition of shots are relatively simple; however, the relationship between sound and picture is extremely complex and not yet well understood. The cause of this complexity is to be found in the relationship between the symbolic quality (of many news images), and the shortness of news stories and their subplots (Glasgow 1976, 30).

To examine the complex process of audiovisual meaning creation in the news discourse, we utilized three units of analysis, which we drew from the journalistic practices involved in fashioning programs. These units were the story, the item, and the segment. The news *story* (or bulletin) is a purely semantic category, defined in terms of the coherence of its subject matter and its relationship to an identifiable event (example: the tabling of the PQ's White Paper in Quebec's National Assembly). As Chapter 3 demonstrated, each news program contained between ten and sixteen stories of different lengths. The longer, top stories appeared at the beginning of the program, the shorter ones lower down in the news hierarchy. Story length was determined by the number of news *items* it contained. Items introduce subplots or 'angles' to the reporting of an event and thus function as both syntactic and semantic categories. Since items are made up of a number of different audiovisual segments, we defined them in terms of the journalistic roles that introduced the subplots (example: the civil servant's disruption of the closed briefing held to acquaint journalists with the White Paper, which was introduced by a reporter voice-over). The third and most important unit of analysis is the *segment*. Segments enabled us to analyse how the various news presenter roles were related to the topics they addressed and to the ways those topics were visually represented. Segments are the smallest building blocks in the audiovisual discourse, and are defined as either 'changes in role' or 'changes in the visual mode' – that is, in particular filmic modes associated with their imaging (Connell, 1980: 140). The segment (example: the shattering of the glass door to the building where the White Paper briefing was taking place), as the smallest unit of audiovisual meaning creation, functioned like a phoneme in a linguistic text. Because segments and how they are assembled in a news discourse specify differences in audiovisual renditions, most comparisons reported in this chapter will focus on the segment level. Our method of deconstructing the television news discourse will provide a potent new tool not only for stylistic analysis, but also for understanding the rhetorical thrust of campaign reporting, which has previously eluded researchers.

In the television discourse that reconstructed the White Paper narrative, speaker roles could be roughly divided into two major classes. There were the *intrastation* speaker roles, which were occupied by journalistic personnel, and the *extrastation* roles, which used legitimated political players' images and voices. The four intrastation roles – anchor, reporter, commen-

TABLE 6.1
Comparison of speaker roles in French and English
newscasts (percentage of all White Paper news
segments)

Role	Percentage of segments		
	Total	French	English
Intrastation			
Anchor	24	24	25
Reporter	41	45	34
Commentator	5	1	11
Interviewer	3	0	10
Extrastation			
News maker	24	26	20
Expert	2	3	0
Vox-pop	1	1	0
Totals	100	100	100

tator, and interviewer – provided what John Hartley calls the 'institutional
voice' of the stations. Previous studies have shown that the institutional
voice frames how stories are to be interpreted and thus provides the general
meaning context for the audience group at hand (Hartley, 1982: 47; Glasgow University Media Group, 1976: 298). On the French stations, as Table
6.1 shows, only two roles were used to construct news accounts: the
anchor (24 per cent) and the reporter (45 per cent). These two roles introduced and appeared in more than two-thirds (69 per cent) of all segments.
The narrative dominance of these roles was further reinforced by the finding (see Chapter 3) that on average, French-language news stories had
fewer items (F2, E2.6) as well as fewer segments (F2, E3.7). Consequently,
French news stories were often shorter in length and visually more
straightforward. Whether they were thus easier for viewers to understand
is a hotly debated issue (Sturm and Greve-Partsch, 1987). The English stations, in contrast, constructed their news discourses using four intrastation
roles – the anchor (25 per cent), the reporter (34 per cent), the commentator
(11 per cent), and the interviewer (10 per cent) – in their reporting of the
White Paper tabling. These varied roles, which have different narrative
tasks to fulfil, added visual and audio variety to the English-language news
discourse. Greater speaker variety also signalled that the English discourse

was going to cover more story angles and give more details. Table 6.1 also shows that among the three extrastation roles, only the news-makers/politicians entered both the French and the English news narratives. They were used to validate the news personnel's reconstructions of events. The same table also demonstrates that the French rendition of the White Paper tabling acknowledged experts and people-in-the-street, but that their voices were not highly valued: they appeared in a mere 4 per cent of all French news segments. The English discourse did not utilize them at all.

Table 6.1 indicates that by the beginning of the 1980s, politicians' ability to speak directly to the Canadian public had diminished. This erosion has continued into the mid-1990s: the duration of items and stories is now even shorter. The fact that politicians' voices appeared in only 26 per cent of the French and 20 per cent of the English segments about the White Paper tabling is evidence of this erosion. Though politicians' voices were part of the White Paper reconstruction as much as the anchor voices, their function in the news discourse was very different. Political actors were *characters* in the news personnel's narration of daily events. Typically, politicians' voices were used to introduce a new story angle or to explicitly validate a point of view that the news personnel had already contextualized. This subordinate role in the news discourse was visually reinforced by middle-distance, often 'profiled' camera treatment (24 per cent of segments). All of this suggests that it has become more difficult for politicians to subvert the journalistic interpretation of political events – an issue that will be dealt with in the final section of this chapter.

Political Events Featured

All political dramas feature sets of events in which party leaders and their followers battle for political ascendancy. Because 'events' refer to the kinds of happenings that the stations featured as referendum items/stories, this variable is conceptually related to what journalists consider newsworthy. Eleven different types of events were distinguishable in the referendum narrative, including meetings, tablings, speeches, and polls. According to Roland Barthes, such events are ordered and mark out different levels of intelligibility in the news narrative (Barthes, 1977: 117–9). A comparison of CBC's *Ce Soir* and *City at Six* coverage of the White Paper tabling demonstrates that the French and English event selections were notably different, just as they were in Montreal's print coverage. On 1 November 1979 a number of newsworthy events occurred. Among these were the unveiling of the White Paper in the National Assembly, the day-long walkout by

Quebec civil servants contesting a wage proposal, the disruption of a closed door briefing, and opposition members' anger over their inability to read the document. The French and English stations' narratives linked and integrated these event reconstructions in very different ways and thus provided the basis for radically different narrative reconstructions for their Montreal viewers.

Our verbatim transcripts demonstrate that French television personnel were fully aware that they were addressing viewers with varied political leanings. Like their *La Presse* colleagues, they therefore contextualized the White Paper tabling in a neutral discourse which stressed that the strike inconvenienced the journalists who were to read the document, but *not* the government, which presented it in the National Assembly at 2 p.m. without further incident.

REPORTER: (Gilles Morin) L'opération *Livre blanc*, planifiée depuis plusieurs semaines par le gouvernement, a été dérangée par des fonctionnaires mécontents. Au nombre de deux à trois milles, ils sont arrivés au Centre Municipal des Congrès ce matin avant les journalistes. Tous ces derniers devaient prendre connaissance à l'avance du contenu du *Livre blanc*. Les manifestants ont brisé une porte vitrée et une fois à l'intérieur, ils ont neutralisé des machines à écrire en leur enlevant les rubans, fait voler les papeteries, bref, c'était sans dessus-dessous. Cette manifestation a davantage dérangé les journalistes que le gouvernement. Le *Livre blanc* a été deposé comme prévu à 14 heures à l'Assemblée Nationale sans autres incidents.

In contrast, the English station personnel already knew that their viewers rejected the PQ's secession option, and made an event selection that acknowledges their viewers' deep suspicion of the Parti Québécois's intentions. The CBC's *City at Six* (story 2, item 1) provided the following narration of the White Paper tabling:

ANCHOR: It was a *miserable* day for a lot of people in Quebec City, certainly for anybody that had anything to do with the distribution of the White Paper. The government planned to hand out copies early this morning to reporters at the Quebec City Convention Centre, but striking civil servants had a plan of their *own*, as Melvin McLeod reports [emphasis in original].

REPORTER: (McLeod) It was *such* a well-planned event. But when the hundreds of reporters showed up to read the long-awaited White Paper at 8:30 this morning, they found hundreds of striking civil servants blocking the entrance to the hall. Outside waited several thousand more. Then, suddenly a door was smashed, and in

TABLE 6.2
Event reconstructions in the French and English White Paper
discourses (percentage of duration in seconds)

	French		English	
	%	order	%	order
Speeches	23	(1)	30	(1)
Parliamentary discussion	11	(4)	22	(2)
Document content	20	(2)	11	(4)
Sources response	15	(3)	16	(3)
Revolts, demonstration	5		10	(5)
Public response	7		3	
Reports presented	9	(5)	0	
Tabling	4		3	
Meetings	5		0	
Public debate	3		0	
Other	1		0	

they poured into the hall the government had *so carefully* prepared for the journalists to digest the White Paper. The room quickly became a shambles as strikers milled around singing union songs and throwing around the foolscap that was supposed to hold the words of wisdom about sovereignty-association [emphasis in original].

The English station's event selection – the civil service strike, the chaos in the convention centre, the journalists' inability to read the White Paper document as planned – enabled English media personnel to create narrative closure around the negative themes of 'chaos' and 'instability' – neither of which were evoked in the French station's account.

The two stations' initial accounts selected the same set of events for the retelling; but as Table 6.2 indicates, the *overall* event reconstruction of the PQ's sovereignty-association proposal and the subsequent National Assembly debate were quite different for the francophone and anglophone stations. Table 6.2, which compares the amount of program time devoted to different events, demonstrates that the French stations covered speeches (23 per cent) and the White Paper's content (20 per cent) about equally, while ignoring the parliamentary discussion (11 per cent). In such a narrative format, the political values of both the pro- and anti-referendum viewers could be accommodated, though through a different strategy from that utilized in the print media. Speeches could feature both advocates and critics of the PQ initiative, as could source responses, which took up 15 per cent of the francophone coverage. The English-language news coverage, in contrast, privileged speeches (30 per cent) and parliamentary discussions (22 per cent) *about* the controversial White Paper, while downplaying the document's content (11 per cent), which anglophone viewers were assumed to reject. Such an event reconstruction was similar to what the *Gazette* did, in that it also emphasized *responses* to the White Paper document, rather than its content. Disapproval of the PQ's secessionist political agenda was also the reason why so much attention was paid to another negative event – the civil servant strike (10 per cent), which received only marginal mention (5 per cent) on the French stations, because it had nothing to do with the document itself.

The differing French and English news reconstructions demonstrate that viewers' political values not only affect a station's event selection, but also the ways in which the station personnel construct balance. The French programs achieved a sense of narrative balance by featuring positive and negative responses from a wide range of different sources, among them other Canadian parties, federal and provincial government agencies, and national and international markets. Such a construction of balance would make the reports acceptable to both the YES and the NO voters in Quebec's referendum campaign. In the English programs, negative events such as the civil service strike were selected and highlighted to illustrate and reinforce *existing* negative public opinion toward the Parti Québécois's White Paper.

Cast of Political Characters

While the different event selections set the broad context for French and English audience interpretations of the White Paper tabling, the cast of characters chosen to speak about these events constituted an important narrative element in the varied meaning constructions that the two language groups created for themselves. The sources for the television news stories were, as in the case of the press analysis, divided into the YES and NO sides. The YES forces included René Lévesque as well as Parti Québécois spokespersons. The NO forces were led by Prime Minister Trudeau and other federal politicians and by Claude Ryan, the leader of the provincial Liberals. Chapter 5's comparison of print media showed that characters and events are intimately connected, and that this modifies the tone of news stories. The same comparison also demonstrated – to our surprise – that the White Paper was overwhelmingly left undiscussed in *La Presse* and the *Gazette*, and that what discussion there was featured NO-side voices.

In the French-language television discourses such a one-sided deployment of characters would have seemed unbalanced. We therefore expected that there would be an equal representation of YES and NO spokespersons in any discussions of the document. Interestingly, there was not. Francophone stations utilized more PQ spokespersons (61 per cent) to speak for the White Paper, while a mere 39 per cent of NO-side characters critiqued its content. Because anglophone and allophone viewers were against the secession option, we expected that the English stations would render the White Paper debate from the NO point of view. This was indeed the case: 73 per cent of all segments featured NO spokespersons, and the remaining 27 per cent featured YES sympathizers. We note here that another comparative study registered a similar disproportion of spokespersons (Caron et al., 1983a: 486). One must conclude from this that news stories are usually told from the point of view of the characters involved. North American viewers do not interpret such a narrative convention as unbalanced, because documentary accounts on which television news formats are based follow similar conventions.

News Stories: Narrative Strategies of Consensus Building

All attempts to analyse the media's role in public opinion formation must account for their *active* participation in this process. Reception theorists argue that this 'activity' goes beyond the media's selection of the events to be narrated and the cast of characters to be covered. What is added from the viewers' perspective is a particular narrative process that creates unique news program scripts with their own plot laws. As 'scripts,' news stories implicitly contain explanations and normative dimensions that project for the audience 'how things work' in their society, as well as the rules about 'how to live.' As a symbolization of the social order, the story world of a television news program thus transmits meta-dramatic understandings of the political and social worlds. The 'scripting' of news stories and of the discourses in which they are embedded has received increasing attention since the 1980s, because it permits us to gain a better understanding of how news narratives persuade viewers through both presentational devices and logics of argumentation (van Dijk, 1988). Components of story construction and argumentation style are designed to provide insight into the rhetorical – that is, 'persuasive' – components of the journalistic discourse. Following Kline (1982: 28–31), we identified eight different kinds of narrative patterns in news discourses – report, description, commentary, narration, opinion, points of view, opinion poll, and fact – all of which we will now illustrate. Together these narrative patterns permit an assessment of the types of interpretations that news stories entail and provide clues to how 'factuality' was constructed in French and English programs during the referendum. The television news narrative, it will be shown, makes use of a number of presentational devices and story formats to implicitly overdetermine and thus *encourage* idiosyncratic ways of understanding the White Paper tabling.

Styles of Speech and Modes of Address in 'News Talk'

The institutional voices of the Montreal television stations 'speak' to us in a particular style that is recognizable and familiar to French and English audiences. As viewers, we do not seem to have any difficulty understanding the news language's special form, fluency, and uninterruptedness. This is because any language is a code based on cultural understandings that are shared by journalists and audiences alike and that involve common frameworks of knowledge and meaning structures (Hall, 1980: 130–1). Speaker and hearer roles, though separate, are thus united by a reflexive commitment to honour the other's existence and interpretation of the situation – otherwise, the communicative exchange would not have made sense.

In television new programs, the news talk as a language system is highly structured, formal, and polite. Many have characterized it as 'rational and bureaucratic' (Dahlgren, 1985a: 358; Altheide, 1985: 12). Such a description is at best partial, since it fails to explain the 'persuasive' quality of this language system, which visually clues the viewer into the same space and time continuum as the station. Studio personnel thus become stand-ins for us, the home viewers; they are also visually rendered in such a way that they seem to be talking to us across our living room coffee table. All of this reinforces the 'windowpane' metaphor that frames the 'unvarnished,' 'brute fact,' 'realistic' discourse the newscast seeks to re-create.

Like other narratives, stories on French and English local and network news presuppose the existence of a storyteller – that is, a subject who does the telling and orchestrates the voices belonging to all the other characters. Erving Goffman (1983: 236) provides an important clue to the mediated nature of the news discourse when he notes that anchors are not ordinary storytellers, but rather 'announce' other people's texts. Anchors merely *suggest* that they have authored what is being said. The viewers who are addressed by the anchor are in a mediated position as well. Though they

TABLE 6.3
Types of 'announcing' and 'modes of address' in the White Paper discourse
(percentage of segments)

Mode of address	Other–Direct	Indirect Interview	Speech	Press conf.	Editorial
Intrastation voices					
Reporter	98	—	2	—	—
Anchor	100	—	—	—	—
Commentator	—	86	—	—	14
Interviewer	10	90	—	—	—
Extrastation voices					
News maker	2	23	41	34	—
Expert	17	83	—	—	—
Vox-pop	—	100	—	—	—
Total	65	15	11	8	1

are verbally addressed and visually recognized as 'phantom' participants in the communicational encounter, they cannot themselves respond audibly. This does not, however, imply that television viewers are 'passive,' as Todd Gitlin claims (Gitlin, 1977: 788). News comprehension studies have demonstrated that viewers are able to distinguish between and interpret the three types of news announcing that the news discourse employs.

Table 6.3 compares the types of announcing and modes of address in the French and English coverage of the White Paper tabling. It demonstrates that in both the French and the English news discourses, the 'direct' mode of announcing was the preferred style of news speech. Combined with what we have called 'face to camera' imagery, this mode simulates a two-person telephone conversation in which the news personnel ostensibly speak to each audience member individually. In the White Paper reconstruction, a full 100 per cent of all anchor interactions and 98 per cent of all reporter statements utilized the 'direct' mode of address, in which the narrator quoted a spokesperson or 'spoke for self.' The 'indirect' modes of address, Table 6.3 shows, were practiced in such situations as interviews, speeches, press conferences, and editorials, and involved 'extra-station' personnel. Both news-makers'/politicians' and experts' statements were heavily inflected. Politicians were able to address the viewer directly in only 2 per cent of all segments, while experts had a little more freedom and addressed us directly in 17 per cent of all segments. Otherwise, the station personnel used their statements to construct their own interpretations. People-in-the-street were never allowed to speak directly: their opinions were always elicited in response to an 'interview' question (100 per cent) and thus were guided along very narrow response routes. These differences in modes of address, as Chapter 5 demonstrated, were also found in the print media, where they manifested themselves as differences in quoting strategies.

Much less often, anchors and reporters/interviewers engage in two other types of announcing. Goffman calls these 'three-way' and 'fresh talk' announcing. The first occurs when the anchor hails one of his own 'team,' such as the reporter, or the sports or weather casters. In the previous section we saw that the *City at Six* anchor hailed the Quebec City reporter by announcing him by name: 'As Melvin McLeod reports ...' 'Fresh talk' announcing is practised by reporters and commentators when they provide voice-over detail about a particular news event (1983: 336–41). Though these occur more rarely, all three types of announcing share the same communicational characteristics. They treat the remote viewer as a visually ratified participant, though they verbally deny the viewer access. Public opinion formation in such a setting will also be one-way, legitimating those who can talk in their own voice over those who cannot. Through the indirect mode of address, extra-station voices become characters in the station's narration. Rhetorically, this means they are in an *indirect* relation to what is being said (Nichols, 1977: 39). They are merely called upon to illustrate a point, introduce a news angle, or present an alternative point of view. Though television news styles vary in Europe, our evidence indicates that both the French and English Montreal stations utilize the same modes of address (Robinson, 1987: 75). Such a finding testifies not only to the unifying influence of professional training across language groups in North American journalism, but also to the fact that there are different stylistic methods for rendering objectivity in the European and the North American news discourses. This requires further investigation.

Presentational Devices

Presentational devices are textual devices that are connected with narrator roles and indicate the strategies and types of contextualization that are characteristic of specific journalistic (intrastation) and other (extrastation) voices in the construction of their argument. Thus, in addition to saying that the anchor role/voice provides the major focus of the story, and that the reporter/voice adds detail, we can now specify the strategies by which argumentation proceeds *within* the story unit and how coherent narrative formats are created. David Morley distinguishes five narrative strategies utilized in news discourses: linking, framing, focusing, nominating, and summing up (1980: 58–9). These clarify the points at which different kinds of interpretation enter the supposedly 'neutral' journalistic discourse. We have added a sixth strategy – the *nominee* category – to this list, in order to clarify the degree of access that outsider voices have to the journalistic discourse and the ways in which such formats as the interview and the discussion constrain these contributions.

Since the modes of address of our French and English stations' White Paper accounts made use of the same types of address and overwhelmingly privileged the interview mode for eliciting information from the outside actors on the political stage, other narrative devices must account for the two station groups' differing argumentation strategies. Chief among these were the narrative presentational activities performed by the station personnel, and the story formats that resulted from these functions. Five presentational devices can be distinguished. 'Linking' provided the textual function of guiding the viewer through the news story, while 'framing' established the topic and its relevance. Add to these 'focusing,' which determined the angle of the story, 'nominating,' which identified the newscaster voices, and 'summing up,' which drew together the main threads of the argument, so that the story's relevance, as well as the context into which it was to be placed, could be assessed by the viewer (Morley; 1980: 58–9). All of these strategies clarified the points at which argumentation entered the supposedly neutral journalistic discourse. The different presentational activities thus acted as a 'skeleton' of persuasion, and so functioned much like the 'nested' quoting practices used by Montreal's newspaper journalists (Zelizer, 1989).

Table 6.4, which compares speaker roles by presentational devices in the French and English news discourse, illustrates the various activities of the news personnel in the persuasion process. It indicates how little the newsmaker/politician as 'nominee' is able to affect the news discourse. The table shows that the anchor, who commands four of the six presentational modes, is most influential in guiding the audiencing process (Ang, 1987). The anchor sets the interpretive stage through a combination of framing (29 per cent), focusing (27 per cent), and linking (22 per cent) activities. The anchor also calls upon or 'nominates' the reporter and commentator, whose purpose is to add further details to the story by introducing new subplots. Reporters most often focus (41 per cent) or frame (32 per cent), while commentators link (32 per cent), frame (32 per cent) and focus

TABLE 6.4
Speaker role by presentational devices (percentage of
presentational devices)

	Anchor	Reporter	Commentator	News maker
Linking	22	7	32	—
Framing	29	32	32	4
Focusing	27	41	29	3
Nominating	20	9	—	3
Nominee	1	1	7	90
Summing up	1	10	—	—

(29 per cent) in almost equal amounts. News makers are rarely able to put their own meaning across, since they frame/focus/nominate in only 10 per cent of their audiovisual appearances. Excerpts from the CBC's *City at Six* program of 1 November 1979 illustrate the news personnel's control over the persuasion process:

ANCHOR: (story 1, item 1)
The White Paper on sovereignty-association has been tabled; but it was almost upstaged by an invasion of civil servants into the room where the document was supposed to be released. We have the full story tonight on the *City at Six*. [linking]

Good evening. I'm Stan Gibbons. George Finstadt is in Quebec City. [nominating]

Just after two this afternoon, Premier Lévesque stood in the National Assembly and tabled the White Paper on sovereignty-association, a document called 'Quebec-Canada, a NewDeal.' [linking/framing]

Don McPherson has spent most of the afternoon reading it and he reports there is nothing in it that is substantively news. But it is different: it's the first time a government of Quebec, not just a party, has outlined a position for negotiating a new relationship with Canada. Here's his report. [nominating/focusing]

The evidence shows that the five presentational devices, in which viewers are explicitly addressed, give the journalistic voices control over which external voices will be permitted to enter the narrative and how their statements are going to be evaluated. According to Genette (1982), stations' narrative voices not only define the types of knowledge that will become available to the viewers, but also establish the legitimacy of all voices within the narrative logic itself. These narrative devices help the journalistic voices construct the strategy and structure of the news story itself. In Brunsdon and Morley's words: 'The structure contains (in both senses: includes and holds within limits) the independent-authentic contributions of the extra-programme participants ... The discursive work of linking and framing items binds the divergent realities of ... varied news accounts into the ... one 'reality for the program' (1978: 61).

From an interpretive standpoint, it can therefore be said that the journalistic voices provide the 'meta-language' of the news program. These voices take charge of the meanings a news story will convey, not only by semantically subordinating other voices, but also by implying that what politicians, experts, and the public say is rhetorically *less believable*. Though these three groups are legitimated political actors in the democratic contest for public opinion, the narrative evidence confirms that media personnel have usurped other actors' interpretive capacities. No wonder politicians are complaining more and more that their messages to the public are being intercepted and quoted out of context.

Story Formats

Story formats are the narrative patterns in which news items are couched. They permit us to explore how balance and neutrality are stylistically rendered. Michael Schudson notes that it is precisely by observing these journalistic obligations that the media achieve their ideological effectivity (1982: 267). Our analysis identifies eight different story formats: report, description, commentary, narration, opinion, points of view, opinion poll, and fact (Kline, 1982: 28–31). Of these eight story formats, only three (descriptions, reports, fact) can be called 'neutral' or 'factual'; the other five (opinion, points of view, commentary, opinion poll, narration) all incorporate varying degrees of interpretation. Appendix C indicates that 'descriptions' refer to stories in the 'you are there' presentational style without commentary, and that 'reports' contain only a bare outline of the news event.

Table 6.5, which compares the types of story formats in the French and English news discourses, corroborates that French and English journalists utilized strikingly different story formats in recounting the White Paper tabling. The French stations' news discourses, which had to appeal to audiences with varied referendum outlooks, used the 'points of view' format (33 per cent) most frequently. This format makes conflict the centre of the story, because it juxtaposes outside sources and contestants with opposing

TABLE 6.5
Comparison of French and English newscasts
by story format (percentage of duration in seconds)

	French (%)	English (%)
Opinion	28	50
Points of view	33	17
Commentary	13	13
Description	12	9
Narration	5	11
Report	10	1

political points of view. Example: during the referendum campaign, the French stations would visually represent and quote sources from the YES and NO sides, without investigating the veracity of their claims to symbolise 'balanced' reporting. Montreal's French-language stations also used the more neutral description (12 per cent) and 'report' (10 per cent) story formats, as did the francophone press, to appear impartial – that is, outside the political argumentation. But in spite of the varied political outlooks of their francophone viewers, even the French stations narrated 28 per cent of their stories in the 'opinion' format, with an outside source providing the focus of the story. The fact that nearly one-third of the total discourse time utilized the opinion format corroborates that all journalistic reconstructions are heavily mediated.

Table 6.5 indicates furthermore that English stations rendered fully one-half (50 per cent) of their stories in the heavily inflected opinion format. Because such stories evaluate an external source (view, opinion, speech, or report) as the pivot of the story, this format works particularly well for representing ideas with which one is *not* in agreement. Another 13 per cent of story narratives were in the commentary format, which assesses an event in relation to its causes or consequences. More than two-thirds (67 per cent) of English-language stories were heavily interpreted in this way, as one would expect considering that the majority of anglophone viewers had already made up their minds to mistrust the White Paper document favouring Quebec independence.

The comparisons show that public opinion formation proceeds through at least four interlocking narrative processes: the exclusion of the viewer as an *active* participant in the communicational encounter; the subjugation of the politicians' and other outsiders' voices in the news narrative; the use of narrative devices to contextualize the subject matter; and the use of unique story formats to couch the narrative. Each of these processes adds narrative elements to the journalistic recounting of events. Clearly, editorializing is a very complex process that enters the news discourse not only through the selection and reordering of events, but also, much more forcefully (yet less visibly), through the narrative process of 'dramatization' itself. These dramatization processes *create* the meaning contexts into which the audience's interpretive hypotheses must eventually fit. These processes are often called 'propagandistic' because they help manufacture public consent by quietly rearranging the meaning context through rhetorical means (Monière, 1980: 108–9). Dramatization created a sense of an orderly political process in connection with the White Paper tabling, and hid or 'naturalized' the news personnel's *version* of what happened behind an orderly recounting process. The persuasive dimension of orderly recounting influences public opinion formation by representing an 'institutional order of power ... as one of consensus and legitimacy, *as if* it were compelling and beyond the argument of rational people' (Gusfield, 1981: 75–6).

Rhetorical Substance: The 'Whatness' of the White Paper Debate and Its Types of Appeal

If every television news program renders politics as a 'theatre of public life,' how were the YES and NO sides rendered? As we showed in Chapter 4, election coverage on North American television follows well-established narrative strategies that use game metaphors and polar oppositions to add drama to ongoing stories. Leader descriptions enter this narrative as audiovisual *dramatis personae*, while diverse social groups, political party representatives, businesspeople, and others become grouped and stereotyped into polarized teams or camps. In the Quebec referendum debate, the leaders' personae became stereotyped into the smoke-surrounded, populist orator René Lévesque, who was signified by the blue Fleur de lis, and his stern, intellectual adversary, Claude Ryan, who was signified by the red Maple Leaf. We had expected that the English stations would privilege the NO characters and the French stations the YES team; we were not prepared for the highly critical meaning inflections that both news narratives attached to the YES side of the debate. These reminded us of the rhetorical strategies developed in the daily press, where most commentators on the White Paper came from the NO side. The next question is this: What types of appeals did the two station groups make to their audiences?

We have already indicated that the French news narrative focused its attention on the YES characters, privileging them strongly (61 to 39 per

TABLE 6.6
Comparison of YES and NO voice presentations by
French and English stations (percentage of segments)

Presentation of Voice	French		English	
	NO	YES	NO	YES
Indirect	63	81	60	66
Direct	38	19	41	35

cent) on the political stage. But on the English stations the NO characters were privileged, accounting for almost three-quarters (73 per cent) of character mentions. This lopsidedness during the referendum debate by both sets of stations was, however, counterbalanced by the ways in which the two news narratives *inserted* the YES and NO characters' voices into their discourses.

Table 6.6 shows that the voices of both sides in the debate were presented mainly *indirectly*. Neither set of stations permitted the different *dramatis personae* to speak directly for themselves; rather, their statements were recontextualized through three narrative strategies. The journalistic narrator either used their statements in a straight commentary, or articulated them as part of a news analysis, or quoted them indirectly, through paraphrases. The major difference between the two stations' renditions is that the French contextualized the YES side (which was also their main focus) *more heavily* than they did the NO side. Table 6.6 confirms that 81 per cent of the YES side's statements were indirectly presented, as opposed to only 63 per cent of those offered by the NO opposition. The comparison also shows that on both the francophone and anglophone stations, treatments of the NO forces were more direct than for the YES forces. Voices speaking against the PQ document were permitted to address the viewer directly in 38 per cent of all NO segments on the French side and 41 per cent of all NO segments on the English side. This direct presentation of NO voices in both Montreal news discourses not only created a more sympathetic tone for this option but also assigned greater credibility to the NO than to the YES voices.

Table 6.7 explores the *use* to which the French and English stations put a character's statements. It illustrates how the NO side's ability to maintain interpretive superiority was enhanced through 'double-contextualization.' The table illustrates how Premier Lévesque's statements were generally used as a basis for *interpretation*, while those of Claude Ryan were left

TABLE 6.7
Use of characters' statements in French and English stations (percentage of segments)

Characters	%	Role	Presentation of voice	Context
Lévesque	25	News maker	Source for self	Source as basis
Ryan	25	News maker	Source for self	Uninterpreted
Clark	31	News maker	Source for self	Source as basis
Trudeau	22	News maker	Source for self	Source as basis
Broadbent	43	News maker	Source for self	Source as basis
Other feds	19	News maker	Source for self	Source as basis
PQ Spokespersons	33	Commentator	Paraphrase	Interprets
Provincial Liberals	100	News maker	Source for self	Uninterpreted
Other provincial	18	Anchor	Paraphrase	Interprets
Civil servants	53	Reporter	Analysis	Interprets
Business People	50	Anchor	Analysis	Interprets
	50	Anchor	Analysis	Introduces topic
Experts	33	Reporter	Paraphrase	Interprets
Other names	16	Expert	Source for self	Source as basis
Unnamed actors	100	Interviewer	Analysis	Introduces topic

completely *uninterpreted*. Though both characters spoke for themselves, Lévesque's statements were recontextualized by the station personnel, while Ryan's were left unmediated. This same treatment was also accorded to the party spokespersons: statements from the Parti Québécois were interpreted while those from the Liberals were rendered verbatim. Because the news personnel of *all* stations not only paraphrased the YES side's statements more frequently, but also used them to further their own narrative goals, one can argue that YES side statements were *doubly* contextualized in the Montreal news discourses. Since viewers learn to consider voices that address them directly as more authoritative, one can hypothesize that the double-contextualization of the YES-side statements likely rendered them less credible to all viewer groups.

We have seen that the same effect was achieved in the French and English newspaper accounts by differences in quoting practices, with the YES side voices reconstructed through reporters' narrations and the NO side voices being directly quoted in the reporters' texts.

A final rhetorical strategy that the French stations used differentially against the YES side had to do with the explanatory context into which characters' statements were placed. Table 6.8, which compares this explanatory context in the French and English news discourses, shows clearly that

TABLE 6.8
'Explanatory contexts' of YES and NO side statements
in the French and English news discourses (percentage
of segments)

	French		English	
	NO	YES	NO	YES
Source as basis	35	24	25	21
Quote as proof	30	14	23	27
Interpretation	9	38	19	24
Introduction	22	22	10	7
Uninterpreted	4	3	17	14
Diminishes	—	—	5	7
Evaluation	—	—	1	—

more YES side statements (38 per cent) than NO side statements (9 per cent) were used in the context of interpretation (that is, the speaker interpreted the significance of the statement, document, or event for the viewers). Also, more NO statements (35 per cent) than YES statements (24 per cent) were used as sources for interpretion, or in the 'quote as proof' mode – a format in which 30 per cent of the NO but only 14 per cent of YES statements appeared. A second interesting point revealed by this table is that the English news discourse seems to have treated the two sides of the debate more even-handedly: the comparison of NO and YES side descriptions indicates differences in treatment of no more than 4 percentage points. About the same percentage of English news segments were rendered in the 'source as basis' (25:21) , 'quote as proof' (23:27), 'interpretation,' (19:24) and 'introduction' (10:7) contexts, or left the segments uninterpreted (17:14).

These findings suggest that the French stations had to work harder to keep their narratives balanced than the English stations, which were reporting to audiences that were generally of the NO point of view. The table indicates that for the French stations, working harder meant having to do more interpreting and use more strategies. A mere 4 per cent of their characters' statements were left uninterpreted, compared to the English stations' 17 per cent. Furthermore, in order to satisfy their politically polarized audience groups, the French stations had to develop two unique kinds of explanatory strategies for the YES and the NO coverage. An *indirect* interpretation strategy using primarily the 'source as basis' (35 per cent of segments) and 'quote as proof' (30 per cent of segments) modes was developed for the NO side statements; and a *direct* interpretation strategy, which relied primarily on interpretation, was developed to contextualize 38 per cent of the YES side segments.

Political Consensus Building and 'Image Politics'

Alvin Gouldner has argued that the relationship between the media and the public is so close that they are mutually constitutive concepts: 'A public consists of persons who habitually acquire their news and orientations from impersonal mass media' (1976: 96). David Chaney adds that the interdependence of public opinion and the mass media clarifies a common feature of them both: 'They are ways of talking about society that are to a significant extent governed by the interests of metropolitan administrative elites' (Chaney, 1981: 116). As our study has demonstrated, there is never *a* public, but rather a potentially *large set* of publics that must be addressed by the media. In Montreal during the referendum campaign, these publics organized themselves by political beliefs that overlapped with language and ethnic origin. English Canadians and immigrants from Italy, Portugal, and Greece, who constituted the majority of ethnic Quebecers at the time, aligned themselves with the antisecessionist NO forces in the campaign. French-speaking Quebecers constituted various publics across the political continuum between those supporting sovereignty, and those who were neutral to or against it.

Montreal's French and English stations, as consensus builders for their particular publics, narrated the White Paper tabling in different ways. This indicates that public opinion is an evocative concept through which authorities and pressure groups categorize beliefs in ways that marshal support or opposition for their respective interests (Edelman, 1977: 50). As in the print media, differing audiovisual renditions of the White Paper tabling were constructed out of differing event selections and differing casts of characters, as well as through the use of differing argumentation strategies. The French stations overwhelmingly covered the YES side characters; the English stations focused on the NO side of the debate. However, the two sets of stations treated the NO side arguments differently and contextualized them less heavily. They used the NO statements as sources for interpretation or in the quote-as-proof mode (in which characters speak in their own voices). Regarding the YES side statements, the station personnel contextualized 38 per cent of all statements directly, paraphrasing or voicing over what had been said by PQ officials or their sympathizers.

Our analysis has also demonstrated the active role of viewers in meaning creation – something that was overlooked in earlier theorizing. Though spatially the different Montreal viewer groups were 'phantoms' in the mass-mediated television situation, *temporally* they were acknowledged in the rhetorical construction of the news programs. Even though the various audience groups could not talk back to the announcers/reporters, their points of view were acknowledged in the White Paper narrations. Viewers themselves, this evidence shows, have an important role to play in the public opinion formation process – a process that is both circular and reflexive. Viewers supply the various 'common stocks of knowledge' about politics in Quebec, and the two media groups act on these in constructing their logics of argumentation. These political outlooks, as we have seen, had become increasingly polarized since the 1960s and consisted of two juxtaposed ideologies by the time of the 1980 referendum campaign: *nationalisme québécois* and 'renewed federalism.' The 1995 debate about the meaning of 'distinct society' indicates that these nationalisms are still in conflict and continue to challenge centralized Canadian political federalism to this day. Michael Schudson correctly observes that 'narrative conventions consequently function less to increase or decrease the truth value of the message they convey, than to shape and narrow the range of what kinds of truths can be told' (1982: 98). In the next chapter we will explore the range of truths that Montreal's media utilized to explain the defeat of the PQ's sovereignty-association option on 21 May 1980.

PART IV

EXPLORING THE ARGUMENTATION:
RHETORICAL PROCESSES IN
PUBLIC OPINION CREATION

7

'The Day After': Explaining the Referendum Outcome to French- and English-Speaking Montrealers

Previous chapters investigated how the Montreal media surveyed the political environment for francophone and anglophone viewers. Here, we will enlarge the analytical framework and explore another aspect of the media's effectivity – namely, their linking function between political élites and the voting public. This linking function is not a one-way but rather a reciprocal process, whereby the media offer a platform for the government to explain its policies, while at the same time shaping citizen roles and knowledges about the political process. Our analyses of the constructions of the Montreal news discourses have indicated that the mass media in industrial and capitalist societies play both a fragmenting and a homogenizing role in public opinion creation. What we mean by this is that the media, through their means of signification, provide a variety of frames of reference, through which different social groups are able to experience and understand their own and others' 'lived reality' (Hall, 1979: 341). In Montreal during the spring of 1980, this lived reality was fragmented as contending forces offered conflicting visions of the province's political future.

Having fragmented political understandings, the media's most challenging function therefore became a reconstruction of the political consensus, so that public life would not deteriorate into civil strife. For democratic governance to remain viable, the media had to organize, orchestrate, and bring together that which they had selectively represented and selectively classified. Stuart Hall speaks of the engineering of this consensus as the creation of an 'imaginary cohesion' on the political stage. This is achieved by transposing real social divisions – of power, ethnicity, gender, class, and interest – onto the symbolic plane of public opinion, where they can be used to rally support for alternative political solutions. In democratic societies, such a transposition is achieved through conventions of narration supplied by the media. In Canadian election reporting, among these conventions are the customs of equality and balance in party coverage, and the ritual whereby leaders publicly accept defeat (or victory) in front of the cameras. This chapter will explore how the Montreal media conceptualized the referendum outcome and thus created the integrative coherence of 'public opinion' that enabled French- and English-speaking citizens to continue their communal existence.

To explore the rhetorical conventions and argumentation strategies that were employed in creating consensus about the vote outcome, we compared the programs of two stations: the French CBFT 2 *Ce Soir* and the English CBMT 6 *City at Six*, both of which aired at 6 p.m. on 21 May 1980 and were designed to put the outcome in perspective. These programs were also part of the composite-week sample we used to systematically explore more general issues such as stylistic and format differences be-tween French- and English-language Montreal programming which were reviewed in previous chapters. In this analysis, the emphasis is on the rhetorical and persuasive dimensions of language – that is, on those properties of television discourse that make communications practices *convincing*. According to classical rhetoric, there are five practices that enhance argumentative composition: *inventio*, which refers to the selection of topics and arguments; *dispositio*, which refers to their arrangement and sequencing; *elocutio*, or style of presentation; *memoria*; and *pronunciatio*, or the art of delivery (Corbett: 1980). To explore the rhetorical strategies used by Montreal's two station groups, we compared the topics (*inventio*) that were selected to explain the referendum outcome. We investigated modes of appeal by scrutinizing René Lévesque's, Claude Ryan's, and Pierre Trudeau's speeches that interpreted the vote outcome for Montreal's YES and NO voters. We then looked at *dispositio* by analysing how the voices of politicians, journalists, experts, and the 'public' were used to construct these explanations. Finally, we considered *pronunciatio*, the art of delivery – in other words, how journalists legitimized their own discourses as 'true' renditions of the 'facts.'

According to Joseph Gusfield, public opinion formation and the engineering of consent involves three types of symbolic activities: 'naming' the problem; giving it 'public status' by assigning responsibility to someone to do something about it; and legitimating a particular way of 'viewing' the problem (1981: 3–6). Our comparative analysis focused on these symbolic processes in order to determine how narrative closure was rhetorically achieved after the referendum vote for Montreal's linguistically and politically varied viewer groups.

TABLE 7.1
Comparison of French and English journalistic reconstructions of
the 'Day After' discourses (21 May 1980)
(by number of arguments)

Topic frames	Ce soir (SRC – French)		City at Six (CBC – English)	
	Yes	No	Yes	No
1 Nature of the campaign	6	11	1	0
2 Ethnic group's response	3	9	0	3
3 Economic implications	1	4	0	6
4 Renewed federalism	4	7	4	14
5 PQ's political future	4	3	0	2
6 'Yvettes'/turning point	0	3	0	0
7 Others	3	9	8	2
Total	21	46	13	27
	(67)		(40)	

Creating the Universe of Discourse: Politicians in Command

In earlier chapters we demonstrated that the 'naming' of the two referendum options was achieved through two party documents. The PQ's White Paper constructed a new sense of the Quebec 'nation' and 'people' and projected a future for Quebec outside the Canadian federation; the Liberals' Beige Paper countered by espousing a 'renewed form of federalism' in which Quebec would occupy a more autonomous place within the Canadian federation. By the end of the referendum campaign, the 'status quo' option had been eliminated, in that both the Parti Québécois and the provincial Liberals now supported some form of special status for Quebec. The White Paper and Beige Paper, which incorporated the French- and English-Canadian versions of nationalism, provided a complex inventory of possible arguments in terms of which the meaning of the referendum outcome could be explained.

Table 7.1 indicates that the PQ's referendum defeat was explained to Montreal's polarized viewers by means of a small subset of six themes, which grew out of the foci of traditional Canadian election reporting. Such coverage, as demonstrated in Chapter 4, tends to focus on polls, party standings, and predictions. Also, it highlights questions of strategy, including backroom party disputes and the tactical motivations of participants. Moreover, Canadian campaign coverage scrutinizes campaign events and makes judgments about their success, and focuses on leaders rather than on party platforms (Mendelsohn, 1993; Fletcher, 1987). Of the six theme clusters – which are ordered in Table 7.1 according to the number of arguments supplied – five were concerned with questions of strategy and with new political scenarios arising from the rejection of the secession option. These five clusters were as follows: speculation about how to achieve renewed federalism; discussion of the nature of the campaign, including winners and losers; the responses of ethnic voters, who had become polarized during the campaign; discussion of campaign events, such as the mobilization of women through the Yvettes campaign; and discussion of the leaders' future roles. Only one theme, 'economic implications,' acquired greater saliency in the referendum situation than had been usual in Canadian electoral coverage. This was because the Parti Québécois was arguing that as the second most populous province, Quebec was able and ready to stand on its own economic feet in a new 'association' arrangement. Since the province planned to use the Canadian dollar and retain other trade advantages associated with federal status as well as retain Canadian citizenship, the economic claims became a major point of contention in the referendum campaign. All of these points had been made clear during the March 1980 debate in the National Assembly and resulted in increased support for the NO side.

Canadian electoral coverage is scripted as a 'game' between contesting political parties rather than as a 'consultation' with the citizenry, and for that reason utilizes polarization to enhance interest and to add colour to the narration. To highlight the narrative implications of these polarizations, we divided the arguments used in explaining the referendum defeat into two types: those advanced by the PQ, and those advanced by the NO forces. Table 7.1 indicates that *twice as many* NO side arguments (73) as YES side arguments (34) were used to explain the YES side's referendum defeat. This is no surprise, considering that both the French and English print and television coverages of the White Paper tabling had utilized mainly NO side voices (see Chapters 5 and 6). Table 7.1 indicates that the most prominent theme, 'renewed federalism,' was used as the basis for eight YES and twenty-one NO arguments, with the YES arguing that federal renewal was 'impossible to achieve' or 'a waste of time' and that the defeat of sovereignty-association was not final. The NO arguments, in contrast, considered what renewed federalism might mean for the future and noted that constitutional change was necessary and that the vote *must* be considered final. The second theme, the 'nature of the campaign,' was the focus of seven YES and eleven NO side arguments. The seven YES side arguments included statements about the PQ's 'grass roots' campaign, about the fairness of the question, and about the fact that the federalists had 'blackmailed' Quebecers by threatening not to negotiate. The eleven NO side arguments used voting statistics, refuted criticisms of federal campaign spending, commented on the unreliability of opinion polls, and noted that the referendum question was badly phrased.

The 'ethnic group' topic produced three YES and twelve NO arguments, among the latter the fact that ethnic groups needed to be reconciled after the divisive campaign and questions as to the conclusiveness of the NO vote outcome. The 'economic implications' topic provided only one YES side argument – that economic uncertainty influenced the vote outcome – but ten NO statements on the negative impact that separation would have had on the Quebec economy. Only the PQ's 'political future' topic generated about the same number of YES (4) as NO (5) side arguments. Among the YES side arguments was the claim that the vote was a personal defeat for Lévesque and that the étapist strategy had failed; at the same time, another argument reaffirmed the PQ's strength as a social democratic party. The NO arguments, for their part, considered whether the NO vote was directed against the PQ's governance or against its option. The 'Yvettes' topic was not discussed by the YES side, but in three NO comments was considered a turning point in the campaign. The 'other topics' category included twelve YES and eleven NO side arguments and mentioned the social divisiveness of the referendum campaign.

The table furthermore demonstrates that the explanations for the referendum loss required a greater *total number* of arguments in the French- than in the English-station discourses. The French program made use of a total of sixty-seven arguments to provide closure for the referendum loss, whereas the English program utilized only forty. This indicates that the French station had to engage in more rhetorical labour in order to satisfy its politically polarized audience groups. Closure about the 'meaning' of the referendum outcome was constructed for the French-speaking viewers around the 'nature of the campaign' theme, which provided 25 per cent of all explanations (17 out of 67 arguments). These explanations related to mistakes in the PQ's campaign strategy, the fairness of the question, and the supposed federal 'blackmail' strategy, with its suggestion that negotiations with the rest of Canada would be difficult. The themes of 'ethnic group responses' (12 arguments) and 'renewed federalism' (11 arguments) rounded out the explanatory agenda. Interestingly, the PQ's re-election potential and women's support for the NO side were only minor themes in evaluations of the defeat. The fact that the four main theme complexes

included both NO *and* YES arguments enabled both NO *and* YES sympathizers to affirm the democratic nature of the referendum process, even
while those two sides disagreed in political terms about the desirability or
undesirability of its outcome.

The English-language *City at Six* reconstructions used only forty different arguments; twenty-seven of these were chosen from the NO repertoire
and thirteen from that of the YES side. As we argued in Chapter 6, less ideological labour was involved in explaining the referendum outcome to this
politically more homogeneous viewer group. On the English-language program the theme of 'renewed federalism' dominated the explanations, providing nearly one half (45 per cent) of the total arguments. These arguments
provided closure around a *futures* agenda in which constitutional negotiations, who should participate in them, the adequacy of Lévesque for the
task, and the PQ's chances in the next provincial election, all became salient
issues. Strangely enough, no mention was made in the English discourse of
the importance of the 'Yvettes' affair in turning around the NO campaign,
or of the role of women voters in the electoral process. This neglect, we will
argue in Chapter 8, had to do with the fact that at the time of the 1980 referendum, the 'gender gap' had not yet been recognized in the electoral literature. This gap would become a powerful force in the 1984 and 1988 federal
election wins of Brian Mulroney (Lemieux and Crête, 1981: 223–5).

Our topic inventory demonstrates that the Montreal media conceptualized their public opinion creation function as one of healing the differences
between the city's francophones, anglophones, and allophones. Healing
was also necessary between French-speaking extended families, some of
whom had voted for opposite outcomes. As we have demonstrated, the
'healing' scenario was argued mainly in two theme clusters: the nature of
the campaign, and the nature of renewed federalism. Together, these constituted the meta-meaning frames for the French and English program discourses. They provided nearly half the arguments (47 out of 107) for
explaining the PQ's referendum defeat.

The evidence indicates that on the level of 'naming' what the referendum
vote was all about, the politicians were clearly in command. The two sets of
provincial politicians (Parti Québécois and Liberal) had drawn up the
opposing party platforms for the campaign. Federal politicians in Ottawa
had in turn set guidelines for those umbrella organizations which were
uniting the business, financial, educational, and trade union groups that
wished to take part in the campaign on one side or the other. Chapter 3 furthermore demonstrated that through the CRTC, federal Liberal politicians

TABLE 7.2
The three leaders' speeches (20 May 1980)
(by topics and arguments)

	Trudeau (NO Side)	Ryan (NO Side)	Lévesque (YES side)
1 Nature of the campaign	0	4	1
2 Ethnic group's response	1	4	1
3 Economic implications	0	0	0
4 Renewed federalism	3	6	1
5 PQ's political future	0	0	0
6 Yvettes/turning point	0	2	0
7 Others	2	2	2
Total	6	18	5

had brought in unprecedented, but 'arm's length,' policies for supervising the media, in order to guarantee impartiality of coverage. The media organizations bowed to these extraordinary demands by not only adjusting the style of their coverage, but also producing internal CBC and Radio-Canada documents that outlined editorial procedures for 'neutral' and 'balanced' coverage. When the vote outcome showed that the majority of francophones as well as other Quebecers had rejected sovereignty-association, it was the political leaders who were called on to place this outcome into perspective.

Table 7.2 indicates that the leaders' speeches May 20, 1980 interpreting the referendum outcome presaged the argumentation strategies of the French and English 'day after' programs that were aired the next day. This is evident both in the topic selections and in the types of arguments the three leaders used in explaining the vote outcome. In the spirit of conciliation, all three speeches called for a renewal of Canadian federalism, but there the similarities ended. Pierre Trudeau, as prime minister of all Canadians, stressed this topic exclusively, implying that the ethnic groups had added their voice to the NO vote (one mention), and pleaded for change and a restructuring of federal-provincial relations (three mentions). Claude Ryan's very long speech to his Liberal supporters also stressed the importance of 'renewed federalism' (six mentions), but provided three additional reasons why the NO won. These were the quality of his campaign (four mentions), support from the ethnic vote (four mentions), and the important role of Quebec women in the NO struggle (two mentions). The

'Yvettes' factor, which arose from Lise Bissonnette's flippant attack on Ryan's wife, had galvanized Liberal women of all ages into staging a huge rally for the NO at Montreal's Forum. René Lévesque's short and emotional acknowledgment of defeat for the sovereignty-association option emphasized history and the long term. He criticized Trudeau's interference in the provincial campaign (one mention), noted ethnic group opposition (one mention), and asked his followers to give federalism one more chance (one mention).

The three leaders 'named' the problem through their particular topic selections. This process was amplified by their differing modes of appeal, which were designed to create emotional closure for party workers and for Montrealers gathered around their television sets. Classical rhetoric distinguishes between *logos*, or rational appeals, *patos*, or emotional appeals, and *ethos*, or ethical appeals (Corbett, 1980: 50–106). In his victory speech, Trudeau made a predominantly ethical appeal; Ryan for his part made a rational appeal, while Lévesque resorted to an emotional one. Trudeau's ethical appeal created closure through a logic of argumentation that equated degrees of democracy with opportunities for citizens to have their voices heard. From his point of view, the use of a referendum to deal with an issue as explosive as national dismemberment placed Canada in the forefront of democratic states:

I have never been as proud as this evening to be a Quebecer and a Canadian. We are experiencing tonight the fullness of democracy with all its joys and sorrows ... All of us have the opportunity to show the whole world that we are not the last colonials on earth, but rather among the first people to free ourselves from the old world of nation-states. And with God's help, we shall succeed.

Ryan's rational mode of appeal focused on the concept of 'equity' in democratic society and its application to *all* citizens. At the Verdun Arena, surrounded by a crowd of Liberal Party supporters, a serious Ryan commented:

This stunning victory took place practically all over Quebec, and among all sectors of the population. It will no longer be possible after tonight to indulge in the kind of subtle distinction that some have tried to make between various categories of Quebecers. We are all once again first-class citizens, equal citizens ... Please accept this verdict as a clear indication of our will to continue to seek our future in co-operation and consultation with you, the other provinces of Canada. It calls for action and change and I do hope that all those who want the progress of federalism in Canada, both in Quebec and in the other provinces, will come together to readjust the federal system to the needs and realities of today.

The framing and closure strategy in Premier Lévesque's emotional appeal was quite different. To comfort his followers, he placed the referendum outcome in a historical perspective and provided emotional closure through the communal singing of 'Gens du pays,' the PQ's anthem. On a virtually empty stage at the Paul Sauvé Arena, he tried unsuccessfully to still the emotional outpouring of his PQ supporters, but was finally able to say:

My dear friends, if I have understood you well, what you are saying is 'until the next time.' But in the meantime, with the same serenity that has characterized our behaviour throughout the whole campaign, we have to accept defeat ... But I have confidence that, one day, we shall have another rendezvous with history. Quebec will keep it. Tomorrow we must go on living together despite the deep divisions that exist between us. And that's why I ask you to sing with me to all Quebecers without exception, our loveliest song ...

Though their modes of appeal differed, as did their closure strategies, all three politicians interpreted the outcome of the referendum vote as a desire for change on the part of all Quebecers. This desire for change, however, meant different things to the three party leaders. For Trudeau and the federal Liberals, it implied a new Constitution that would affirm Canada's statehood: 'It is upon this desire for change that we must build a renewed Canadian confederation which will give the people of Quebec and the whole country more reasons to proclaim proudly that we are Canadians.' For Ryan and the provincial Liberals, it meant the renegotiation of Canadian federalism with special status for Quebec: 'It will be necessary that we be given before long the opportunity to say under what conditions this renewed federalism can be achieved.' For Lévesque and the Parti Québécois, it signified postponement of sovereignty until another rendezvous with history could be arranged. (With hindsight, we know that this date was to be 30 October 1995; on that day the PQ under Jacques Parizeau came within a whisker of winning a majority for secession.) Reiterating a basic tenet of *nationalisme québécois*, Lévesque noted: 'Let us never lose sight of an objective which is so legitimate, so universally recognized among the peoples and nations – political equality. I must say that this year, 1980, will remain as one of the last manifestations of the old Quebec.'

Journalistic Engineering of Consent

Two additional processes are involved in public opinion formation. They are, according to Joseph Gusfield (1981), the assignment of ownership to a particular social élite, and the legitimation of a particular way of thinking about public problems. In Chapters 5 and 6 it was demonstrated that the Montreal stations, through their production and editing practices, provided different ways of thinking about referendum issues for their francophone and anglophone viewers. However, the role of the Quebec media as generators of consensus still needs to be pieced together, because it is complex and fairly invisible. On the institutional level, the media's 'ownership' of campaign reporting is legitimated in the *Canadian Broadcasting Act*, which also codifies performance practices such as equal time for all party spokespersons. These codes are translated into journalistic performance characteristics such as 'neutrality,' 'objectivity,' and 'timeliness,' which affect story structure and news characteristics, as was demonstrated in Chapters 4 and 6. Yet beyond these stylistic characteristics, there are additional narrative properties of the journalistic discourse that are the outcome of the rhetorical use to which the voices of politicians, experts, and people-in-the-street are put. Because narratives operate on two levels – the linguistic and the dramatic – three rhetorical elements must be distinguished: the selection of voices, the selection of frames, and the selection of elements of argumentation. During the referendum, all of these selections, which were made by the editorial team, limited the spectrum of meanings available to viewers for making sense of the outcome.

Table 7.3 analyses *dispositio*, or the journalistic sequencing of topics. It demonstrates the obvious – namely, that the news personnel were in control not only of the sequencing, but also of the hierarchizing of topics in terms of which the referendum outcome was explained. Huge teams of news personnel were marshalled by both the French and the English stations to cover this culminating referendum event. Eleven reporter voices were active in the French discourse and fourteen in the English. The more extensive use of reporter voices and the greater number of sequences initiated by the anchor only (3 out of 8) underscore the stylistic differences between the French and English news discourses that we discussed in Chapter 3. The table also demonstrates that the sequences were ordered according to the political importance of the four types of participants in the public debate. The French program's eight sequences began with federal politicians in Ottawa, followed by the provincial political actors and inter-

TABLE 7.3
Journalistic sequencing of topics and voices (21 May 1980 newscasts)

Radio-Canada: *Ce Soir* (French) (31 voices)	CBC: *City at Six* (English) (47 voices)
BULLETIN NATIONAL	Anchor: G. Finstad/Rep: Johnson (2 anchor/reporter) Sequence 1: The 'No' Committee (1 politician)
Anchor: Paul Racine (1 anchor) Sequence 1: Le gouvernement fédéral Trudeau/Clark/Broadbent (3 politicians)	
	Anchor/Rep: Moscovitz (2 anchor/reporter) Sequence 2: The 'Yes' Committee
Reporter: D. L'Heureux (1 reporter) Sequence 2: Le comité parapluie du Non Ryan (1 politician)	
	Rep: B. Stewart (1 reporter) Sequence 3: Federal Politicians (2 politicians)
Reporter: M. Poulin (1 reporter) Le comité parapluie du Oui	
Lalonde/Chirac (2 politicians) Anchor (1 anchor) Sequence 3: Réactions internationales	Rep: C. Kinch/S. Firestone (1 politician) (2 reporters) Sequence 4: 'No' Committee
Anchor (1 anchor) Sequence 4: Les réactions du marché boursier (autres nouvelles) (1 expert)	Rep: M. Macleod/Rep. T. Kennedy (2 anchor/reporter) Sequence 5: 'Yes' Committee
	Vox-Pop (8)
BULLETIN RÉGIONAL	Sequence 6: Reactions of the business sector
Reporter: C. Desbiens (1 reporter) Sequence 1: Répartition du vote selon les différentes circonscriptions électorales	Rep. Bigeault: Stock market (1 expert) Rep. Fryer: Conseil du Patronat (1 expert) Rep. Desmarais: Chambre de commerce (1 expert) Rep. Rivet: Retailer's Association (1 expert)
Reporter: C. Gervais (1 reporter) Sequence 2: Réactions de différents organismes satisfaits: Conseil du patronat, Chambre de commerce (2 experts); déçus: 3 grandes centrales syndicales; neutres: L'Union des municipalités, le maire (1 politician)	Anchor/Rep. T. Rowe (2 anchor/reporter) Sequence 7: The pollsters
Reporter (1 reporter) Sequence 3: Vox Pop (9 public)	Anchor (1 anchor) Sequence 8: Mayor Drapeau's reaction (1 politician)

TABLE 7.3—*Continued*

Radio-Canada: *Ce Soir* (French) (31 voices)	CBC: *City at Six* (English) (47 voices)
Reporter (1 reporter) Sequence 4: L'atmosphère le soir du vote D. Levasseur – Camp du Non (1 reporter) N. Lessieur – Camp du Oui (1 reporter) A. Dumas – rules (1 reporter)	Anchor (1 anchor) Sequence 9: People's reactions Vox-Pop (10) Anchor/Rep. D. Bjarnason (2 anchor/reporter) Sequence 10: International reaction Anchor Sequence 11: (1 anchor) The 'No' Committee Anchor Sequence 12: (1 anchor) Federal politicians Anchor/Rep. Johnson, Moscovitz, MacPherson (3 reporters)

national reactions. In the second part of the program, the vote outcomes in important electoral districts were recounted, responses from various experts representing interest groups were sought, and the public's thoughts were canvassed. This structural logic seemed 'fair' to both supporters and critics of the sovereignty option, because it conformed to the *usual* news format conventions, which place the most important voice or group at the top of the line-up.

The English program's twelve sequences began with the local Quebec NO and YES committees, moved on to the federal politicians' assessments, and returned again to the provincial NO and YES leaders. Each of these sequences was interspersed with vox-pop interviews. The reactions of the Montreal business community were then solicited. In the second part of the program, the pollsters were queried; Mayor Drapeau refused an interview; people-in-the-street were again questioned; and international reactions were recorded. The program ended with a sequence in which provincial NO committee and federal politicians constructed past and future political actions from the NO point of view. These format characteristics served not only to symbolize the levels of importance assigned to different political players, but also as 'genre markers' by which television audiences would be able to read the content as 'news' and not as 'make believe.' According to David Altheide, formats in this way underlie frames and refer to the internal organization or logic of a shared symbolic activity – that of 'news' producing and news viewing as a sense-making activity (Altheide, 1985: 9, 14).

Dispositio includes not only of the sequencing of topics, but also the sequencing of voices. Again, voice sequencing varied between the two news discourses. The French station (see Table 7.3) recounted the referendum outcome using 31 different voices, of which nearly half (12) were those of station personnel. Of the remaining 19 voices, 7 belonged to politicians, 3 to business and professional interest groups speaking as experts, and a remarkable 9 to people-in-the-street. These voices occupied different positions on Montreal's political spectrum. The sequencing logic of the news discourse 'naturalised' the differences in socio-political power status of these voices, through visual representation formats and rhetorical strategies that were implicit in the news discourse, though they were not obvious to viewers. High-ranking politicians and experts were allowed to speak first and were given the opportunity to 'narrate' aspects of the situation from their own perspectives; the lower-ranking people-in-the-street were consulted last and were used mainly as narrative colour. The evidence indicates that in the French discourse, the voices of station personnel played the key role in delineating how the vote outcome was to be interpreted; as a result, the opinions of politicians and experts were stripped of much of their importance. Furthermore, the public's voice was not used to explain differences in political outlook, but merely to visually signal the democratic nature and balance of the news account as a whole.

The English network's recounting used a different rhetorical logic. Table 7.3 documents that faced with an audience that overwhelmingly rejected Quebec sovereignty, the English program included more voices than the French news discourse and structured them in a more egalitarian manner. The 'City at Six' account featured 47 voices, which were evenly distributed between the three groups of legitimated players in the Canadian political arena. The 19 news personnel voices contextualized the referendum outcome; politicans (6 voices) and experts (4 voices) explained it; and people-in-the-street (18 voices) signified the importance of the people's voices in public opinion formation. In sum, a more egalitarian voice distribution was used to legitimate the balance of the station's account.

The evidence reiterates what previous chapters have indicated: that in the struggle for control over how political occurrences are to be defined, the journalists are clearly in command. They not only select which voices will be heard, but also reconstruct the interpretations of all voices, through sequencing and rearrangement. Note this especially: although in the French discourse politicians' and experts' voices represented about the same proportion (10) as those of journalists (12), the journalistic voices intercepted what politicians were trying to convey to the electorate. In Gusfield's sense (1981), journalists 'own' political problems by having the power to define and edit them. This does not imply, however, that the journalists' definition of the situation will automatically be accepted by the station's viewing public, which requires rhetorical convincing.

This rhetorical convincing involves a third process, which is the journalistic legitimation of a particular way of *viewing* a problem or public event. In public opinion formation, this process culminates in what Stuart Hall (1979) calls the creation of 'imaginary cohesion.' This is based on a reflexive though not necessarily symmetrical relationship between the message creators and the message interpreters. Three factors affect this relationship: knowledge frameworks, the types of rhetoric utilized, and the status of the voices in the news discourse and in political life. The next table compares the topics and the types of argument that the French and English Montreal stations selected for their respective viewer groups. Clearly, since the topics selected and the arguments utilized depended on the perspective from which the vote outcome was viewed (i.e., YES or NO), the interpretative strategies and closure patterns also differed.

Table 7.4 correlates the inventory of topics with argumentation styles on the two news programs. This comparison shows that although different voices were used in the narration, journalistic selection severely limited the *kinds* of arguments that *all* types of voices were able to make in the respective news discourses. *Ce Soir* and *City at Six* programs both treated the topics of 'renewed federalism' and 'provincial elections' as interrelated. That being said, they presented the topics in inverted order, and the types of arguments they used to convince the French and English-speaking audiences were quite different. Within its first two program segments, *Ce Soir* used five different arguments to the English program's three, and chose these from *both* the YES and NO repertoires to signify narrative balance. The two NO arguments noted that negotiations for renewed federalism should take place rapidly (N1), and that the PQ might block the process (N4F). From the YES repertoire came a call for negotiations (Y4C), and the

TABLE 7.4
Sequencing the elements of argumentation (21 May 1980)
(first two topics only)

Radio-Canada: *Ce Soir* (French)	CBC: *City at Six* (English)
S.1 Federal politicians	S.1 The 'No' Committee
T.1 Renewed federalism	**T.1 Provincial elections**
1.1 Processus de négociation (Y4C)	1.1 Voters must now choose which
1.2 Nécessité d'agir rapidement (N1)	provincial party is best suited
1.3 Blocage éventuel de la part du	to work for renewed federalism
gouvernement du PQ (N4F)	(Ryan) (Y4E)
1.4 Appel au PQ à participer loyalement	
au renouvellement du fédéralisme	1.2 The ball is now in Lévesque's
(Y4E/a)	court; it is up to him to respond
1.5 Participation des partis de	to Quebecers' demands for renewed
l'Opposition au renouvellement de	federalism (Ryan) (N4F)
la constitution (Y4E/b)	
	1.3 Informal talks between Claude Ryan
S.2 Le comité parapluie du Non	and the provincial premiers should
	precede formal constitutional
T.1 Élections provinciales	negotiations (journalist)
1.6 La balle est dans le camp du PQ	
2.1 Le PQ ne peut se maintenir au pouvoir	**T.2 Renewed Federalism**
s'il conserve l'option que la population	2.1 Rejects Trudeau's proposal for
vient de rejeter (Y4C)	formal constitutional talks before
2.2 Le PQ ne peut pas défendre adéquate-	summer; informal discussions
ment le fédéralisme renouvelé (Y4F)	needed (Ryan) (N4C)
2.3 Ryan réclame des élections provinciales	2.2 Ryan will meet with premiers to
au plus tard à l'automne (N4C)	acquaint them with his position
1.7 Ryan s'engage à rechercher le compro-	spelled out in White Paper (journalist)
mis nécessaire pour élaborer un projet	2.3 These will be private meetings
précis de nouvelle constitution	preparing for the day when he takes
	over from Lévesque (journalist)

announcement that opposition parties would have a role to play in renewed federalism (Y4E/b), as well as a call for the PQ to loyally participate in the debate (Y4E/a). Closure in the French narrative involved the creation of 'imaginary cohesion,' which was sought through arguments that made sense of renewed federalism in *national* terms, as a co-operative *process* in which both provincial and federal leaders would have a role to play. Because this closure did not offer detailed proposals for the future, it was ideologically acceptable to all supporters irrespective of which side they had voted for.

Quite a different rhetorical strategy was utilized by the English station, which was sure of its audience's political preferences. It created closure around Claude Ryan's persona (N4E), and around his agenda, which included future consultations with provincial premiers and the federal government, to achieve renewed federalism (N4F). *City at Six* drew its arguments from the Beige Paper, which advocated special status for Quebec; also, it emphasized the need for consultation with the other premiers before Trudeau's constitutional talks were to begin (N4C). This rhetorical closure strategy, which was based mainly on journalistic editorialization (3 out of 6 arguments were presented by them), was possible only because the journalists felt they were stating the obvious.

The evidence shows that the journalistic engineering of public consent took place through processes of reduction and sequencing that restricted opinion access across all three levels of the news narrative. On the pragmatic level, reduction and hierarchization legitimated the voices of politicians and the public as most relevant to 'public opinion creation,' while downgrading those of the experts. The contributions of news personnel were 'naturalized' stylistically by being presented as standing outside the spatio-temporal universe of the referendum story itself. Their editorial comments were narratively transmuted by being presented as extra-diegetic statements (Nichols, 1976/77: 38). Finally, argument selection was restricted by the nature of the linguistic group that was being addressed and by the viewers' political values. All of these interpretive frameworks worked together to legitimate a kind of rhetoric that gave more credence to the journalistic voices than to the other actors in the political realm. How this came about will occupy our attention in the next section.

Journalistic Legitimation Strategies: The Rhetoric of Scientism

Since news programs both *constitute* and *legitimate* the world of democratic politics, we must now explore how this legitimation is accomplished. John Searle (1969) has pointed out that speech acts can be of different kinds: promising, accusatory, congratulating, and asserting. News discourses consist almost exclusively of assertions, which Goffman (1983) differentiates into three types of 'announcing' on the grounds that news personnel are not ordinary storytellers, but announcers of other persons' texts. News assertions, which are updated on a twenty-four-hour cycle, need to be made intelligible, as well as 'convincing' for the diverse viewer groups to whom they are addressed. Over the years many authors have tried to explain how the persuasive dimension of the journalistic discourse actually functions. One of the first to consider this question was Bernard Roshco, who noted that because this discourse is 'time bound' and there-fore ephemeral, it differs fundamentally from 'knowledge,' which aspires to longevity. With Robert Park, he therefore concluded that the journalistic discourse provides 'acquaintance with' rather than 'knowledge about' the world (Roshco, 1977: 13–14 Park, 1952). Paul Corcoran made the addi-tional point that electronic communication technologies have affected the 'art' of persuasion – its performance techniques as well as its verbal con-tent. In Corcoran's opinion there is a return to the medieval distinction between the *lingua franca*, the 'vulgar tongue,' and the learned official lan-guage used skilfully only by those in the corridors of power (1979: 201). Peter Dahlgren draws yet another useful distinction when he notes that 'official discourse' is based on 'rationality,' while 'unofficial discourse,' which is used with friends and family, is grounded in a person's values and emotions. Each of these discourses has its own performance and repression criteria (1985a: 34).

These insights indicate that the news rhetoric is not limited to the usual figures of speech, but incorporates strategic devices that enhance truthful-ness, plausibility, correctness, precision, and credibility. Journalists trans-late these criteria into 'factual reporting' conventions that exhibit a form of, and are informed by, 'scientific rationalism,' which makes these discourses into universal forms of neutral description. Timothy Reiss (1982) notes that what he calls the 'analytico-referential discourse' of positive science is based on two assumptions. First of all, that the syntactic order of semiotic systems (particularly language) is coincident with the logical ordering of 'reason.' Second, that these two orders are identical to the structural orga-nization of the world, given as 'exterior' to these two orders (1982: 13). The notion that the procedures of reason and rationality as embodied by sci-ence are welded to the actual structure of the physical universe is what guarantees that the analytico-referential discourse has access to the truth and will speak this 'truly' and without distortion.

In the 1950s and 1960s, both of these axioms began to be questioned. In *Science in a Free Society*, Paul Feyerabend provided evidence for the social foundation of scientific rationality and in doing so demolished science's claim to superiority over other means of intellection (1978: 19–20). In turn, Thomas Kuhn (1962/70) and others undermined the idea of the isomor-phism between reason and the universe's structural order. Different institu-tional and social settings, Kuhn found, give rise to competing scientific theories about the *same* set of facts. Together, these critics demonstrated that scientific discourse itself is a *rhetoric*, a form of persuasion, not a *neutral description* of the world. Science, then, is used to legitimate both a particular way of speaking about the world, and the people who do the describing.

It is our contention that journalists, in their drive for professionalization, have appropriated this rhetoric of scientism to upgrade the authority for their particular descriptions of public events, with the strategic goal of eliminating critiques of these descriptions. Michael Schudson (1978) investigated the development of journalistic discourses since 1890, and demonstrated that reporting styles are time-bound and that they have defined 'objectivity' in at least five different ways. Like other 'scientific' discourses, they can therefore not claim to be universal or neutral. An analysis of what rhetoriticians call the three aspects of the 'mode of address' provides us with a way of exploring how the contemporary television rhetoric of scientism is constructed. Mode of address distinguishes between two narrative aspects: the way something is talked *about*, or the attitude of the teller to the material, and *how* something is talked about, or the attitude of the teller to the audience. This concept enables us to isolate three formal textual characteristics that provide journalistic voices with narrative power and credibility. These are the distinction between narrators and characters, the locus of the line of argument, and the construction of the position of knowledge. Each of these elements is used to set up the triple-identity between the semiotic order of language, the logical ordering of reason, and the origin of the external world, as demanded by the analytico-referential discourse.

Our analysis has already shown that intrastation journalistic voices have a different function in the television narrative than extrastation voices. As *narrator* voices, they exist outside the spatio-temporal narrative. They are 'extra-diegetic,' that is, they represent the collective points of view not only of their profession, but also of the particular French and English stations on which their programs appear (Nichols, 1976/77: 39). Our 'day after' program comparisons show that these discourses were ideologically stratified in relation to whether they had to address a YES audience, or a NO and neutral audience, or both. Extrastation voices were used as *characters* in the discourse – as individuals representing their own social roles. They were inside the referendum narrative; in that sense the voices of Lévesque and Ryan signified *themselves* as well as their *leadership roles* in the political contest. The narrative work of the double-contextualization of character voices is hidden and naturalized by the division of labour of the journalistic speakers. As we have seen, anchor voices not only make manifest the logical principles that order the topics they introduce, but link, frame, and focus those topics in relation to other topics and to the program as a whole (Morley, 1980). Reporter voices provide elaborations of selected angles using statements offered by such character voices as experts, politicians, and people-in-the-street (Nichols, 1976/77: 42). Character voices, in whichever way they are represented, always serve to legitimate the topic selection made by the news personnel.

Control over the line of argumentation in a discourse offers yet another means for legitimating the rhetorical superiority of the journalistic speaker voices. In classical narration, the narrative voice carries the line of argumentation. In the television discourse, the argument is marshalled through the editing and juxtaposing of various character statements (Nichols, 1976/77: 40). The Chapter 4 discussion of broadcast rules pinpointed three kinds of television program conventions that pulled the fragmented line of argumentation about referendum events together into a coherent, signifying whole: the 'election' frame, the politico-ideological juxtaposition of the YES and NO sides envisioning Canada's future, and the oppositional narrative approach. All of these rhetorical devices contributed to erasing the journalistic meta-contextualizations in the referendum narrative. The electoral 'game' framing excluded voters from the dialogue and made them 'bystanders,' who were acknowledged only in crowd scenes, or in people-in-the-street interviews where, as *characters* in the narration, they were permitted to state their opinions but not the 'facts.' The Manichean oppositional approach offers an even more important strategy for creating cohesion between juxtaposed character comments. It narrates news events in a dramatic mode and in terms of a two-valued logic of good and evil; this makes it easy for campaign teams and their leaders to be classified as heroes or as villains. The Manichean rhetoric facilitates meaning accretion to character voices diachronically through time and synchronically in opposition to each other. This happened to both Lévesque and Ryan as party leaders: as early as November 1979 they were dichotomized into the 'emotional' and the 'rational' leaders respectively. Furthermore, the oppositional approach utilizes a logic of argumentation that *confirms* each side's point of view rather than *refuting* the arguments advanced by either side. Such a logic presents adversarial sets of statements as hermetically sealed off from each other in the journalistic discourse, so that their truth never has to be tested.

As was demonstrated in Chapters 4 and 6, through these narrative strategies the journalistic voices are able to legitimate their own position of knowledge as 'superior.' The narrator's knowledge of how things *really* are becomes the meta-language for evaluating the character contributions (McCabe, 1974: 11). Yet here there is a chink in the journalistic armour. By utilizing the *direct* mode of address, which explicitly acknowledges the viewer's existence, the journalistic discourse opens itself to the possibility of being interpreted as a *personal* opinion statement.

To avoid this suspicion, journalists follow the strategies of science, arguing that their narration is superior because of the rationality of its *form* and the authoritative *methods* through which it has been generated. Formal rationality is stylistically indicated in print through the use of numbers, creditable persons and institutions, and the eyewitness accounts of direct participants. Their statements are reconstructed through five different quoting practices, which, as we have seen, hierarchize and interlink them into a complex relevance structure where a range of opposing views can be stated without any need to investigate their truth value (Zelizer, 1989). On television, the same fact/interpretation distinction is achieved by juxtaposing character voices and 'action visuals,' which purport to let the viewers 'see for themselves.' The institutional reporting and production methods through which the authoritative news discourse is created, are additionally legitimated by being presented as the product of careful checking and verification of the 'raw facts' of the case.

Journalists thus base their credibility on a rhetoric of 'scientism' that mimics the stylistic features of reasoning and rationality. 'Like science and ideology, this rhetoric is grounded in a culture of careful discourse, one of whose main rules calls for *self-groundedness*, which implies that ... the speaker's conclusions do not require premises other than those s/he has articulated' (Gouldner, 1976: 42). It is a rhetoric that stresses what Frank Stark calls the elocutionary and delivery side, rather than the truth value of its content (Stark, 1984: 12). Through this rhetoric, the 'artful realm of the public' is re-created in a novel way in post-industrial society.

'Vox-Pop' Interviews: Their Role in the Constitution of Public Opinion

Hovering behind most TV news analysis is the theme of democracy and the role of the media in constituting the public sphere. This public sphere is variously described as the place between the state and the people where public opinion formation takes place and where the popular will is given expression (Dahlgren, 1987: 39). It has been widely argued that the medium of television and its bureaucratic structure have invaded this sphere and changed the formats and modes of persuasion. 'Image politics' is said to have relegated voters to passivity and also to have made it difficult for them to acquire the information necessary for serious political decision-making. While a more detailed investigation of these issues will have to wait till Chapter 8, one aspect of this debate can be addressed here. It concerns the symbolic rendition of the 'public' as the fourth legitimated player on the political stage, and the treatment of that public in the 'day after' reportage on the two Montreal stations. Previous sections showed that people-in-the-street interviews were an important *visual* component of French and English news programming. These voices, however, were much more heavily mediated than the *character* voices of other legitimated players in the public sphere. Reporters use vox-pop interviews to ground their reporting practices and to buttress their story angles. That being said, our analysis indicates that in two out of its three renditions the 'public' lacks a mode of address and therefore cannot communicate verbally at all. As stand-ins for the station's viewers, people in news stories are often seen but not heard. In a sense, they are used as 'atmosphere.' This is well illustrated in the use of the public as a 'crowd description' or a 'voting statistic.'

The 'crowd description' is an interesting stylistic and rhetorical feature of television news discourses, in that it renders 'people' audiovisually but does not permit them to address the viewer. Crowds can clap, shout, and sing, but they cannot make a reasoned argument, as evidenced by Cynthia Kinch's television report of the NO camp's victory party at the Verdun Arena. She noted: 'Everyone knows Claude Ryan is in the building [flag waving, cheers]. Ryan steps into the arena [chants of Ryan, Ryan ... NO theme song]. Once at the podium ... Ryan greets the crowd. Victory is his.' Yet all the crowd was shown to be doing was cheer and wave flags; in this way, these Montreal citizens were reduced to a visual backdrop for their leader's speech. Another audiovisual means of curtailing the public's ability to speak, is to render it as a voting statistic. In this rendition, people become social objects that politicians' and journalists' voices can manipulate at will. A classic example of this reporting style was the segment on *Ce Soir* where the reporter's voice announced: 'Et nous allons maintenant revenir chez nous pour parler du référendum, plus particulièrement dans la région métropolitaine. Tel que l'ont indiqué à peu près tous les sondages, ce fut un balayage presque complet de l'action du NON.' The legitimate role of the public in political life was here rendered as a 'sondage' rather than the outcome of discussion, group pressure, or voter action. Polling statistics detailed the numbers of votes cast by anonymous Quebecers against the sovereignty-association proposal, but without telling the viewer anything about *why* the votes were cast the way they were. The audiovisual 'crowd' renditions, and the accurate voting percentages, were thus rhetorically used not to legitimate the public as a key player in the political decision process, but rather to legitimate the scientific accuracy of the news discourse as a whole.

Only 'vox-pop' interviews, which use individuals to stand for political groupings, offer members of the public an opportunity to speak in their own voices. Yet even here there are structural and content constraints on the ability of ordinary voters to discuss political issues. Our transcripts (Appendices D and E) indicate that there were a total of nine interviewees on the French and eighteen on the English 'day after' programs, which suggests that vox-pop interviews are important formats for demonstrating that public consultation has occurred and that diverse views on an event exist. As such, they dramatize the ideal 'marketplace of ideas' from which informed public opinion in democratic politics is supposed to emerge. On both programs journalistic 'timeliness' and 'neutrality' requirements mandated that the news discourse include both YES and NO supporters.

Predictably, on the politically united English-language program more NO than YES supporters were interviewed (12 to 6). On the French program, which was addressed to a politically fractured public, a more equal number of YES and NO voices (4 and 3) were allowed to speak. Two respondents representing stances between the two political options were also heard. In this way, vox-pop interviews constituted ritual enactments of the democratic order, which like the marketplace of ideas was represented as open and egalitarian.

Vox-pop answers are constrained by both topic and question format. Charlotte Brunsdon and David Morley found that participants of low status tended to be questioned only about their feelings on well-defined issues and were quickly cut short if they moved 'off point' (1978: 65). This British-style élitism was not evident in the referendum interviews: participants were treated even-handedly in both the French and English discourses. What *is* evident, however, is that French and English journalists used quite different question formats, which Hanni Woodbury calls the 'inquiry' and 'control' modes of questioning. The 'control' mode raises detailed questions, to which only assent or dissent is possible; this makes it easier for the narrator voice to impose its own topic orientation on the interviewee (Woodbury, 1984: 199–204). The narrative effect of this mode is well illustrated in the way Cynthia Kinchs fused two distinct quotes into a narrative sequence that validated her segment introduction: 'As the crowd disperses ... many people mill around talking about what happened' (in the NO victory camp). The first respondent (#1) noted, 'We are still part of Canada.' The second (#2) answered Kinch's 'how do *you* feel' question outside the Verdun Arena with the response, 'Oh! I feel great with this here' (see Appendix D).

The vox-pop interviews on *Ce Soir* on 21 May 1980 were rendered quite differently, using the 'inquiry' mode of questioning (see Appendix E). This questioning strategy permits respondents to develop their explanatory agenda in a more personal manner. This was particularly evident in the comments offered by respondents #1, #5, and #9, who seemed to be offering their own interpretations of the NO side loss. Each of these voices represented a different point on the Montreal political spectrum. The woman on the NO side, possibly remembering the Yvettes campaign, noted 'Je me sense mieux en tant que femme parce qu'en plus, le vote des femmes est majoritairement sur le côté du NON.' The man on the YES side opined, 'Je pense que les Québécois sont prêts à se faire hara kiri.' A seemingly uncommitted bystander joked, 'Il faut avoir un référendum pour avoir de belles températures au Québec.'

Rethinking the 'Active Audiencing' Link

At the beginning of this chapter we noted that the media are able to link political élites and the voting public only if one assumes that 'active audiencing' is possible. Such a possibility occurs because news discourses are more than textual descriptions; they are also forms of social interaction between all participants in the public communication enterprise because they share common linguistic and cognitive frames. It is these knowledge frames that make news stories understandable. Members of a given society build up these common frames out of attitudes toward everyday life, which constitute the competent citizens'/viewers' means for making sense of what politics is all about and how it works in Quebec and Canada. News producers as well as viewers reflexively co-constructed the political assumptions underlying the varied French and English versions of referendum events and issues.

On the production side, discourse theory indicates that the reproduction of news events involves complex forms of text processing, as well as cognitive strategies and forms of narration. These forms of narration differed both textually and visually on Montreal's French and English stations, because there were divergences in how the anchor and reporter

roles were deployed. Teun van Dijk notes that besides a mental representation of the various source texts, journalistic narrations also construct a
'model' of the situation – that is, an episodic, subjective knowledge structure of what the source texts are about (van Dijk, 1988: 180). The construction of these models is sustained by general knowledge scripts, such
as the 'election as game' with its topic and argument restrictions. Added
to these are political attitudes and ideologies, which during the referendum entered the news narrations through the 'points of view' from which
vote outcomes were narrated. Our comparison indicated that these points
of view favoured the NO over the YES arguments by a margin of two to
one. This in turn produced a rhetoric that constructed consensus around
two themes: 'campaign mistakes' to explain the referendum loss on the
French program, and 'renewed federalism' as the task for the future on
the English program.

Our comparisons suggest that on the understanding and reception side,
the efficacy of a news discourse depends both on the representations proffered and on the interpretations suggested by rhetorical means. Even
though news discourses seemed to use a 'fact' based narrative style and did
not argue for a specific position or opinion, they presupposed ideological
stances in the ways in which they constructed explanations. Current work
on news understanding therefore suggests that readers/viewers do not
remember news reports or create new interpretations, so much as they
update previously existing models of already known situations (van Dijk,
1986). Our discovery that the referendum outcome was recounted through
a very restricted and oft-repeated repertoire of news topics, suggests how
such updating might be accomplished. Also, the use of a restricted set of
simple, two-valued, YES/NO 'canonical formulas' to argue referendum
issues adds credence to the experimental research on 'schemata,' which has
demonstrated that people remember best what they already know
(Crocker, Fiske, and Taylor, 1984: 315–37). No wonder, then, that the
description of the referendum outcome involved emotionally charged
speeches by Pierre Trudeau, Claude Ryan, and René Lévesque.

The fact that the structures of news reports can be systematically linked
to the cognitive processes of news making and to those of understanding,
suggests that viewers/readers do not passively absorb subliminal text
'inputs,' but actively and discursively 'make sense' and produce readings.
The discussion of the Yvettes mobilization in the final chapter will illustrate this in greater detail. Reader response theorists argue that audiencing
behaviour cannot be 'read off' from social categories such as age, race, class,
and gender, though these do help determine the interpretive competencies

of different reader groups (Fiske, 1989: 160). Interpretive differences, the Montreal comparisons suggest, are not grounded in individual psychological make-ups; rather, they arise from membership in interpretive *communities* that are politically and linguistically defined.

8

Rethinking News, Public Opinion, and Democratic Politics in Quebec and Canada

This book started from the common sense assumption that the media play an important role in democratic political life. The question now is this: How much power do they exercise in our complex, pluralistic, and fragmented modern society? This has been hotly debated. Media power in traditional public opinion research was conceived in political terms, in the context of influence and attitude change (Katz, 1995). Yet there are, of course, other forms of power, such as the power to define what the political system is all *about*. This type of power affects citizens as much as government decrees and court decisions (which Colin Sparks refers to as powers exercised in public social relations; see 1995: 45). The previous chapters of this book explored how the Montreal media's *definitional* powers affected in real if complex ways how the 1980 referendum was described and enacted by French and English media in Quebec. This chapter will open by summarizing the major findings of our comparative study, and then address two additional but related issues: the media's capacity to mobilize a given subset of the public, and the media's changing role in democratic politics.

The Media and Public Opinion Formation

In post-industrial societies, media influence is a function of five intertwined activities: the media as providers of socially relevant information; their 'agenda setting' and 'priming' functions; their political linkage role between élites and the population; and their direct influence, through news coverage, of political actors. We will summarize how these media-political relationships constituted themselves in Montreal during the 1980 referendum. It is important to remember here that all media systems are embedded in unique social and political matrices that structure their activities at a particular historical place and time. Robert Hackett (1991) describes how Canada's 'news net' encompasses both a set of institutional relationships, and specific collection and distribution *flows*, which are selective and do not cover all regions and events equally. In Canada this news net has three main characteristics: it is hierarchically organized; it is concentrated around two nodes; and it functions in two languages. The net's hierarchical organization refers to the fact that Canadian media outlets are organized geographically, into national, regional, and local news distribution systems. Electronic media are found on all of these levels, though their agenda-setting 'effectivity' is greatest on the national and regional levels, because of the country's size and low population density. Newspapers, in contrast, have their greatest 'effectivity' on the local scene, where they monitor city politics. The news net is concentrated around two urban nodes, Montreal and Toronto, in large part because about 75 per cent of Canadians reside within the Montreal–Toronto–Ottawa triangle, and because the former two cities are headquarters both to the public and private broadcasters and to the CP (Canadian Press) national news agency. Through this triangle, Canadian national news producers are connected to global suppliers, such as Reuters and Agence France Presse (of Europe), and Associated Press and United Press (of the United States) (Robinson, 1981: 188–214).

Our evidence indicates that Montreal and Toronto have acquired additional prominence because they function as the hubs for the country's French and English news flows, and because they are the home towns of the country's two 'national' newspapers, *Le Devoir* and the *Globe and Mail*. In the 1980s these linguistically separate news networks were held in place by media ownership patterns in which francophone and anglophone interests did not intersect. In English Canada at the time, two press conglomerates held sway: Thomson owned 34.2 per cent, and Southam 12 per cent of Canada's daily newspapers. In Quebec, three other conglomerates dominated the print market: Francoeur's Unimedia (11.7 per cent), Péladeau's Quebecor (2 per cent), and Desmarais' Power Corporation (3.4 per cent) (Raboy, 1992: 83–7). In broadcasting a similar division held sway in both the public and private domains. Radio-Canada is administratively separate from the English CBC, and Télé-Métropole (TVA network and Vidéotron) offers services similar to those offered by the Ontario-based Global network. Since the 1980s many of these Quebec and Canadian media empires have been further concentrated into multinational corporations, which today cross linguistic as well as national boundaries. That being said, language and ownership bifurcation, and the dominance of Montreal and Toronto as the country's two news hubs, provided the structural framework in which the varying Quebec French- and English-Canadian news agendas and ways of talking about referendum issues were constructed in the 1980s.

During the referendum campaign, the Montreal media's gate-keeping and agenda-setting roles were in the hands of a highly trained corps of journalists, both French and English, who according to Armande Saint-Jean had rapidly become professionalized in the two decades leading up to 1980. Chapter 2 explained how unionization and a series of strikes improved Quebec journalists' working conditions and substantially increased their salaries. But these strikes also signalled an end to hopes for autonomy in news production. As a result of the strikes some outlets, including the Parti Québécois's *Le Jour* and the popular weekly *Québec-Presse*, were forced to close, and this meant that francophone outlets for critical political reporting on the model of the European party press had been eliminated. By 1980 it was clear that the Quebec market could not support an alternative press financed by subscription, and that Quebec journalists would have to submit to North American industry norms. In both languages, newspaper competition decreased, and the publications that were still alive began retructuring themselves to offer information as a commodity for a largely undifferentiated readership. In such a climate, journalists were treated more and more as 'employees' by the media conglomerates, which set out to make money rather than to champion particular political causes (Demers, 1989). No wonder, then, that Quebec newspaper owners chose to align themselves with the NO rather than the YES side in the referendum campaign.

After the 1976 election of the Parti Québécois and the party's subsequent announcement that it would hold a referendum on sovereignty-association, print and broadcast outlets were forced to scrutinize their professional practices and attitudes even more carefully than before. In the House of Commons, vigorous debate opened as early as February 1977, when Prime Minister Trudeau stated that he was 'very concerned about the possibility of CBC/Radio-Canada propagandizing separatism' (in Rose, 1993: 176). As the referendum debate heated up, Montreal newspapers began to formulate editorial 'neutrality' policies, and the Conseil de presse du Québec began debating the social role of journalists. In the spring of 1980, Yves Gagnon, whom the FPJQ had commissioned to survey the press coverage of referendum issues, reported that the majority of Quebec papers and journalists subscribed to the notion of 'équilibre' or 'balance,' but that the doctrine of balance was practised differently in francophone and anglophone papers (1980: 174–5). Our detailed findings on these narrative differences will be discussed shortly. More to the point here is the implicit suggestion that francophone journalists were somehow less trustworthy than their anglophone counterparts in fulfilling their 'neutral' reportorial role (Clift, 1980). Fuel was added to this assumption by Pierre Godin's discovery that 79 per cent of francophone journalists had voted for the PQ in the 1976 election, and that 66 per cent had declared themselves to be sovereigntists (1979: 39).

The argument that a relationship existed between a journalist's 'private' political preferences and her or his performance of 'public' reportorial duties seems plausible on the surface. In fact, as Saint-Jean and other Quebec media scholars explain, two socio-political events make such a conclusion quite untenable. The first was the vivid memory of the War Measures Act and its consequences in 1970, and the second was the newspaper owners' declared opposition to the sovereigntist project. The War Measures Act had required that all francophone Radio-Canada programming be submitted to pre-censorship by CBC headquarters in Toronto, and had culminated in the dismissal of a number of francophone reporters (Robinson, 1975: 152–3). Self-censorship was also fostered by the conflict in political views between francophone journalists and the newspaper owners they worked for – a conflict that made it impossible for journalists to play a critical role for fear of being branded 'non-objective' (Lachapelle and Noiseux, 1980: 138–40). Chapter 2 documented that only a small handful of Quebec francophone and anglophone journalists demanded the right to be politically active, while at the same time fulfilling their professional obligations. Their demands were rejected by newspaper managements, who during the campaign suspended six journalists at *La Presse* (1), *Le Soleil* (1), *Le Nouvelliste* (2, and the *Gazette* (2). Some of these journalists were suspended with pay and some without, depending on their contracts (Leblanc, 1981: 123).

According to Évelyne Dumas, who had worked at *Le Jour*, this professional double-bind resulted in referendum coverage that lacked all historical perspective and that featured a small number of arguments made over and over again (*Le Devoir*, 7 November 1979). Our analysis of *La Presse* in Chapter 5 gives some credence to this assessment, but the reasons behind it were more complex than Dumas suggests. Far from becoming obvious participants in the political process and practising sensational coverage, as was claimed during the constitutional crisis of 1990–2 (Taras, 1993: 141), Quebec journalists at the time of the 1980 referendum took enormous pains to perform their professional role in the same competent and 'neutral' manner as their English-speaking colleagues. Though simplistic claims of ideological bias have always been made to explain the different ways that francophone and anglophone Montreal media constructed the referendum news agendas, our comparative study demonstrates that quite the opposite is true. News reports, especially in the electronic media, are not produced by single individuals; rather, they undergo an organizational editing process. It follows that differences in news agendas during the referendum were grounded in audiovisual *production* decisions made by French and English language stations, and in the news frames that Montreal's producers and viewers *co-constructed* to explain what particular referendum events were perceived to be *about*.

To explain these differing audiovisual production decisions, and how Montreal's three politically polarized viewer/reader groups were narratively addressed, we developed a dramaturgical analysis scheme based on Goffman's notion that politics in post-industrial democratic societies unfolds on a public and mediated electronic discussion stage. This stage is peopled by four kinds of legitimated players: politicians and their party supporters, news personnel, experts, and the public. The setting in which these players appear affects not only how they are able to speak and behave, but also the authority their voices will carry in the news discourse. In the news drama, journalists perform two types of roles. There are the 'in studio' roles of anchor, commentator, reporter, and interviewer, where journalists are *in charge* of constituting the news program. Additionally, journalists' voices are in charge of *retelling* the daily news events, thereby legitimating the station's narrative thrust. In such a set-up the three 'outside' players – politicians, experts, and people-in-the-street – are part of the supporting cast. Like a Greek chorus, extrastudio voices are used to illustrate or comment on the events selected by the news personnel.

Chapter 3 explored the audiovisual configurations of Montreal's French and English stations to demonstrate how audiovisual production decisions affected the *renditions* of people and events in the news discourse. According to Teun van Dijk, unique *style* characteristics prescribe what types of audiovisual combinations are permissible in this discourse (1988: 25). To our surprise, the two station groups made very different production decisions concerning the selection and choreographing of their news presenter roles, as well as their audiovisual imaging techniques. On the francophone stations, the anchor role was supreme. It constituted and carried the news program almost single-handedly, with minor assistance from the reporter role. It also accomplished most of the interpretive work in the narrative, by being visually present in more than half (56 per cent) of all story items. In contrast, anglophone stations constructed their story accounts around three in-station roles, which practised a visual and argumentative division of labour. The anchor role, which was present in 29 per cent of all items, introduced and framed the story; and the reporter role (40 per cent) linked the different subplots together; while the interviewer role (20 per cent) provided focus and detail. When and why these stylistic differences arose is a question that cannot be answered from our evidence. Only historical comparisons of archival news program material from the 1950s onward will be able to illuminate these issues.

The different news presenter role selections led to differences in audiovisual imaging combinations, because each role is associated with a particular visualization technique. Through routinization of work practices, these visualization techniques become combined into audiovisual paradigms. Because the anchor role predominated on the French stations, visualization was achieved mainly through the frontal piece-to-camera mode and through graphics. Such a discourse seems visually more uniform and (some researchers argue) easier for the viewer to decipher, because camera changes are kept to a minimum. In contrast, the English stations provided many more visual possibilities because they constructed their news accounts through three roles. These included the reporter's film-and-voice-over mode, which was visually located outside the studio, and the interviewer's filmed interview mode, which rendered politicians, experts, and people in public spaces at middle distance.

The differences in choreography and in audiovisual imaging techniques led to differences in narrative structures and story flows. The francophone stations created shorter stories, which on average were made up of two items or subplots; while the anglophone story lengths averaged nearly three subplots/items per story. Also, the camera handling within the subplots was slower in the francophone discourse, averaging two different camera angles to the anglophones' four. Because news reports were visually retold through the eyes of the anchor and utilized fewer camera changes, francophone story flow seemed more tranquil. The English stations' narrative flow was enlivened by the reporter and interviewer roles, which brought outside voices (politicians, experts, the public) into the discourse. Thus, anchor/piece-to-camera accounts were interspersed with studio/film or location/film visual renditions. Furthermore, more frequent intercutting, zooming, and camera changes speeded up the anglophone news discourse and made it somewhat more difficult for viewers to follow. We shall demonstrate that these narrative and audiovisual differences gave rise to different ways of constructing 'balance' and 'verification' criteria within the two news discourses – a point suggested but not analysed by Yves Gagnon in 1980. Our evidence indicates that in spite of these narrative and audiovisual differences, the francophone and anglophone news discourses both created their story flows between news personnel roles, which means that news personnel voices were in charge of constructing the meaning contexts through which Montreal's YES, NO and undecided citizen viewers made sense of referendum events.

After exploring the regulatory and journalistic settings in which the referendum news discourses were created, Chapter 4 focused on how the media 'mapped' referendum events. This mapping went beyond the 'agenda setting' and 'priming' functions documented in the 1970s, to create the political *meaning context* in which the links between élites and the public in the political process could be imagined. In post-industrial democratic societies, the media must symbolically constitute this reality to make ethnically diverse peoples feel that they are participating in one and the same political enterprise. The resulting political maps in the first instance have cognitive impacts, but attitudinal consequences are likely to follow. Recent scholarship has argued that the media, both print and broadcasting, have three types of involvement in public meaning and opinion creation. The media's news programs *selectively construct* social knowledge and thus provide a frame of reference through which different social groups are able to understand their own and others' 'lived reality.' Furthermore, they select the issues and thus provide an *inventory* for understanding what the referendum campaign was all about. A third and even more difficult function of the media is to fashion public consensus on major issues of the day. As we shall see, this consensus had to be made visible so that diverse citizens' groups would be able to view themselves as part of the same public.

Our comparative case studies demonstrated that both station groups engaged in three types of classificatory activity to selectively reconstruct the referendum maps for Montrealers. This selective reconstruction involved a substantial political *redefinition* of what was happening in Quebec. The Montreal and Canadian media did not describe the PQ's referendum proposals as one of the most important constitutional challenges to Confederation since the nineteenth century; nor did they describe them as a federal/provincial struggle over the decentralization of powers. Instead, the Montreal media, like the media in English Canada as a whole, labelled this extraordinary plebiscite as an election. Identifying the referendum as an election helped to naturalize and defuse this politically explosive challenge and to associate it with normal and routinized Canadian democratic processes.

Montreal journalists benefited from the 'election' designation in the sense that it offered them a set of familiar scripting possibilities. 'Scripts,' according to Goffman (1974), have complementary functions for journalists and for viewers/citizens. For journalists, scripts make it easier to select and identify newsworthy events; for citizens/viewers, scripts make selected events narratively comprehensible. All of this is discernible in our comparison. The 1979 and 1980 federal elections marked a turning point in Canadian electoral history, and political events could have been narrated from at least three different points of view. The first scripting option arose from the fact that 15 per cent of the electorate were new voters; their participation could have been acknowledged as a 'competition between newly emerging interest groups.' The second scripting option had to do with the fact that substantial population growth in British Columbia and Alberta had redistributed voting 'weight' to the West. In 1979 and 1980, the two provinces received 9 new seats to give the West a total of 77, which meant that the West for the first time had more seats in Parliament than Quebec, with its 75. Such a redistribution could have given rise to a scripting in which the election was interpreted as a 'dialogue between elected officials and citizens' about the future of the country. The third scripting option related to the appearance of a new set of opposition leaders; their arrival on the scene made it possible to contextualize these elections as a partisan game played by Ed Broadbent (NDP) and Joe Clark (PC) against the Trudeau Liberals (Mendelsohn, 1993: 150). Walter Soderlund and colleagues, as well as Fred Fletcher, found that in fact, the Canadian print and broadcast media did adopt the 'game' script in both 1979 and 1980. Such a framing removed the national unity issue from the news agenda, while highlighting economic issues, especially in Western Canada (Soderlund et al., 1984: 53–7; Fletcher, 1981a: 295, 313). Our comparison indicates that the same game scripting was carried over into the referendum campaign, where it affected the choice of referendum topics.

By choosing to recount the preceding Canadian elections as a partisan game, the media restricted their narrative focus and rendered it more adversarial, to the point that they highlighted only four topics. Two of these were the activities of the party leaders, and the polls and standings, in which the media showed an abnormal interest. These topics highlighted campaign events and questions of strategy rather than the substance of what Quebec secession would mean for Canada's federal political system. In a later section we will discuss the implications of such contextualizations for the functioning of Canadian democracy. For now it is important only to note that the CFCF case study demonstrates the narrative implications of these topic foci. The focus on leaders took Lévesque and Ryan out of the March 1980 National Assembly theatre, where the advantages of sovereignty were being debated, and showed them 'on the road' being queried about the latest poll results. As we saw, these leader interviews did not explore the *reasons* for the vote shift toward the YES option at the time; it merely used them to visually contrast the 'emotional' and 'rational' leader personae. The focus on backroom strategy turned the coverage of the PQ's White Paper, with its critique of federalism, into a discourse about its use as a tool for propaganda. Together, the comparisons we have made demonstrate that the media's three reportorial strategies – redefining the plebiscite as an election, and framing it as a game, and focusing all issues through an adversarial reporting lens – not only narrowed the discussion agenda but also made it more negative. What we mean by this is that the referendum coverage became focused on the YES and NO options, on the strategic wins and losses of the two teams, and on their positive or negative performances. Lost in all of this were media discussions of the range of political options available to rebuild the Canadian federation, and of different voter groups' more nuanced understandings of the issues of the day. Such a narrowing of the agenda also implied that consensus building, which is the outcome of the process of public opinion creation, would become more and more polarized over time.

The final way in which the symbolic map of referendum issues was selectively constructed for Montreal viewers, was through the political alternatives proposed by the PQ and the Liberals in the White Paper and Beige Paper documents. Chapter 5 explored what the referendum was considered to be *about*, politically speaking. It also clarified the alternative political futures that 'sovereignty-association' and 'renewed federalism' offered to Quebecers in 1980. The chapter illustrated that the 'political grid' of the referendum map was co-constructed by Montreal journalists and citizens' groups, who were engaged in a common public communication interchange. The news discourses functioned both as 'texts' and as forms of 'social interaction,' which reminds us that strategies of persuasion depend on a communicative partnership between those who create the message stream and those to whom it is addressed. Through persuasive strategies, the French and English journalistic discourses encouraged citizens/viewers not only to understand what was being said, but also to accept the assertions as 'truth' – or at least as possible versions of the truth regarding what the referendum was *about*.

Chapter 5 showed that the 'sovereignty-association' and 'renewed federalism' options constructed opposing political rhetorics using three key terms: the 'state,' the 'nation,' and the 'people.' The PQ's White Paper developed a rhetoric of 'destruction of dependence' for the *peuple québé-*

cois through a YES vote, while the Beige Paper argued that the destruction of dependence implied a cost, namely, the 'destruction of a country' that Quebecers had helped found and continued to share. Renewed federalism should be embraced, the Liberals argued, on the grounds that the federal structure had constituted a positive resource for francophones since Confederation (Monière, 1980: 102–8). Public opinion polls at the time indicated that these rhetorics had different appeals for Montreal's three citizen groups, with anglophones and allophones overwhelmingly attracted to the Liberal proposal and francophones divided among all three political options. The city's French and English station groups consequently had to construct very different political 'pitches' to account for and address their politically differentiated viewer communities.

The second type of ideological labour engaged in by the media in public opinion creation involves presenting an inventory of values. Consensus building through scripting leads to a narrowing of the public discussion agenda on the textual level; and implies as well that an overdetermination of sense will occur on the cognitive level – this process has rarely been carefully documented. Scripted news discourses implicitly contain explanations and normative prescriptions, which represent for a given viewer community 'how things work,' as well as rules about 'how to live' in society. Montreal's French and English TV discourses constructed and distributed metadramatic understandings of Quebec's political and social aspirations, which had to be differentially conceived for the city's linguistically and politically stratified viewer/reader groups. Chapter 6's comparison of French and English language reconstructions of the White Paper tabling analysed how the two station groups utilized the rhetorical strategies to achieve cognitive 'overdeterminations' of meaning.

Barbie Zelizer's work on journalistic quoting practices provides essential clues for unravelling the complex and reflexive interrelationships between textual features and the interpretive opportunities they offer news viewers/ readers. Zelizer points out that quoting practices are an important means for journalists to draw audiences toward an ideologically specific point of view. For journalists, quoting practices have a number of useful functions. To begin with, they permit the reportorial storyteller to separate ideas from their context of utterance and to reincorporate them within new, ideologically specified contexts without an overt stance having to be taken. Quoting practices furthermore are media-specific; they can be adapted to print as well as to broadcast discourses. In addition, they are flexible and can be tailored to different reader groups. Finally, quotes perpetuate the illusion that journalistic discourses are collective activities and therefore constitute superior narratives, as well as superior 'veracity' and 'neutrality' (1989: 382–4). Quoting practices, as collective and therefore authoritative types of 'saying,' mimic the 'scientific' discourse of rationality grounded in Enlightenment thinking, which was discussed in Chapter 7.

Our Chapter 5 and 6 comparisons demonstrated how quoting practices helped construct particular types of understandings about 'how things worked' in Quebec City during the White Paper tabling. These understandings, as indicated above, had to account for Montreal's francophone, anglophone, and allophone political stances in order to be intelligible to the city's differentiated reader/viewer groups. Canadian democratic theory considers four groups of roles and voices as equally legitimate in the political arena: politicians, experts, news personnel, and the public. Our comparisons demonstrated that every French and English journalistic retelling of the White Paper tabling constructed a separate point of view about what had happened and why. Three types of rhetorical devices – narrative linking, modes of address, and textual formatting – contributed to these separate understandings. From an interpretive point of view, narrative devices define the types of knowledges that will become available to viewers, and also determine the legitimacy of all voices within the narrative logic itself. The evidence shows that both in print and on television, the journalistic voices were in control and relegated politicians, experts, and the public into 'character' positions, where they could speak only for themselves. Cognitively, this meant that these voices could contribute nothing more than their 'personal opinions' to the story line, and that therefore they lacked the interpretive authority of the journalistic voices (Nichols, 1976/7: 38).

The different ways of distributing the presentational devices of linking/ framing between in- and extra-station voices affected how ideological consensus was created in the White Paper accounts, both in print and on television. Our print comparison made it clear that the narrative devices affected the selection of story sources and the 'tone' of the articles. To our surprise, both *La Presse* and the *Gazette* selected NO side spokespersons to comment on the White Paper tabling, with the result that the quotes utilized by the reporters were overwhelmingly negative in tone. In contrast, the linking/framing devices utilized on television did not affect *which* events were selected for coverage, but rather *how* these events were evaluated. In the French news discourse, the tabling in the National Assembly was recounted as having proceeded according to the PQ government's plan in spite of the civil servants' strike; in the English discourse, the tabling was contextualized as chaotic. Here the disruption that the civil servants caused during the reporters' attempts to read the document before it was tabled, provided a negative frame of reference when it came to interpreting *all* tabling events.

The narrative practice of 'mode of address' further reinforces the hierarchization of the politically legitimated voices. It permits the storyteller to orchestrate the voices of the other characters in the story. Our comparisons of *La Presse* and the *Gazette* indicated that most stories were told from the point of view of the reporter, who either paraphrased the quotee's words, or used them directly, to illustrate the line of argument being taken. In the television discourse, through imaging techniques, the character voices were mediated even more strongly than in print. Anchor and reporter accounts in both Montreal television discourses utilized the direct mode of address, in which the narrator speaks for himself or herself, or quotes another spokesperson. On the other hand, extra-station voices represented in interviews, speeches, and press conferences were cast in an 'indirect' mode of address. Politicians and experts were able to address the viewer directly in only 2 per cent and 17 per cent of all segments respectively, and were otherwise 'quoted.' The 'public,' in turn, was never permitted to speak directly to viewers. In the French discourses, PQ spokespersons recounted the tabling events (61 per cent), while in the English discourses, NO side spokespersons predominated (73 per cent). Thus, modes of address, both in print and on television, not only legitimated those who were selected as spokespersons, but also gave extra weight to what they had to say.

The third and final set of devices utilized by journalistic voices to justify their knowledge superiority related to 'format' characteristics. These textual features are used to signify stylistically to readers that the text is 'true' and 'factual.' Both in print and on television, the discourses made use of such formatting, though in different ways. Based on the types of knowledge they convey, different story formats signify different degrees of truth. In the press we found that document reprints carried greater authority than regular articles, because they offered the reader unmediated textual access. Ninety-two percent of *La Presse*'s space for White Paper coverage was devoted to document reprints; the *Gazette* gave only 59 per cent of its coverage space for reprints. Because different article types represent different attitudes of the writer to his or her subject matter, the choice of both article types and their proportions are capable of acting as legitimation strategies. *La Presse*'s virtually exclusive use of document reprints without commentary signified 'neutrality' through the act of 'publication,' in the sense that journalistic voices detached themselves from the actual content of the document. Neutrality was signified by permitting the newspaper's politically fragmented reader groups to make up their own minds about the White

Paper proposals. The *Gazette*, which knew that it was addressing a politically homogeneous readership, constructed neutrality through its article mix. Its coverage was half reprints and half different kinds of reports that offered readers information about the document's content and how it was being received by provincial premiers and the business community. Zelizer (1989) calls this an 'oral' legitimation strategy in the sense that it is grounded in the statements of other political players. In verbal terms, the television discourses were even more heavily interpreted than in the press. The majority of the tabling events were rendered in the 'points of view,' 'opinion,' and 'commentary' formats, which lend themselves to the reproduction of opinions with which the writer is in disagreement. These heavily inflected formats were naturalized through television's 'transparent' imaging techniques, which showed both YES and NO characters talking *about* the White Paper document.

Our comparative evidence demonstrates that presentational devices that contextualize the subject matter, modes of address that indicate the narrator's attitude toward the material, and story formats that offer different types of knowledge to readers/viewers, all add narrative and persuasive elements to the journalistic recounting of events. Clearly, editorialization is a complex process that shapes the news discourse not only through the selection and ordering of events, but much more forcefully through the narrative process of dramatization. Dramatization created the meaning contexts into which the viewers' interpretive hypotheses about the White Paper tabling had to ultimately fit. Through narrative as well as visualization techniques, it also naturalized the reporters' voices and consequently their versions of what happened. These versions provided two unique ways of describing referendum events and thus presented Montreal viewers/readers with an 'overdetermined' point of view about 'how things worked' during the White Paper tabling.

Our analyses suggest that throughout the referendum period, the Montreal media were extremely effective in providing varied frames of reference for francophone and anglophone citizens to understand their own linguistically polarized political realities, but not necessarily the political realities of other groups with different cultural backgrounds and political experiences. Consequently, the media's most challenging public opinion function after the rejection of the sovereignty-association option, became the reconstruction of consensus so that public life in Quebec and Canada could continue. Furthermore, this consensus had to be made visible so that diverse citizen groups could view themselves as part of the same democratic public. In Chapter 7 we compared the ways that the outcome of the referendum was interpreted, and analysed how this narrative closure was rhetorically achieved for Montreal's polarized viewer groups. Our comparison focused on the persuasive capacity of television discourse. Three rhetorical practices were involved here: *inventio*, which determines topic and argument selection; *dispositio*, which is the arrangement and sequencing of these arguments; and *elocutio*, which is the style of their presentation. Together, these constitute the narrative processes of dramatization. We have already demonstrated that the 'election as game' perspective narrowed the reportorial frame in terms of which all referendum events were narrated. We were not prepared, however, to find that by the end of the campaign, the referendum reporting focus had been reduced to a mere seven topics. These topics included the nature of the campaign, ethnic group responses, economic implications, renewed federalism, the PQ's political future, and the Yvettes phenomenon. The seventh, 'other' category accounted for less than 5 per cent of the total arguments advanced. All seven topics together provided an inventory of 107 arguments, in which the NO versions predominated over the YES by two to one and the French news discourses utilized more explanatory arguments than the English (67 to 40).

The above topic inventory makes it clear that the Montreal media conceptualized their consensus creation function as one of healing the differences between francophone and other citizens, and that they perceived 'conciliation' as achievable through the renewal of Canadian federalism. However, Quebecers' desire for change meant different things to the three party leaders, as they indicated in their speeches of 20 May 1980. For Pierre Trudeau and the federal Liberals, it implied a new Constitution that would affirm Canadian statehood. For Claude Ryan and the provincial Liberals, it meant the renegotiation of Canadian federalism with 'special status' for Quebec. For René Lévesque and the PQ, it signified a postponement of sovereignty until another rendezvous with history.

Because news stories are narrated by a cast of storytellers, a comparison of the voices through which the news discourses were constituted provides another method for comparing argumentation strategies. In Chapters 5 and 6 it was found that the French stations utilized fewer presenter roles, and that their news discourses employed fewer voices as a consequence. The francophone 'day after' accounts employed 31 voices compared to the anglophone accounts' 47. Eleven of the 31 voices in the French discourse were station personnel; of the remaining 20 voices, 7 belonged to politicians, 4 to experts, and a substantial 9 to people-in-the-street. In the English explanatory discourse, news personnel also played an important mediating role. Nineteen voices belonged to station personnel, 6 to politicians, and

4 to experts; the remaining 18 represented the public. This distribution indicates that both news discourses legitimated the referendum outcome
by highlighting and reproducing a large number of vox-pop interviews.

A third rhetorical process through which consensus was created can best
be described as 'meta-communicational.' It consisted in the rhetorical
acknowledgment of knowledge frameworks that were common to both
message creators and message interpreters. Our comparison showed that in
the French 'day after' accounts, both consensus and closure were constructed through arguments that made sense of renewed federalism in
national terms. Renewed federalism was described as a co-operative process in which both provincial and federal leaders would participate.
Because this closure strategy offered no explicit proposals for the future, it
was ideologically acceptable to French-speaking voters, both sovereigntist
and federalist. In contrast, the English-language stations used Claude
Ryan's persona and his constitutional agenda to create closure. Among
other things, this agenda argued for special status for Quebec in a reconstructed Canadian federal system.

The rhetorical evidence indicates that the media's role in public opinion
formation is multilayered and reflexive, and involves politicians, news
personnel, experts, and people's voices. However, the contribution these
voices make to the construction of meaning in the news discourse is not
egalitarian, but hierarchical. In this sense-making hierarchy, contemporary
news personnel inhabit social roles that are narratively more powerful than
those of politicians, and the voices of citizens are at the bottom of the pyra-
mid. Contemporary journalists inhabit what Marshall Sahlins (1976) calls
the 'synaptic space' of artists and advertisers, and this thrusts them into a
contradictory position in the political arena – something that is reflected in
the present electoral laws, which since the mid-1970s have permitted parties 'free time' access to the electorate and allowed the use of paid campaign
'spots.'

The 'Public' as Symbolically Contested Space: The Yvettes Phenomenon

A variety of linguistic and political collectivities were called into being
through the referendum rhetoric; democratic theory assumes that these
collectivities then made themselves felt in the political realm. But the means
by which such effectivity is achieved are difficult to establish empirically,
and for that reason are hotly debated. Spin doctors and campaign strate-
gists argue that advertising helps mobilize the voting public (Lee, 1989: 42).
Campaign workers contribute to this process through riding association

meetings and doorbell ringing. All of these campaign practices are predicated on the notion that there is a 'public' to be reached and mobilized. Yet, as John Durham Peters (1995) notes, the 'people' who are supposed to take part in political discussion and decision making cannot today be assembled in one physical place, except in the 'place' the media provide. Consequently, he argues, the modern 'public' has become a 'robust fiction' (1995: 15–16). What he means by this is that the public today is a social fiction, and that only in very specific circumstances, where mobilization takes place, is it an objective fact.

Contemporary evidence indicates that such a mobilization fact began to happen after the National Assembly debate of March 1980, which was televised live for one week from Quebec City. During the debate, Parti Québécois MNAs systematically explained the political and economic implications of their sovereignty-association project, and suddenly galvanized a specific group of individuals – women – into taking an active stand (McGee, 1975: 241). Two sets of polls indicated that the Liberal Party's comfortable lead was narrowing and that the YES and NO sides might soon be in a dead heat. The first showed that the National Assembly debates had finally convinced 60 per cent of decided francophone voters to support the PQ – a support level that placed victory within a two percentage point reach. The second indicated that the least likely groups to support sovereignty-association were anglophone voters and Quebec women. The person selected to change this situation for the PQ was Lise Payette, Minister for the Status of Women, who addressed a partisan crowd in Montreal on 9 March 1980. Women, she proclaimed, should stop being afraid of change. All women in Quebec, she went on, had been brought up to be 'Yvettes' (the dutiful little girls represented in Quebec's primary school readers), and it was time to reject that role. So far, Payette was on politically uncontentious ground; but in responding to a question from the floor about Claude Ryan's leadership of the NO campaign, she spontaneously added that he was the kind of man who wanted Quebec full of Yvettes. Then in a blunder of all blunders (as she later admitted), she added: 'Moreover, he is married to an Yvette' (Payette, 1982). In the case of Madeleine Ryan, this was certainly inaccurate, since Mme Ryan had been a well-known activist in education and other social issues. The response in the French press was swift and scathing: Lise Bissonnette of Le Devoir commented that by attacking Madeleine Ryan through her husband, Mme Payette was signalling her readiness to 'descend to the depths of sexism in her fight for the Yes option' (10 March 1980).

There is usually a division of labour between politicians and the media in the process of forming public opinion. The 'Yvettes affair' was a unique example of an exception. In the Yvettes affair, both the definitional and the diffusion roles were played by Lise Bissonnette of *Le Devoir*, who not only identified Payette's words as a 'gaffe politique,' but suggested that they had insulted not only Madeleine Ryan but also Quebec women as a group. Even though her explanation of why the province's female voters had suddenly become mobilized was largely incorrect, it was widely repeated in Montreal's press and by broadcasters, and also by such national opinion makers as the *Globe and Mail* (Dandurand/Tardy, 1981a: 25, 30–2).

In hindsight it is more accurate to explain this mobilization as the outcome of a complex web of factors, which include differences in the influence that women members had in the two provincial parties, differences in party responses to the 'gaffe,' and contested meaning structures about gender, women's place in politics, and nationalism and motherhood. Up to this point, all of the above factors had been dormant in the referendum campaign. The first reason for the NO side's mobilization advantage must be sought in how the two contending party organizations integrated their women members. After the 'gaffe,' one would have expected both parties' women members to rally: PQ women to the side of Payette in order to keep the francophone mobilization going; and Liberal women to a search for counterstrategies to retain the support of Quebec women. The evidence shows that a rally was not as easy to accomplish in the PQ as in the Liberal ranks. An important reason is that the PQ, like many reformist parties, had fewer women members to draw on than the Liberals. In 1979, women were only a little more than one-third (37.5 per cent) of the total PQ membership of 211,474. Also, women members of the PQ were younger and more militant and were drawn from different political groupings. At first, this political variety had been an asset for the PQ, which provided a relatively open forum for women to influence social change through direct input on the party platform (Tardy, 1980: 200). For instance, in 1973 the PQ was the first party to include women's issues (day care, violence against women, abortion and so on) in its party platform; it also promised to revise the Civil Code. In 1976, it had elected four women, rather than a token woman, to the National Assembly. In 1978 it became the first party to create a Ministry for the Status of Women and to promote a women's policy: *Pour les Québécoises: égalité et indépendance.* Furthermore, feminist party members (which included Lise Payette) had acquired top positions in party councils (Dumont, 1995: 156).

Roberta Hamilton (1995: 143–4) notes that in spite of this initial openness, PQ women did not support a unified political agenda, and this ultimately hampered them in their drive for party influence during the referendum. Some championed social democratic ideals of equal pay and equal work opportunities; others were of a clerico-nationalist background and subscribed to French-only cultural and linguistic ideals; still another group embraced feminist values. These divisions had already surfaced by 1980, and women's influence within the PQ's male hierarchy was on the wane. The party reverted to a pro-life ideology in conjunction with its nationalist agenda. The male élite, including René Lévesque, vetoed the abortion clause in its new platform document, and Jacques Henripin, the dean of Quebec demographers, supported day care not for equity reasons but because it might encourage women to have that third baby, which would supposedly guarantee the survival of francophone society. In such a setting, certain groups of women PQ members became disaffected, and several women's committees in PQ ridings disbanded and tried to establish an autonomous women's network. However, this effort was short-lived (Dumont, 1995: 157).

In the Liberal Party, women's involvement was proportionally greater. Almost half (47 per cent) of Liberal Party members were women, and they were organizationally better distributed and ideologically less polarized than PQ women. Futhermore, 51 per cent of women Liberals were home-makers and thus had time to participate in mobilization strategies (Tardy, 1980: 200). In contrast to their PQ sisters, Liberal women had gained their political identity independently from the male power structure – in 1950, when federation committees were set up in most local ridings. These had laid the groundwork for future solidarity through the championing of widely accepted civil and educational goals. By 1971 the federation, with its 25,000 members, was wielding substantial political power; at this point it was asked to join the official party structure (Dumont, 1995: 157). It did so on the condition that two members of every Liberal riding association would be women and that women would have equity on delegations to party conventions, where they would have a voice in platform building (Maillé, 1990: 90, 112). Though Liberal women were less strongly identified with feminist causes, they were organizationally better en-trenched in the Liberal Party structure, in which they filled positions everywhere except in the top councils.

Though women were present in the councils of both parties, until the Payette gaffe both parties had made gendered assumptions about women voters' lack of interest in political issues; both had therefore failed to develop 'citizen-centred' strategies to rally women to the referendum cause. How can such an oversight be explained? One possible reason relates to the sexist assumptions regarding women's 'essential nature' – assumptions that coloured the campaign strategies of both the PQ and the Liberals. The PQ unveiled its 'essentialist' prejudices in its October 1979 rally for housewives, which had as its theme 'La politique, c'est l'affaire de toutes les femmes.' This was supposed to be followed by 'kitchen assemblies' across the province, which were, however, not very effective because they presumed that women needed 'special instruction' in citizenship (Tardy, 1980: 196–7). This presupposition seemed also to inform Lise Payette's discourse. Throughout the referendum campaign the PQ combined its paternalistic 'women's approach' with a much more successful 'regroupment' strategy that mobilized supportive organizations and individuals into close to 8,000 groups: taxi drivers, families, employees in factories, economists, scientists, and so on. These supporters were often awarded certificates – often by Premier Lévesque himself. These mobilization strategies were, however, largely ignored by the Montreal media. Even the PQ's counter-rally of 26 April 1980, which brought out 15,000 men and women to commemorate women's suffrage in Quebec, could not stop the party's slide in the polls.

Denis Monière gives another reason why PQ women did not come to Lise Payette's aid: PQ campaign strategy was administered from the premier's office, without input from lower-ranking members (Monière, 1980: 102–3). Until the fateful gaffe, the disciplined nature of the National Assembly debates about sovereignty-association, and the success of those debates among voters, had seemed to support such a top-down strategy. After the gaffe, the PQ found itself at a huge disadvantage, which Roberta Hamilton (1995: 146) explains under four headings. First of all, the media amplified the blunder by pronouncing the Yvettes movement as antifeminist. This selective interpretation failed to give credit to the PQ for its other mobilization strategies, and thus contributed to the party's stalled approval ratings (Dandurand/Tardy, 1981a: 27). Second, Payette's male colleagues in cabinet failed to support her; instead, they responded with anger and silence, as did Lévesque himself (Lévesque, 1986: 303). Third, the minister, noting that she had lost her credibility both inside and outside cabinet as a spokesperson for women, dropped out of the campaign during its most fateful period, which left the party without a women's mobilization strategy (Payette, 1982). Fourth and finally, many women members of the PQ felt disillusioned, and were unhappy that Payette had used the feminist cause to further clerico-nationalist goals. Denise Riley (1988) examined the problematic nature of the term 'woman' for feminists and for nationalists, and pointed out that though it may be a necessary ground for political mobilization, it is not a sufficient one. In the case of the PQ campaign, the identification of 'national survival' with motherhood offered only *one very restricted* manner in which Quebec women could define themselves as 'good' citizens. Few younger Quebec women were willing to assume this role identification at the time; this tended to marshal women's votes for the opposition.

The Liberals had also ignored their female constituents, but in this case because of general overconfidence. The certainty of a NO side victory had pushed the need for mobilization into the background in party councils; it had also delayed the formation of the special umbrella committee that was to spearhead the final mobilization drive. When the gaffe occurred in March 1980, Pierre Bibeau had just begun to organize his twenty-two-member strategy committee. The Liberals' strategy planning was also hampered by tensions between the federal and provincial leaders over the role of the Canadian Unity Information Office (CUIO), which Trudeau had established in Ottawa in 1979 (Fraser, 1984: 220–1). It was this office that had initiated the health and public service advertising campaigns that suggested 'NO merci' as a proper response to drunk driving, and reminded Quebecers that 'there was so much to stay for' in Canada, touristically and otherwise (Rose, 1993: 186–91). It was also responsible for scripting Trudeau's four carefully timed speeches in Ottawa (15 April), Montreal (2 May), Quebec City (7 May), and the Paul Sauvé Arena (14 May). Together with the Yvettes initiative, these speeches were credited with focusing the referendum debate and with ensuring a victory for the NO side (Fraser, 1984: 224). A number of Quebec researchers, following Betty Zisk (1987), downplay the role of the Yvettes and instead attribute the referendum win mainly to the federal government's superior ad campaign, which cost no less than $5 million and may have cost over three times that. In contrast, the two umbrella committees' advertising expenditures were roughly $4 million (Monière and Guay, 1996: 10–11). Yet all of our evidence indicates that money of itself cannot buy interpretive advantages, unless these interpretations are congruent with people's own understandings of events.

With its lack of organization, it is no wonder that the Liberal party's strategy committee took three weeks to ponder how to make use of Payette's gaffe, and how to respond to the disastrous 16 March 1980 poll, which showed a thirteen-point slip in women's intentions to vote Liberal (Lévesque, 1986: 303). It is not quite clear whether it was Andrée Richard, the wife of a Quebec City Liberal organizer, who came up with the winning mobilization strategy, but certainly it was she who organized the first of the hugely popular 'Yvettes brunches' held on 28 March 1980. Liberal women operatives must therefore be credited not only with devising a new mobilizing strategy, but also with winning back the women's vote by addressing them as qualified citizens. The women organizers understood what the media and the male party stalwarts did not: that women not only had an interest in their own political future, but needed no instruction to fulfil their obligations as citizens. The accuracy of their estimation is attested to by a strategy committee document which showed that by 5 May 1980, 42,760 women from all over Quebec had participated in a Yvettes brunch. The brunch initiative was augmented a week later, on 7 April 1980, by a rally of Yvette sympathizers in Montreal, which was organized by seasoned activists Louise Robic and Diane Fortier, and which attracted 15,000 cheering women to the Forum (Tardy, 1980: 201). Though the discourses of this mass meeting were mainly in the 'public' domain, in that the Liberal speakers addressed political rather than private themes, stereotypical notions continued to play a part. According to Lise Bissonnette, three types of themes were intertwined: a political one against sovereignty-association; a feminist one on the citizenship responsibilities of women; and a third that was oriented around the essentialist notion of women's 'conserver' role in society (Le Devoir, 9 April 1980).

For whatever reason, a 25 April 1980 poll confirmed that the Liberals had benefited from women's mobilization. However, *why* women were mobilized was still unclear to both Liberal and PQ operatives. Evidence provided by Janine Brodie and Celia Chandler (1991) on changes in voting behaviour among North American women since the 1950s suggests that the strength of the Yvettes mobilization was not due mainly to 'emotional outrage,' as Lise Bissonnette and the media claimed; rather, two other social processes were key factors. These were first, the fact that by the late 1970s women were slightly more likely to vote than men, and second, that in 1980 women tended to prefer the Liberals over other parties by about six points vis-à-vis men (Everitt, 1996). Quebec women perceived the Liberal Party as more likely to protect social services such as child support, day care, and health insurance – all of these essential to women, who were entering the labour market in ever-increasing numbers (Brodie and Chandler, 1991: 23; Burt, 1995: 93). This 'gender gap,' coupled with Tardy's finding that women voters were not more conservative than men when social variables such as age, education, and employment level were kept constant, provides a sounder explanation for the success of the Yvettes campaign. Tardy's reanalysis of the Hamilton/Pinard poll of 15 May 1980 demonstrates that about half of the gender variance in women's vote intentions could be eliminated by utilizing representative sampling methods; also, that the remaining differences would have disappeared if the missing evidence from the 14 per cent who refused to reveal their preferences had been distributed more carefully by the major polling firms (Tardy, 1980: 194–6). This interpretation is supported by other studies, which confirm that gender gaps in Canada have increased since the 1970s, and that such gaps are strongly influenced by socio-demographic variables such as education level, paid employment, and the influence of the women's movement (Rinehart, 1992; Shapiro and Mahajan, 1986).

Furthermore, more recent research by Brodie and Chandler (1991) indicates that between December 1979 and May 1980 the total number of women planning to vote had increased, but that their *intentions* had not changed. It also shows that women's preference for the NO side remained stable at about 44 per cent, which was about six percentage points higher than among males. Brenda O'Neil's recent longitudinal study (1995) confirms that women attach greater importance than men to social welfare, and that consequently they display higher levels of support for social welfare programs (Everitt, 1996: 13). All of this suggests that the gender gap was indeed surfacing in the 1980 referendum campaign, during which health and educational transfer payments as well as old age pensions became key issues.

How then to explain the journalists' adherence to the essentialist arguments about women's *inherent* lack of interest in politics (Siltanen and Stanworth, 1984: 95)? Part of the answer must be sought in the media's arbitrary assignment of the Yvettes event to the 'private' domain, because it involved women. Kress (1988) argues that the media's classification of events as *public* or *private* affects how stories are covered, as well as the types of explanations offered and the motives assigned for actions. This is documented in Dandurand and Tardy's survey (1981a) of Montreal newspaper coverage, which revealed that the media explained the Yvettes mobilization in 'personal' terms. The four preferred interpretive 'tropes' were that housewife Yvettes were personally 'insulted' by Lise Payette and that their responses amounted to a 'backlash to feminism.' Furthermore, it was claimed that women's reactions were 'spontaneous' and that they had been 'manipulated' by the Liberal Party. Each of these interpretations sought the causes of the Yvettes' behaviour in their personal and domestic life experiences, rather than in their knowledges and actions as competent citizens. The journalistic misassignment also led to a misconstruction of brunch participants' motives. The brunch in St-Georges-de-Beauce was reported as having created 'fellowship' among the women, rather than 'an opportunity to make an active choice for a particular political option,' as Madeleine Ryan explained it to *La Presse* (28 April 1980).

Our analysis of the Yvettes phenomenon indicates that it was the media in conjunction with the two Quebec parties, rather than the participating women themselves, who obliterated and misinterpreted women's political mobilization for the NO side at the end of the referendum campaign. Mistaken topic assignment, as well as stereotypical reporting angles, created these misinterpretations. They also ignored the fact that the Yvettes brunches were a new means for mobilizing a particular constituency, women, in a political campaign. As a result, the media descriptions were not only inaccurate but also misleading. Their misassignment of the Yvettes brunches to the *private* domain of 'ladies' teas' undervalued the *public* impact of these activities and ignored their mobilization potential. As Chapter 7 demonstrated, from an interpretive point of view persons assigned to the public domain are represented as social agents in active roles, while those assigned to the private domain are represented as unable to affect the public good. Underlying this division is an unexamined journalistic convention that declares the *private* to be a domain beyond social theory, and beyond ideology, and therefore devoid of power. The reporting on the Yvettes demonstrates that during the referendum, the public/private dichotomy became a highly charged signifier ripe for ideological deployment and exploitation (Kress, 1988: 400). Politicians and the media exploited the Payette gaffe for their own ideological purposes, but without understanding that the stereotypical descriptions masked the fact that women were developing a voting consensus around issues of social welfare, and that this would ultimately benefit the provincial and national Liberals in the 1980 referendum. This helped derail the PQ's referendum strategy, not because women *qua* women were more conservative than men, but because as citizens they believed that the party's social platform would be compromised by secession.

The Media's Changing Role in Democratic Politics

Since the 1980s, many attempts have been made to reassess the role of the media in democracies. Three strands of research within sociology, history, and communication studies have begun to synthesize some of the scattered findings, out of which a more reasoned consideration of the media's current role in the political process can be developed. One of the key findings of these inquiries has been that in the move from industrial to postindustrial society, both media technologies and social processes have undergone drastic and interrelated changes. This move was initially described in economic terms, as a transformation from a production to an information based economy; it is now, at the end of the twentieth century, more care-fully diagnosed as a move from 'classical' modernity to 'high' modernity. According to Anthony Giddens, in this move the *consequences* of four modernizing processes are becoming heightened and universalized (Gid-dens, 1990: 3). These processes are the rise of capitalism as the dominant mode of economic organization, the development of the nation-state as the modal unit of political administration and action, the ending of religious monopolies over thought and knowledge, and the emergence of a more fragmented and contested cultural field in which contending discourses struggle for public visibility and authority. In all of these processes, the communications media have been centrally implicated as public meaning organizers of contemporary life. In 'high' modernity, the economy and the polity produce the major institutional rules and resources that organize grounded experience; while the formations of knowledge and culture pro-vide the discursive and representational resources that invest experience with meaning (Murdock, 1993: 523–5).

In Canada the institutional relationship between electronic media and politics began to change in the 1970s, when computers were linked to cable and satellite technologies. By the time of the referendum these interactive capabilities had transformed the country's political culture, including the strategy, conduct, and functioning of Canadian electoral campaigns. Over-night public opinion surveys, interest group targeting, and the 'real time' monitoring of campaign events from a distance not only shortened politi-cians' response times, but also made them more dependent on a new breed of advisors, campaign consultants, and pollsters. The work of 'spin doc-tors,' such as Martin Goldfarb for the Liberals and Allan Gregg for the Progressive Conservatives, displaced activities previously carried out by riding groups and positioned this new group of professionals between the populace and the leader. Although policy itself was and still is gener-ated by party conventions, the choice of which policies to emphasize has fallen out of the hands of regional party organizers and into the hands of pollsters, who stratify and respond to voter's concerns through focus group and polling strategies (Lee, 1989: 18–44; Fletcher, 1981: 287–91). High-tech campaigning, Gary Selnow argues, has threatened the ability of leaders to weigh local needs against the national public interest, because it 'tailors' voter appeals and depersonalizes the political process (Selnow, 1994: 167–71).

In the realm of public meaning creation, interactive communications capabilities have reintroduced questions of how political discourse is orga-nized and who has the 'licence' to speak on whose behalf. In the process, new media are helping to reconfigure systems of power and networks of social relations. In 'high' modernity, Murdock explains, public meaning creation, which used to be dominated by a single agency, the state, is now being dominated by two institutions with different agendas: the state, and industry. The former is concerned mainly with the management of mass political participation, addresses its viewers as rational citizens concerned with the public good (Murdock, 1993: 526). Industry, on the other hand, utilizes the North American media primarily to co-ordinate markets and sell goods. It addresses its viewers as consumers and offers personal solutions to public difficulties through consumer choice.

As we noted in Chapter 3, in the political domain economic considerations have also infiltrated electoral rules, since Canadian voters switched to television as the main source of campaign information. Since 1971 both the electoral coverage rules and the balance between the three types of campaign flows have changed. Since that year, as Fred Fletcher demonstrates, party investment in unmediated messages such as 'campaign spots' and free-time broadcasts has vastly increased (1981: 285). There has also been more use made of 'partially mediated' information streams, such as leader debates and TV interviews, which were not introduced to Canada until the 1974 election. In the interim, the availability of 'heavily mediated' news programming flows has hardly changed. According to Fletcher, the regulatory changes demanded by the arrival of television have flowed from reinterpretations of the 'right to respond' clause inherent in the concept of free speech and from the introduction of the Charter of Rights (1987: 348). Since 1974, electoral rules have restricted paid advertising to the final half of the campaign, regulated the allocation of free-time party appearances, and limited campaign spending, while offering 50 per cent reimbursement for the cost of radio and television spots purchased by registered parties. By 1980 these rule changes had led parties to spend 76 per cent of their advertising budgets (roughly $4.6 million) on television spots; this vastly increased their unmediated access to the voting public. At the same time, print expenses remained relatively stable (Fletcher 1987, 351).

The institutional tensions that arise when people are viewed as 'citizens' in the political realm but as 'consumers' in the industrial realm, Murdock argues, are mapped on to the political systems of representation, which are increasingly becoming commodified and taking on what Graham Knight calls a 'tabloid' style. As a distinct news idiom, tabloid news is rooted in earlier scandal and gossip sheets, in human interest magazines, in the sports press, and in the yellow and muckraking journalism of the early twentieth century. 'Moral disorder' and 'personalization' are the primary tropes of this style, which has earned political reporting a negative reputation for exaggeration, overdramatization, and sensationalism (1989: 94–5). Four things give tabloid news its idiomatic flavour: essentialism, hyperactivity, hyperrealism, and populism. Each of these was found in the referendum coverage. In Chapter 3 we saw that French and English Montreal stations used graphics and flags to identify their referendum reports. These blue and red symbols polarized and simplified the YES and NO options and helped viewers orient themselves in the political debate. Yet they also, as we have seen, reinforced the 'two camps' interpretive scheme, which over-simplified the political divisions within Montreal's viewing public. *Hyper-activity* was evident in the White Paper tabling analyses, where the English-language station used video images of smashed windows to signify the 'disorder' surrounding the event. No such imagery was present on the French station's news accounts. By the late 1970s, *hyperreality* had begun to make the narrator as well as the technical apparatus of the television dis-course more visible. An example of such demystification of the authorial presence was the use of newsmakers' close-ups on a large video screen behind the anchor in the studio setting. Such a framing makes closed-circuit interviews seem more like conversations; it also increases opportu-nities for viewers to identify with the station personnel's interpretations of events. *Populism* was manifested both in the less formal speech patterns of the station personnel and in their rhetorical approaches. Since tabloid jour-nalism speaks for the people, it uses the 'common sense' address of real persons. Furthermore, viewers are legitimated by a 'realistic' narrative that contrasts the 'family's point of view' on events with that of the powerful, who are assumed to be the creators of the 'moral disorder' of the contem-porary world.

Knight argues that tabloid populism, while celebrating people as bearers of positive values, is intrinsically conservative (1989: 107). Chapter 7 dem-onstrated that during the referendum it cast 'the public' in a mainly passive light, as recipients of and reactors to politicians' interpretations. In news reports, 'the people' can speak only in response to reporters' questions; in their other renditions as 'the crowd' and the 'voting statistic' they are speechless. The advertising-based tabloid discourse, with its individualistic frame and moral-disorder focus, is based less in logic than in emotion. Tab-loid news discourses also transpose the egalitarian 'citizen' relationship between news producers and viewers, into an inegalitarian special-interest 'client' relationship. The Yvettes coverage demonstrated how this client mentality transposed a public issue – the political mobilization of Quebec women – into a private event of good fellowship among housewives at the brunches. In the process, respect for citizen's personal competence to judge public matters was eliminated from the political reporting agenda, and the importance of women party operatives was underestimated in the campaigns of both sides.

Hovering behind these analyses are two queries that must now be explicitly addressed. They concern the interrelated issues of whether, and how, the processes of 'tabloidization' affect voter comprehension and the practice of democracy itself. There are two major theories about the role of the media in democracy. The first, which is based on the work of German media theorist Jürgen Habermas (1989), argues that the media old and new have been instrumental in creating an *egalitarian* space for public discussion. Habermas contends that the development of early modern capitalism brought into being an autonomous arena of public debate. The economic independence provided by private property, the critical reflection fostered by letters and novels, the flowering of discussion in coffee houses and salons, and, above all, the emergence of an independent, market-based press, created a new public engaged in critical political discussion. Habermas locates the evolution of the 'bourgeois public sphere' between the seventeenth century and the first half of the nineteenth. He conceptualizes this sphere as a 'neutral zone' where access to relevant information affecting the public good is widely available, where discussion is free from state interference, and where all those participating do so on an equal basis. According to Habermas, the media play a vitally important role in the processes of self-government, not so much as providers of information, but as facilitators of public opinion.

Feminist and critical theorists have argued that in 'high modernity,' the regimes of late capitalism, as well as class and gender divisions, have vitiated the media's ability to create and sustain an equal and gender-free discussion space (Fraser, 1992: Curran, 1992). According to Fraser, participatory parity is better achieved by recognizing and dealing with enduring inequalities such as gender, class, and race, not by theorizing them away (Fraser, 1992: 122). The Yvettes reporting was an especially good example of the inability of counter-publics to influence the political discussion agenda on their own terms, unless they behaved 'oppositionally.' Such a requirement, Lisa McLaughlin argues, is particularly onerous for women's groups, which are consequently marginalized by the media and co-opted by other political interest groups (1993: 614). In 'high' modernity, new corporatist systems of power relations were established between Canada and Quebec and their respective media conglomerates – from which the public was increasingly excluded. As we have seen, during the referendum period all Montreal print media aligned themselves with the NO side, and even the CBC abrogated its 'national unity' mandate to live up to its professional goal of 'neutrality.' In this setting, the media ceased to be an agency of empowerment and rationality, and co-operated with state and economic interests to mold mass opinion.

Regarding the role of the media as facilitators of public information, Paddy Scannel (1992) provides a middle-ground position between the Habermasian and critical poles of thought. He agrees that oligopolist tendencies do exist, but also notes that the twentieth-century media have enlarged the public discussion space. This has come about, he argues, because new delivery technologies have fractured 'national' network practices, thereby weakening the links between the state and industry. Local, regional, and specialty channels are providing new outlets for unique audience experiences and forms of address. Scannel documents that since the turn of the century, newspapers and the electronic media have created a multiplicity of new public discussion spaces for a variety of audience groupings. Both radio and television extended access to previously restricted forms of entertainment, such as lectures, musicals, religious services, and political reports. In the process, the media gave a voice to previously voiceless groups and created communicative entitlements that had not existed before. There has been little research about Canada's experience with forums for public discourse; even so, scholars like Mary Jane Miller (1987) and Mary Vipond (1992) are beginning to document these novel communicative entitlements.

Scannel agrees with our findings that station personnel control the *construction* of the public discourse, but he also points out that media personnel do not control the *communicative context*. It is this context of home and family that the broadcaster must acknowledge in order to create a successful 'audiencing' interaction (Morley, 1986). Broadcasters have done this in the past fifty years by ascertaining at what times of day their listeners are available and adjusting their program schedules accordingly. They have also created new forms of participatory entertainment (game shows and so on) to hold their viewer groups' varied interests, and have created more relaxed and spontaneous communicative styles to match. Because radio and television are interactive with other family activities, their discourses must seem ordinary, accessible, knowable, familiar, shareable, and communicable for a range of different population groups. To establish these discourses, a communicative ethos must be developed that celebrates 'ordinariness' – that is, ordinary people doing ordinary things.

This trend toward relaxed, natural, and spontaneous modes of address and forms of talk has resocialized the public and private domains of communication. Far from debasing political culture, as Knight suggests (1989), the 'populist' style of television recreates the public discourse as a 'conversation' between equals – one that is based not on powers of logical persuasion *alone*, as Habermas contends, but on considerations of clarity, sincerity, relevance, and informativeness, which are communitarian values (Scannel, 1992: 340–1). Scannel's analysis does not overlook that communicational boundaries continue to exist in the public discussion realm between those entitled to express opinions and those who are entitled to express experience (as the referendum 'people-in-the-street' interviews in Chapter 7 showed). He is aware as well of how class, gender, and ethnicity continue to structure the realm of political discussion. Yet he argues that the resulting narrative entitlements are not immutable, but are themselves evolving, as is indicated by recent socio-political developments in Canada and elsewhere. The most visible new Canadian interest group is the First Nations people, who played a decisive role in rejecting the élite-brokered Meech Lake (1990) and Charlottetown (1992) accords, and will be key players in the constitutional debates of the late 1990s.

Let us grant, then, that television has provided a new and enlarged stage for public opinion creation in 'high modernity.' Yet in spite of this the rhetoric of tabloid journalism can be attacked on the grounds that it no longer fulfils its social function of informing the electorate. As we have shown its pseudo-scientific rhetoric, induces belief through its *style* and its *structure* rather than through the veracity of its content and its sources. In that sense, it has contributed to the rise of 'image politics.' The rhetoric of image politics shares many of the formal features of advertising presentations, including juxtaposed voices, the highly selective use of images, and emphasis on simple slogans, clichés, and slang. Kathleen Jamieson (1992) argues that tabloid rhetoric makes it more difficult for viewers/citizens to spot the propaganda dimensions of political discourse. She adds that the elections-as-game rhetoric (which she refers to as the 'strategy script') offers few practical links, in action or in thought, between citizens/viewers and the socio-political environment of everyday life. As a result, the viewers' sense of political empowerment is also reduced. Jamieson concludes by noting that viewers do not realize that the concept of 'race' is an inappropriate metaphor for democratic politics, and that spectatorship is an inappropriate role for the electorate (1992: 165). That the 'games' approach has become an acceptable way of framing Canadian electoral coverage is deeply troubling.

Cognitive psychologists point out that explanatory schemas function as 'cognitive maps' and, because they mediate cognition, affect how viewers perceive new information, remember old, and determine the characteristics of ideal candidates (Crocker, Fiske, and Taylor 1984: 315–37). Cognitive learning experiments have furthermore demonstrated that without varied kinds of informational exposure, viewers cannot develop large enough interpretive repertoires for sorting the different kinds of information that are necessary for understanding contemporary life (Graber 1980). Though the interactive media have enlarged the average person's access to political information, as we have already noted, the *style* in which this information is purveyed is flawed. To regenerate its democratic information potential, electoral reporting would as a minimum have to switch from the 'strategy' schema to what Jamieson calls the 'problem-promise-performance' schema. This explanatory schema would focus on identifying politicians who have successfully combatted social problems or uncovered, created, and found solutions for current political issues. The role of journalists in this exchange would be to contribute to meaningful public discussion by verifying politicians' statements, summarizing their key ideas and checking the accuracy and fairness of their statements (Jamieson, 1992: 192–3).

A 'performance' approach would also require journalists to rethink their responsibilities in public meaning creation, which in 'high modernity' grounds itself increasingly in bureaucratic principles emptied of any public purpose. Because television stations' trade codes demand that they not criticize other news programs or personalities, broadcast personnel are today the only visible public players who retain some measure of public respect. Yet this respect is built on bureaucratic rules rather than on professional integrity. David Hallin and Paolo Mancini (1987: 835) contend that North American journalists' role conceptions, which stem from the Progressive era (Schudson, 1978), as well as their conventions of political reporting, have two potentially adverse effects for political democracy. The tradition of 'independent' journalism, which prevails in Quebec and Canada to this day, has created a profession that sees itself as autonomous and independent from the political order, with the result that journalists' loyalty is to journalism itself (Saint-Jean, 1993). In contrast, European journalists view their social role as anchored in a political party or other social institution, such as a labour union or a religious group. The North American role conception thrusts journalists into a curiously contradictory position in the political arena. Although *outsiders* to the political order, they nevertheless claim that their special training and practices enable them to produce 'accurate' and 'unbiased' accounts of political events. Yet as political players, their evaluative and watchdog functions must be symbolically erased if they are to live up to the conventions of reportorial neutrality.

214 Rhetorical Processes in Public Opinion Creation

For the processes of political democracy, such a contradictory position-ing has the following destabilizing effects. First, as we have seen, it leads to an adversarial narrative stance vis-à-vis politicians, which interferes with the media's political 'linkage' role in the democratic communication pro-cess. This adversarial stance, Clive Cocking explains, 'is not to praise but to criticize. There is a tacit understanding among journalists that to write favourably ... if not perverse [is] at least gutless. Criticism, charges and accusations produce the most jolts on television news and the biggest head-lines in the papers' (1980: 111). Fletcher documents that during the 1979 federal election, this attitude led to a 'capriciously negative' rather than a 'discriminating' coverage, and tended to bring the entire electoral system into disrepute (Fletcher, 1981: 320). Our case studies, while not specifically investigating negativity, do show how in certain situations, such as the English-language coverage of the White Paper tabling and the 'Yvettes affair,' polarization led to increased negativity as well as to misrepresenta-tions (for example, of women's electoral mobilization for the NO side). Increasingly, politicians are attempting to regain control over how their voices are used in the public discourse, by employing counter-propaganda strategies such as party-prepared news spots and prime-time leader appear-ances, and also by seeding the protection of libel and other laws, to quell the most flagrant forms of journalistic editorialization. In addition, the apolitical stance of journalists is potentially destructive of the democratic rights of other political players, especially those of 'the people.' Our com-parisons have shown that in electoral coverage the tradition of 'indepen-dent' journalism has substituted a rhetoric of governance by élites for one of public consultation. As we have seen, people-in-the-street interviews are narratively so restricted that in no circumstances can they shift the journal-istic agenda. The present-day rhetoric undermines the assumption that there is a competent democratic public that uses the media to arrive at rea-soned conclusions about alternative public goals (Carey, 1995: 388–91).

The referendum evidence has shown that through editing, journalists are able to maintain total control over their own performance space and over how they reveal themselves as personalities (Meyrowitz, 1985: 322–4). In effect, of the three public-meaning creating groups (the other two being politicians and experts), only news personnel are positioned to claim that they stand outside of politics and that they carry no social responsibility. While the individual reporter needs to be protected by the equivalent of the First Amendment, a whole industry should not be allowed to hide behind this amendment when its reportorial styles and practices of accuracy, com-pleteness, and fairness are found wanting. Jay Rosen (1991) argues that journalists would improve the dignity of their profession by opening their own practices to the same public scrutiny reserved for the other political players.

In the 1990s Canadian journalism has begun to scrutinize itself. During the two most recent electoral campaigns, all the major Canadian dailies featured examinations of media performance that went beyond questions of 'objectivity' to consider the profession's role in creating public opinion. Journalists such as Chris Cobb of the *Ottawa Citizen* and MaryLou Finlay of CBC Radio's *Now the Details* cover media practices as a regular 'beat.' In the same vein, there is also the *Papermaking* column of the Saturday *Globe and Mail*. And the Canadian Association of Journalists publishes *Media* magazine to sensitize its members to public responsibility issues. Major national monthlies such as *Saturday Night* and *This Magazine* have recently published articles interrogating media practices. All of this indicates that journalists, who have long played a key role in creating public opinion, are beginning to open their own practices to public scrutiny and are laying the groundwork for institutionalizing professional performance criteria. This will help create greater transparency concerning journalistic work practices and the role of journalists in public opinion creation. David Weaver and Cleveland Wilhoit, who for years have studied the evolution of American journalism, have found that contemporary journalists vary greatly in how they perceive their roles: about one-third of them embrace fully both the interpreter role (62 per cent) *and* the disseminator role (51 per cent), and only a minority (17 per cent) consider the adversarial role important (1991: 116). Research by Armande Saint-Jean and myself indicates that in Canada, journalists follow North American practices and stress their information-gathering role over their adversarial role. They also tend to be more critical of certain types of reporting methods. Canadian journalists hold themselves to stricter standards than their American colleagues concerning the use of confidential documents, the badgering of sources, and the use of personal documents without permission (1997: 360–70). What this means is that broadcast journalists in the 1990s are coming under increased public scrutiny as instant satellite transmissions and replay capabilities are making television news programs ever more immediate, transparent, and (seemingly) viewer-friendly. In such an environment, the news profession must pay greater attention to ethical issues.

Coda: Some Commonalities in the Referenda of 1980 and 1995

Eighteen years after the 1980 referendum, and with a third referendum promised after 1998, it is time to pause and to reflect whether anything was learned from the first experience. More specifically, have our analyses provided any useful insights for understanding the continued public debate about Quebec's nationalist goals and how these are argued for Montreal's francophone and anglophone voters? A number of tentative observations emerge from the 1980 case studies. These demonstrate that the PQ's nationalist ideology has changed little in the intervening years, and also that referendum electioneering requires a new rhetoric to mobilize the politically uninvolved.

As we have seen, even though the referenda of 1980 and 1995 were both labelled as electoral contests, in political terms referenda serve vastly different purposes than elections in democratic governance, and involve different constituencies. Four considerations explain the mobilization differences between elections and referenda. To begin with, referenda are public consultations; they do not select candidates to form a government, but present politicians as standard bearers for alternative visions of the state and society. Furthermore, there are no 'lost' votes in a referendum, as there are in an election, because all votes cast are included in the determination of the final outcome. These ground rules encourage the contending parties to mobilize as many people as possible, including that part of the population which is usually uninvolved in electoral issues. In a referendum these voters thus acquire potentially more power than they would have in a typical election. Moreover, referenda are not about personalities but about ideologies, as witnessed in Chapters 5 and 6. Ideological debates draw on various other spokespersons, such as constitutional lawyers and business and banking experts, to assess the socio-economic outcomes of secession (Pinard, Bernier et Lemieux, 1997: 69–101). Denis Monière and Jean Guay assert that these differences confer greater interpretive power on the media during referendum periods than during elections (1996: 14–15). However, political theorists such as Graham Murdock (1993), as well as our own 1980 case studies, indicate that increased media effectivity is generated not through changes in media *practices* during referendum campaigns, but rather through the narrative *styles* and modes of argumentation that the media have adopted in 'high modernity.' The commodified 'tabloid' style that we have identified and described is particularly well suited for attracting the attention of uncommitted voters. As Chapter 4 demonstrated, this is because of its focus on 'moral disorder' and the 'personalization' of political events.

Detailed comparative studies of the 1995 referendum rhetoric have not yet been performed; even so, there is some evidence that the audiovisual presentation differences between the French and English news programs that we discovered in 1980 were still in play in 1995. According to a non-representative comparison of French and English Montreal stations, in 1995 as in 1980 the French stations carried a smaller total number of referendum 'stories' than the English. In the six weeks between 20 September 1995 and 29 October 1995, two French stations (CBFT and CFTM) aired only 387 stories, compared to the English station's (CFCF) 486 (Monière et al., 1996: 79–80). These discrepancies arose, as in 1980, from the fact that the French stations were still programming only two news shows daily against the English station's three. As in 1980, the two station groups also continued to use different presentational styles. Chapter 3 demonstrated that francophone news discourses are made up of shorter audiovisual components and use the anchor role more extensively than English stations (see Table 3.7). Chapter 4 showed that the referendum coverage of 1980 focused on party leaders rather than on the local riding members – a focus that the 'tabloid' style of 1995 accentuated (Monière et al., 1996: 84). The chapter furthermore documented that the focus on leaders was a by-product of Canadian electoral reporting strategies that use 'game' metaphors to heighten viewer interest in what are otherwise relatively uninteresting daily accounts of campaign speeches, lunches, and meetings with different voter groups.

There were also narrative and thematic similarities in the 1980 and 1995 referendum coverages. In Chapter 7 we assessed the YES and NO side coverage of the French and English stations during the final referendum week, and showed that the 1980 defeat was reconstructed in terms of only six theme clusters (the seventh was 'other'). For both station groups, the top four theme clusters were these: renewed federalism, the nature of the campaign, ethnic group responses, and economic implications (Table 7.1). The 1995 researchers used a more elaborate thematic grid with twenty-one categories, yet even they found that the thematic coverage was remarkably restricted, as well as remarkably similar, in the two Montreal stations they compared. The top four themes were these: partnership, federalism, employment, and money. Only the English station acknowledged the importance of the women's vote (Monière et al., 1996: 92). When we translate these findings into our own, more inclusive categories, we find that renewed federalism with its partnership aspects, and the economic implications of secession, were high on the discussion agenda of 1995. This is quite understandable, in light of public opinion surveys that had indicated that outright sovereignty was supported by less than 40 per cent of the Quebec electorate. Consequently, the PQ had to wage its campaign in such a manner as to capture the 'soft nationalist' vote, or what Pinard and Hamilton refer to as the 'neo-federalist' PQ supporters (1984a).

The same unrepresentative comparison furthermore revealed that issues of reporter neutrality and objective coverage were as important to the Montreal media in 1995 as they were in 1980. Once again, referendum accounts dominated the Montreal news agenda, with nearly one-third of stories (28 per cent) and program time (31 per cent) devoted to referendum issues. The same researchers claim that while the French stations (CBFT and CFTM) provided even-handed coverage for the contending forces, the English station supposedly provided less coverage for the YES than for the NO side. Only 25 per cent of CFCF's stories were devoted to the YES, as opposed to 31 per cent of all stories for the NO (Monière, 1996: 81–2). While story number and story times may be adequate criteria for determining some issues, they are insufficient, as Chapter 6 demonstrated, when it comes to determining the 'objectivity' of a news discourse that includes rhetorical features. Only a cross-tabulation of numbers of stories with their respective argumentation approaches and a survey that includes the CBC's English programming would be able to determine *how* the French and English station groups constructed their 'balance' and 'neutrality' criteria, and what types of quoting practices they employed.

Our 'day-after' analysis in Chapter 8 furthermore demonstrated that the Parti Québécois was troubled by the procedural mistakes it had made in the 1980 campaign. Party workers believed they had lost the first referendum becase they had failed to mobilize their supporters *overall*. In particular, they felt they had failed to convince Quebec *women* to support the YES side. This 'in-house' analysis played a prominent role in the planning of the 1995 campaign. Premier Parizeau was clearly aware of the long-term importance of mobilization when he outlined three preconditions for success in his renewed quest for sovereignty. These included, first, the election of Bloc Québécois candidates to the federal Parliament, which was accomplished in 1993 so overwhelmingly that the new party became the official opposition in Parliament. A year later, in 1994, to keep the momentum going, the PQ had to make an equally good showing in the provincial elections. This it did not do: it won the Quebec election with only a slim majority of 15,000 votes and only 44 per cent of the electorate – not enough to unequivocally legitimate its secessionist aims. Parizeau's third precondition – that of referendum mobilization – was hampered by the same ideological barriers as in 1980, when poll results showed that a majority of the electorate was against a rupture with Canada (Venne, 1996). Once again, therefore, strife within the party and inadequate voter support for sovereignty were affecting both the setting of the referendum date and the formulation of the referendum question, on which the outcome of the vote would depend (Pinard and Hamilton, 1986; Morin, 1991). By the fall of 1994, Parizeau's electoral promise to hold the referendum six to eight months after his reelection was being doubted; at the same time, questions about the constitutionality of the National Assembly's vote on the sovereignty declaration had undermined the party's ability to formulate a 'winnable' question (Guay, 1996: 181–3; Lemieux, 1988). As in 1980, the controversy about *when* the referendum was to be held was intricately related to internal polls, which were informing the PQ that francophone voters were deeply uncertain about *what* they would be supporting by voting YES. Would they be assenting to the PQ's nationalist agenda to redress long-standing grievances, or would they be indirectly supporting a platform that would ultimately result in outright secession? Only a complex and subtly misleading referendum question would be able to capture both groups of PQ supporters.

To illuminate the process by which francophone Quebecers were won over to the YES side in 1980, Maurice Pinard and Richard Hamilton reanalysed a series of public opinion surveys. These contained information on ethnic grievances and voter intentions between 1963 and 1980. The surveys demonstrated that there were three categories of ethnic grievances whose saliency had increased over time, and that it was these which had encouraged undecided voters to vote YES in 1980. These categories were as follows: concerns about cultural life (that is, the survival of the French language and cultural institutions); fears of increasing minoritization within Canada; and grievances about the federal political system, linked to a desire for greater self-determination in the Canadian federation (Pinard/Hamilton, 1986: 235–6). The reanalyses showed that despite substantial improvements in their socio-economic position after the late 1950s, by 1980 most francophones continued to share a number of these grievances (1986: 239). Ethnic grievances were therefore part of the necessary preconditions in the cyclical revivals of independentist fervour in Quebec.

Yet ethnic grievances per se do not explain why nationalist fervour was triggered in 1980 and again in 1995. To answer this question, Pinard and Hamilton (1984, 1986) and Pinard et al. (1997) documented the existence of two very different types of PQ supporters: the 'sovereigntist' and the 'neo-federalist' YES voters. These two voter groups, the evidence shows, voted YES for different reasons, which sheds light on the often mentioned 'ambivalences' among francophone voters. The sovereigntists said that their primary intention in voting YES in 1980 was 'to see the realization of the sovereignty-association' agenda. The researchers called these voters the 'hard core' separatists. In contrast, the neo-federalists had voted YES 'to set in motion negotiations for a renewed federalism.' Pinard and Hamilton conclude that the sudden surge in PQ support in the run-up to the 1980 referendum was attributable to an increase in the number of neo-federalist voters who were voting YES either out of political expediency, or (more frequently) because they were highly confused. Neo-federalist YES supporters were not at all sure what they had supported by their vote, and in the surveys offered three different explanations for their YES vote. Some were voting YES in order to improve economic conditions in Quebec; others were in favour of constitutional renewal; and a third group believed that the vote outcome would not affect their personal situation, and therefore supported the PQ 'strategically' in order to boost its strength when it came to negotiating an 'association' with Canada (Pinard and Hamilton, 1986: 254–5).

Pinard, Bernier, and Lemieux (1997) demonstrate that francophone voter confusion was once again in evidence in the run-up to the second referendum. In 1995, YES support surged from a low of 42 per cent on 6 October 1995, to a high of 49 per cent by the end of the October campaign. Four political processes fueled this surge. Among them were the Meech Lake and Charlettetown defeats, the Liberal Party's narrowed federalist agenda, the rising popularity of the PQ after its reelection in 1994 and the 'Bouchard' factor (1997: 313–4). Reanalyses of voting statistics indicate that the Liberal Party contributed to the PQ surge by its misguided scare offensive about the economic consequences of secession, while the PQ garnered support with the abandonment of the hard-line Parizeau plan and the appointment of Lucien Bouchard as 'chief negotiator' for the post-referendum discussions on economic union. Bouchard's personal popularity, furthermore, rallied the middle generation of Quebec voters to the YES side, even though he was not able to eliminate the 'gender gap' (1997: 314; Guay, 1996: 198–202).

The wording of the referendum question was another crucial factor in the success of the campaign. A 1994 study by Maurice Pinard had demonstrated that popular support for the PQ option depended on the terminology used. Questions utilizing the term 'sovereignty' or a 'sovereign Quebec' would increase voter acceptability by seven percentage points, over questions containing the words 'separation' or 'independence.' The PQ referendum question heeded these warnings and was worded as follows: 'Acceptez-vous que le Québec devienne un pays souverain, après avoir offert formellement au Canada un nouveau partenariat économique et politique, dans le cadre du projet de loi sur l'avenir du Québec et de l'entente signée le 12 juin 1995? OUI ou NON.'* Pinard's post-1995 refer-

* "Do you agree that Quebec should become sovereign, after having made a formal offer to Canada for a new economic and political partnership, within the scope of the bill respecting the future of Quebec and of this agreement signed on June 12, 1995?".

endum analysis indicates that confusion continued to reign as to what the question *really* implied. While about half of the YES voters remained confused or ignorant after the 1980 referendum, about one quarter were in this position in 1995. Furthermore, this ignorance favoured the YES side by at least 5 percentage points. Furthermore, according to Pinard, this confusion had a greater impact on the vote outcome than any strategic considerations that might have been involved (Pinard et al., 1997: 349–51, 353).

Careful reanalyses by Pinard et al. indicate that the 1995 surge in PQ support was once again achieved through the mobilization of 'neo-federalist' voters. As in 1980, these voters were captured by the 'partnership with Canada' offer because they favoured renewed federalism over outright secession (1997: 348–53). A July 1997 CROP poll commissioned by the Centre for Research and Information on Canada (CRIC) provides confirmation of Pinard's analyses by showing that 'renewed federalism' sentiments among PQ supporters continue to exist to this day. Even in 1997, one in three YES supporters would switch their vote if Quebec were formally recognized or if Confederation were rebalanced to give more powers to all provinces (CRIC-CROP survey, July 1997).

There is yet another similarity between the two referenda to consider: the importance of the 'gender gap,' which was first discovered around 1980. In Canada, as in the United States, women are more likely to vote than men, and prefer the more liberal over the more conservative parties by a margin of six points. This gap, contemporary studies confirm, increased in the 1980s and has become even more salient in the last decade of the century (Everitt, 1996). The Parti Québécois would have been wise to develop a special strategy for attracting women to the YES side in 1995. It made some steps in this direction through an ad campaign that featured many Quebec women artists and performers, and through its regional consultation committees, which it organized to mobilize Quebecers from all over the province (Monière et al., 1996: 145). Yet in 1995, as in 1980, the PQ failed to place women's social concerns on an equal footing with those of men. Instead of designating a special consultative committee on women's issues, as it did for young people (under 25) and for older voters (over 65), the party again overlooked women's concerns. Survey results from 1995 indicate that even though 50,164 people were reached in this largest-ever exercise in direct democracy, the consultation initiative did not increase women's YES support, which continued to hover around 41 per cent vis-à-vis men's at 49 per cent at the end of March 1995 (Guay, 1996: 195).

The PQ did not address women's concerns, our 1980 case study argued, because its outlook and practices were patriarchal. Party documents from 1995 show that this did not change after Lucien Bouchard was chosen to spearhead the campaign. In his appearance of 14 October 1995 before a few hundred women in Montreal, Bouchard like Lévesque relegated Quebec women to a 'procreative' rather than a 'citizenship' role in the sovereignty campaign. He argued that Quebec had the 'lowest birthrates among all white races,' and added that this 'placed a heavy responsibility for Quebec's future on women's shoulders.' He then encouraged his female listeners to get out and 'make a difference on October 30th.' The reemergence of the gender issue indicates that a basic contradiction exists in the sovereigntist platform, which on the one hand preaches the inclusive values of a multicultural Quebec, yet on the other refuses to grant its own women constituents more than a procreational role in the making of the new society. No wonder Liberal leader Daniel Johnson could accuse Bouchard of doubling Quebec women's sense of guilt: for failing to produce more children, and then for contributing to the possible defeat of the YES side (Venne, 1996: 52–3). These accusations carried echoes of the 1980 'Yvette gaffe,' and indicate how important women's mobilization remains in the 1990s. Gender comparisons of the 1995 vote indicate that the 'Bouchard factor' was much more effective with males, 61 per cent of whom were willing to vote YES by the end of October 1995 as against women's continued reticence (43 per cent). A similar 12-point rise in YES vote intentions on the part of Quebec women would have clinched the PQs 1995 referendum win and indicates that no party will be able to ignore gender in future mobilization efforts (Pinard et al., 1997: 315).

Quebec voters' long-standing habit of voting for different parties federally and provincially indicates that the province has engaged in a renegotiation process on constitutional matters since at least the 1960s (Lemieux and Crète, 1981: 223–34), when a new, technocratic middle-class with social democratic ideas took over political power and modernized the province. Marc Renaud argues that the logic that developed under their hegemony 'has endowed the inevitable expansion of the state with hopes and expectations far beyond what could be delivered in a capitalist economy and under the present system of national government' (1989: 75). No wonder, then, that this new political class is willing to gamble on further constitutional restructuring as a way out of the dilemma. Whether the Liberal Party under the stewardship of Jean Chrétien will be able to accommodate the goals of these élites during the 36th Parliament has become one of the most important issues for the survival of Canada into the twenty-first century. Clearly, the media will play a strategic role in explaining this political change and in amplifying the 'Charest' impact on the Quebec electorate.

Chronology of Events Leading to the Referendum*

Year		Quebec		Ottawa
1970	29 April	Liberals win 44.4% of vote, PQ 23.1% in Quebec elections	16 October	War Measures Act invoked
1971	26–28 February	René Lévesque wins presidency at 3rd PQ convention.	16 June	Victoria Charter tentatively agreed upon
1972	21 May	Claude Morin joins PQ.	30 October	Liberals, led by Pierre Trudeau, win federal election and form minority government
1973	29 October	Liberals under Bourassa win Quebec election, PQ takes 6 of 110 seats with 30.2% of vote		
1974	15–17 November	PQ convention adopts referendum idea to be used as means of ratifying constitution	8 July	Trudeau Liberals win majority (141 seats) in federal election

* Based on Fraser, 1984: 362–78.

Year	Quebec		Ottawa
	if independence negotiations fail		
1975	October	CROP poll shows PQ leading for first time (29%); Liberals have 24% and 33% are undecided		
1976	15 November	PQ wins 71 of 108 seats in Quebec with 41% of vote	10 May	Trudeau says separatism is dead in Quebec
	25 November	Lévesque becomes premier of Quebec		
1977	26 August	Bill 101 passed	4 March	Trudeau asks CRTC to conduct inquiry into CBC mandate
	2–4 November	Lévesque addresses National Assembly in Paris		
1978	15 April	Claude Ryan becomes Liberal leader.	20 February	Cullen-Couture agreement signed giving Quebec partial responsibility for screening potential immigrants to the province
	10 October	Lévesque first speaks of sovereignty-association		
1979	19 February	Liberal Justice Minister Marc Lalonde says 4/5 of PQ program realizable within Confederation	25 January	Trudeau disagrees with Pepin/Roberts report on Canadian unity, which proposes that language policy be left to provinces, while economic powers remain centralized
	23 February	PQ publishes first manifesto on sovereignty-association, D'égal à égal		

Year		Quebec		Ottawa
			22 May	Progressive Conservatives led by Joe Clark win majority (136 seats) in federal election
	21 June	Lévesque says referendum to be held in spring 1980; question to be known before Christmas		
	1 November	White Paper tabled in National Assembly	21 November	Trudeau resigns as federal Liberal leader
			13 December	Clark Government falls on vote of no confidence
1980	10 January	Quebec Liberals publish Beige Paper	18 February	Trudeau Liberals win majority (146 seats) in federal election
	4–20 March	National Assembly debate advances YES vote	15 April–14 May	Trudeau makes four referendum speeches promising 'renewed federalism' for NO
	9 March–7 April	Liberal 'Yvettes' movement formed in response to Payette's 'insult'	8–12 September	Provincial premiers meet Trudeau in First Minister's Conference
	20 May	NO vote wins the referendum	20 October	Trudeau announces he will proceed with unilateral patriation and amend BNA Act by approving a Charter of Rights
	14 October	Lévesque and dissident premiers meet, take first steps to resist unilateral patriation of BNA Act		
1981	13 April	PQ wins 80 seats	21 January	British Foreign

Year	Quebec		Ottawa
	(49% vote), Liberals 42 seats, (46%) in Quebec elections.		Affairs Committee recommends rejection of Trudeau's repatriation request
16 April	Lévesque and dissident premiers sign own agreement for patriation of Constitution	28 September	Supreme Court ruling on provincial challenges to unilateral patriation not upheld
		2–5 November	'Night of the Long Knives' Agreement reached on repatriation between Ottawa and nine premiers; Quebec excluded and refuses to sign.

APPENDIX B

Visual Content Categories

I. Visual Modes

A. *Live studio*: Report coming directly from the studio
pc piece-to-camera (camera addressed directly)
r reporter talking from the studio
i interview from the studio
d debate from the studio

B. *Live location*: Reports presented directly from location

C. *Actuality film*: Filmed reports, including videotaped reports
f film of an event appearing without commentary
fv film with voice-over commentary
fc film with captions
e stock (library) footage
pc film, news personnel address camera directly
r filmed report
i filmed interview

D. *Stills and graphics*: Often used in studio reports; may appear as background for news presenter or alone with voice-over commentary

II. Presenter Roles

A. *News presenter*
a anchor
c commentator

r   reporter
i   interviewer

B. Interviewees
e   expert
n   news maker
p   person-in-the-street

III. Visual Paradigms

PC & A	piece-to-camera/anchor
PC & A & SB	piece-to-camera/anchor/stills in background
PC & A & GB	piece-to-camera/anchor/graphics in background
PC & C & SB	piece-to-camera/commentator/stills in background
PC & C & GB	piece-to-camera/commentator/graphics in background
LSPC & R	live studio/piece-to-camera/reporter
PC & R & SB	piece-to-camera/reporter/stills in background
PC & R & GB	piece-to-camera/reporter/graphics in background
PC & A & R	piece-to-camera/anchor/reporter
SVO & R	stills/voice-over/reporter
GVO & A	graphics/voice-over/anchor
GVO & R	graphics/voice-over/reporter
FILM FN	film/news maker/piece-to-camera
FV & A	film/voice-over/anchor
FV & R	film/voice-over/reporter
FLM & CAPS	film/captions
FLMPC & R	film/piece-to-camera/reporter
FLMRPT & R	film/report/reporter
INTEXPRT	interview/expert
INTNMAKR	interview/news maker
INTPERST	interview/person-in-the-street
FVO & CAPS	film/voice-over/captions
INTV & CAPS	interview/captions

The Coding Scheme

Stephen Kline points out that the central task in unravelling how news is constructed and signifies is to explain the relationship between explanation and narrative in news stories. To get at this narrative pattern, both semantic and rhetorical, we developed four major categories: *speaker roles; cast of characters, events,* and *components of argumentation.*

Seven speaker roles are divided into two major groups: four of these are news presenter roles (anchorperson, reporter, commentator, interviewer), and three are outside sources (news maker, expert, person-in-the-street). Each of these is known to be situated in a particular relationship to the camera that recreates visually the social hierarchy of the station and its relationship to politicians.

The *characters* – that is, the sources of referendum news stories – are divided into the YES and NO forces, and thus represent the two identifiable political positions in the referendum campaign. The YES forces include Premier Lévesque and PQ spokespersons. The NO forces include Prime Minister Trudeau and other federal politicians, and Claude Ryan and other provincial Liberal Party spokespersons. Those other characters who are not readily identifiable with either side in the referendum debate have been excluded from the analysis. They appear in about one-third of the anglophone (36 per cent) and francophone (38 per cent) news segments studied. Characters and *events*, which are intimately related, are handled separately in our analysis. Events include the kinds of happenings covered as referendum items/stories. The variable is conceptually related to what is considered 'newsworthy' and is thus based on journalistic practice. Eleven different types of events are distinguished; these include meetings, tablings, speeches, document content, and polls and other data.

Components of story construction and *argumentation style* are designed to provide insight into the rhetorical – that is, 'persuasive' – components of the journalistic discourse. They include *story format*, which refers to the narrative pattern that characterizes a news item. Eight of these were identified, following Kline (1980: 28–31): report, description, commentary, narration, opinion, points of view, opinion poll, and fact. They permit an assessment of the type of interpretation found in a news story and provide clues to the different ways in which the 'factual' discourses were constructed in the French and English news discourses.

Presentational devices are textual devices that are connected with narrator roles; they indicate the strategies and types of contextualization that characterize specific journalistic and other roles in argument construction. Thus, in addition to saying that the anchor role provides the major focus of the story, and that the reporter adds detail, we can now pinpoint the strategies by which argumentation proceeds *within* the story unit and how coherent narrative formats are created. David Morley distinguishes five strategies: linking, framing, focusing, nominating, and summing up (Morley, 1980: 58–9). These clarify the point at which interpretation enters the 'neutral' journalistic discourse. To this, we have added a sixth strategy, the *nominee* category, which clarifies the degree of access that 'outsiders' have to the journalistic discourse and the ways in which narrative formats, such as the interview or discussion, constrain these contributions.

Presentation of *voice* and *context* code the source and the manner in which news personnel utilize outside sources in building up their argumentation. The presentation of voice refers to either an *indirect* or a *direct* manner of presentation of a character or a source's voice. It is thus a verbalization of the credibility dimension and indicates who gets to speak when, and what sources and topics are ignored. The interpretative use of the source's statement by the narrator, or the *context* in which the character's statement is used, is included as a variable to further refine the notion that positions in the debate are treated differently in French and English story construction. There are seven different types of contexts for statements or attributions to characters: evaluation, diminution, interpretation, quote as proof, uninterpreted, source as basis, and introduction. These are similar to what Barbie Zelizer (1989) calls 'quoting practices.' *Audience links*, finally, refer to the anchor's use of a direct reference to the audience through such personal pronouns as *we, you, one, our*, and *your*. It offers a linguistic clue to the inclusion of the audience in a news account and thus another way of assessing how journalists map an audience's position vis-a-vis their interpretation.

SPSS-X subprograms were used to compute the results of this analysis. BREAK-DOWN was used for analyses in which the dependent measure was length of the segment in seconds. Where the dependent measure was the number of presentational devices used, the MULT RESPONSE subprogram was employed. The CROSSTABS subprogram was used for analyses where the number of segments was the dependent measure. Intercoder reliability was 89 per cent.

English Vox-Pop Interviews (*City at Six*, 21 May 1980) Speaker Questions and Answers

Speaker	Questions and answers	Answer specificity	Topic No./ Arg.
Cynthia Kinch (Verdun Arena) 20 May 1980	As the crowd disperses (from Verdun Auditorium following the Ryan speech), many people mill talking about *what* happened here.	Very open	
#1	We're still part of Canada. I love Canada. It's the greatest country in the world.		4 N4B
C.K.	How about you? *How* do you feel?	Very open	
#2	Oh I feel great about this here. I was hoping to win and I'm really glad it turned out. And it's ... I don't know. I'm pretty speechless. I just love it. Our country is still together.		1 N4B
#3	I'm really tired. I worked all day for the No.		1 N1H
#4	It's the greatest thing in my life that I ever heard before when I heard Mr Ryan say,		1 N1H

Speaker	Questions and answers	Answer specificity	Topic No./ Arg.
	'We're there, we're there!' and we'll always be there, we all agree.		
#5	I agree! We need a change in the Constitution, we've got to be one country. We can't do it alone. United Canada, Together!		4 N4C
Malcolm Macleod (Paul Sauvé Arena)	The polls predicted a defeat for the Parti Québécois but every political campaign creates its own optimism, optimism that survives any poll. Some were more realistic or if they had any doubts, they weren't willing to admit them.		
	(Which side will win?)	Medium	
#6	I think the YES will win.		1 Y1F
M.M.	By *how* much?	Very open	
#7	(five per cent)		1 Y1F
M.M.	*What* do you think is going to happen?	Very open	
#8	Right now, I couldn't make any prediction. I'm just nervous about it. My hands are wet and I just hope for the best.		1 Y1F
M.M.	But you're not so sure.	Yes/No constrained	
#8	No, I'm not. (laughs)		

Speaker	Questions and answers	Answer specificity	Topic No./ Arg.
M.M.	Can I ask you?	Yes/no constrained	
#9	It's the same. I hope it's going to be YES.		1 Y1F
M.M.	But you're not so sure?	Yes/No constrained	
#9	No.		
#10	Frankly, I don't think the YES will pass this time.		1 Y1F
M.M.	*What* do you think will be the result?	Very open	
#10	I don't know. A majority for NO.		
M.M.	That man of course was right. But the crowd didn't know it yet...		1
M.M.	After the speech they filed out quietly and most said they weren't giving up. (*How* do they feel?)	Very open	
#11	Well, I feel down, but I have much hope for the next time.		4 Y4E
#12	Well, it's just an *étape* in our history, it's normal. It's the verdict of the population of Quebec. And now I say in ten years, the next *étape*.		4 Y4E
M.M.	By 10:30 only the		

Speaker	Questions and answers	Answer specificity	Topic No./ Arg.
	reporters and crew men were left to wrap up the evening ...		
George Finstad 21 May 1980	There was no shortage, however, of people who (unlike Mayor Drapeau, who would not talk about the vote) were willing to talk about the referendum results. Israel Sinman was in Phillips Square this morning and had no trouble getting reactions.		
I.S.	*What* do you think about the referendum results?	Open	
#13	I think it's a good result for the federalist forces but I don't think the question of Quebec separatism will go away. I was watching the enthusiasm of the Lévesque supporters versus Mr Ryan's supporters and I think that they'll regroup in some way. We'll see some other form of strategy.		1 N1O
#14	I think it's good this way. I mean we started off as one and now we stay as one. You know,why separate? What's it going to prove?		4 N4H
#15	We in Quebec are quite normal Canadians. We're not extremists and some		7 O

Speaker	Questions and answers	Answer specificity	Topic No./ Arg.
	are and some aren't but we're just normal people and we just like living in Canada.		
#16	I think everyone in the business community is very pleased with it.		3 N3B
I.S.	*Why* do you say that?	Very open	
#16	Well it's more certain now what the future of Quebec will be than at this time yesterday.		0 O
#17	English Canadians on the other side should not take this as a victory. They should understand it's for everybody in Quebec and help us to make this country a friendly country for everybody This is not very difficult when we see the problems of this world actually.		4 N4J
#18	I feel ashamed about Quebec. And I hope that we don't stop the work René Lévesque has done. I hope he still continues what he has done.		1 Y4E
David Bazay (downtown) 21 May 1980	The downtown parks were full of spectators, including a young YES supporter who dismissed last night's	Very open	

Speaker	Questions and answers	Answer specificity	Topic No./ Arg.
	violence as an isolated incident. *What* did you think about last night's events?		
#19	*Je pense que les gens vont l'accepter. Peut-être c'est moins facile pour les gens qui sont tellement fanatiques pour le OUI.*		1N1H
D.B.	This man says even the most fanatic YES supporters will follow René Lévesque's suggestion and give the federalists a chance to renew confederation.		
D.B.	Daniel Boudreau, an unemployed labourer, is disappointed but not embittered.		
#20	*Je respecte les opinions des autres.*		
D.B.	He said he would respect the opinions of the winners. But he wouldn't accept the status quo and he'll keep on working for the Parti Québécois.		

French Vox-Pop Interviews (*Ce Soir*, 21 May 1980) Speaker Questions and Answers

Speaker	Questions and answers	Answer specificity	Topic No./ Arg.
C. Gervais	Maintenant, qu'en pensent les gens de la rue? Il y a André Lavoie qui est allé recueillir les réactions ce midi. On l'écoute à ce sujet.	Very open	
Femme #1	Je me sens mieux en tant que Québécoise franco-phone. Je me sens mieux en tant que femme, parce qu'en plus le vote des femmes est majoritairement sur le côté du NON. J'ai eu deux attitudes. La première, ça a été de me dire, je lâche tout, je m'en vais ailleurs, ça ne vaut plus la peine. Je pense qu'après l'attitude de Lévesque hier, je me suis dit NON. C'est une étape, c'est vrai. C'est de la relève, on est encore là, cette affaire continue.		4 YYE
Homme #2	Je ne sais pas, il me semble que ...		0

Speaker	Questions and answers	Answer specificity	Topic No./ Arg.
Femme #3	C'est à éclairer les gens de voter. Si M. Lévesque se représente, je voterai pour lui, mais s'il y a d'autre monde qui se présente, je pense que je ne vote pas du tout.		1 Y1F
Homme #4	Je suis un ancien combattant du gouvernement canadien durant la guerre alors je touche une grosse pension et je sais pertinemment que si j'aurais voté pour lui et que si lui aurait rentré, je me suis résigné. J'ai été à Ottawa puis ils m'ont dit qu'il y aurait une forte chance qu'ils auraient coupé tout.		3 N3A
Homme #5	La situation était très mauvaise du point de développement industriel, du point de vue des affaires. Et maintenant qu'on a une décision qui est claire, l'atmosphère va s'éclaircir.		3 N3D
Homme #6	Je pense que le Québec va gagner à long terme avec le résultat.		3 N3D
Femme #7	Je suis très découragée.	Very open	0
A.L.	Pourquoi si découragée?		
Femme #7	Je trouve que les Québécois sont prêts à se faire hara-kiri.		0
Femme #8	Extrêmement déçue, on se demande si ce matin NON ça veut encore dire OUI. C'est ...		0

Speaker	Questions and answers	Answer specificity	Topic No./ Arg.
Homme #9	Il faut avoir un Référendum pour avoir de belles températures au Québec.		0
Anchor	Et nous allons maintenant revenir à cette soirée du Référendum, si vous le voulez bien. Danielle Levasseur était à l'aréna de Verdun avec les partisans du NON et elle nous décrit l'atmosphère qui régnait dans le camp vainqueur.		

Bibliography

Allen, Robert C., ed. 1987. *Channels of Discourse.* Chapel Hill: University of North Carolina Press.

Altheide, David L. 1985. *Media Power.* Beverly Hills, CA: Sage.

Ang, Ien. 1987. 'Stereotyping the Audience: And How to Avoid It.' Unpublished paper presented at ICA Conference, Montreal, Quebec.

Barthes, Roland. 1977. 'Introduction to the Structural Analysis of Narratives.' In *Image-Music-Text*, translated by Stephen Heath, 79–124. Glasgow: Fontana Collins.

Bauch, Hubert. 1979. 'A house of cards – Ryan.' *Gazette*, 2 November.

Bissonnette, Lise. 1980. 'C'est pourquoi il faudrait dire non à ce courage-la.' *Le Devoir*, 11 March, 4.

– 1980. 'L'Appel aux femmes.' *Le Devoir*, 9 April, 2.

Bourdieu, Pierre. 1979. 'Public Opinion Does Not Exist.' In *Communication and Class Struggle*, edited by A. Mattelard and S. Siegelaul, 1 (Spring): 124–9.

Brodie, Janine, and Celia Chandler. 1991. 'Women and the Electoral Process in Canada.' In *Women in Canadian Politics: Towards Equity in Representation*, edited by Kathy Megyery, 252–70. Toronto: Dundurn Press.

Brodie, Janine, and Jane Jenson. 1984. 'The Party System.' In *Canadian Politics in the 1980s.* 2nd ed. Edited by M.S. Whittington and G. Williams. Toronto: Methuen.

Brown, Craig, ed. 1988. *Histoire générale du Canada.* French edition edited by Paul-André Linteau. Montreal: Boréal.

Bruck, Peter. 1985. 'Power Format Radio: A Study of Canadian Current Affairs Radio.' PhD dissertation, McGill University.

Brunsdon, Charlotte, and David Morley. 1978. *Everyday Television: 'Nationwide.'* London: British Film Institute, Educational Advisory Service.

Burke, Kenneth. 1973. *The Grammar of Motives.* Los Altos, CA: Hermes.

– 1954. *Performance and Change: An Anatomy of Purpose.* 2nd rev. ed. Los Altos, CA: Hermes.

Burt, Sandra. 1995. 'Gender and Public Policy: Making Some Difference in Ottawa.' In *Gender Politics in Contemporary Canada*, edited by François-Pierre Gingras, 86–105. Toronto: Oxford University Press.

Camp, Dalton. 1979. *Points of Departure.* Toronto: Deneau and Greenberg.

Carey, James. 1995. 'The Press, Public Opinion, and Public Discourse.' In *Public Opinion and the Communication of Consent*, edited by Theodore Glasser and Charles Solomon, 373–402. New York: Guilford Press.

Caron, André. 1981. *Les télévisions au Québec: leurs programmes et leurs publics.* Montreal: Université de Montréal, Cahiers de recherche en communication.

Caron, André, and Marie Couture. 1976. 'Images of Different Worlds: An Analysis of English and French Language Television.' In *Violence in Television, Films, and News: Report of the Royal Commission on Violence in the Communications Industry.* Vol. 3. Toronto: Queen's Printer for Ontario.

Caron, André, Chantal Mayrand, and David E. Payne. 1983. 'L'imagerie politique à la télévision: les derniers jours de la campagne référendaire.' *Revue canadienne de science politique* 16, no. 3 (September): 473–88.

Caron, André, Luc Giroux, and Chantal Maynard. 1983. 'French-Speaking Canadians and English Language Television: Viewing Trends from 1976 to 1981.' Ottawa: Government of Canada, Department of Communications.

Carty, Richard Kenneth. 1986. *National Politics and Community in Canada.* Vancouver: UBC Press.

Chaney, David. 1981. 'Public Opinion and Social Change: The Social Rhetoric of Documentary and the Concept of News.' In *Mass Media and Social Change*, edited by Elihu Katz and Tomas Szeceskö, 115–36. Beverly Hills, CA: Sage.

Chaput-Rolland, Solange. 1987. 'Une crise majeure.' In *Le Québec, 1967–1987. Le Québec du Général de Gaulle au Lac Meech*, 59–62. Montreal: Guérin.

Charland, Maurice. 1987. 'Constitutive Rhetoric: The Case of the "Peuple Québécois."' *Quarterly Journal of Speech* 73 (May): 133–50.

Clarke, Debra. 1981. 'Second Hand News: Production and Reproduction at a Major Ontario Television Station.' In *Communication Studies in Canada*, edited by Liora Salter, 20–51. Toronto: Butterworth.

Clarke, Harold, Jane Jenson, Lawrence LeDuc, and Jon Pammett. 1984. *Absent Mandate: The Politics of Discontent in Canada.* Toronto: Gage.

Clift, Dominique. 1982. *Quebec Nationalism in Crisis.* Montreal: McGill-Queen's University Press.

– 1980. 'French Journalism in Québec: Solidarity on a Pedestal.' In *Canadian Newspapers: The Inside Story*, edited by Walter Stewart, 205–10. Edmonton: Hurtig.

Cocking, Clive. 1980. *Following the Leaders: A Media Watcher's Diary of Campaign '79.* Toronto: Doubleday.

Cohen, Bernard. 1963. *The Press and Foreign Policy.* Princeton, NJ: Princeton University Press.

Connell, Ian. 1980. 'Television News and the Social Contract.' In *Culture, Media and Language,* edited by Stuart Hall, Dorothy Hobson, Andrew Lowe, and Paul Willis, 139–56. London: Hutchison.

Cooke, Peter G., and Myles Ruggles. 1993. 'Balance and Freedom of Speech: Challenge for Canadian Broadcasting.' *Canadian Journal of Communication* 17, no. 1: 37–60.

Corbett, Edward P. 1980. *Classical Rhetoric.* 2nd ed. New York: Oxford University Press.

Corcoran, Paul. 1979. *Political Language and Rhetoric.* Austin: University of Austin Press.

Cowan, Peter. 1980. 'Federal Council Key to Success of Plan: Ryan.' *Gazette,* 11 January, 4.

– 1979. 'PQ Document Attacks Deadlock in Federation.' *Gazette,* 2 November. A1.

Crocker, J., S.T. Fiske, and S.E. Taylor. 1984. 'Schematic Bases of Belief Change.' In *Attitudinal Judgement,* edited by J.R. Eiser, 197–226. New York: Springer.

Cubitt, Sean. 1991. *Timeshift: On Video Culture.* London: Routledge.

Curran, James. 1992. 'Mass Media and Democracy: A Reappraisal.' In *Mass Media and Society,* edited by James Curran, Michael Gurevitch, and Janet Wollacott, 82–117. London: Edward Arnold.

Dagenais, Bernard. 1990. *La crise d'octobre et les médias: le miroir à dix faces.* Montreal: VLB Éditeur.

Dahlgren, Peter. 1987. 'Ideology and Information in the Public Sphere.' In *The Ideology of the Information Age,* edited by Janet D. Slack and Fred Fejes, 24–46. Norwood: Ablex.

– 1985. *Tuning In the News: TV Journalism and the Process of Ideation.* Stockholm: Journalisthogskilan Skrifserie.

Dandurand, Renée, and Évelyne Tardy. 1981a. 'Le phénomène des Yvettes à travers quelques quotidiens.' In *Femmes et politique,* edited by Yolande Cohen, 21–54. Montreal: LeJour.

Darnton, Robert. 1975. 'Writing News and Telling Stories.' *Daedalus,* no. 104: 175–93.

Davey, Keith. 1970. *The Uncertain Mirror: Report of the Special Senate Committee on Mass Media.* Vol. 1. Ottawa: Queen's Printer for Canada.

De Lauretis, Teresa. 1979. 'A Semiotic Approach to Television as Ideological

Apparatus.' In *Television: The Critical View*, edited by Horace Newcomb, 107–17. New York: Oxford University Press.

Demers, François. 1989. 'Journalistic Ethics: The Rise of the "Good Employee's Model": A Threat for Professionalism?' *Canadian Journal of Communication* 14, no. 2: 111–22.

Desrosiers, Richard. 1993. Interview. In *Histoire du nationalisme québécois: entrevues avec sept spécialistes*, edited by Gilles Gougeon, 111–27; 131–43. Montreal: VLB Éditeur de la Société Radio-Canada.

Dion, Léon. 1961. 'Varieties of Nationalism: Trends in Quebec.' In *French Canada Today*, edited by C.F. McRae, 89–99. Sackville, NB: Mount Allison University.

Douglas, Mary. 1966. *Purity and Danger: An Analysis of Concepts of Pollution and Taboo*. London: Routledge and Kegan Paul.

Dumas, Éveline. 1979. 'Une sérieuse réflexion au syndicalisme.' *Le Devoir*. 7 November.

Dumont, Fernand. 1993. *Genèse de la société québécoise*. Montreal: Boréal.

Dumont, Micheline. 1995. 'Women of Quebec and the Contemporary Constitutional Issue.' In *Gender Politics in Contemporary Canada*, edited by François-Pierre Gingras, 153–74. Toronto: Oxford University Press.

Edelman, Murray. 1977. *Political Language*. New York: Academic Press.

Everitt, Joanna. 1996. 'Changing Attitudes in Changing Times: The Gender Gap in Canada, 1965–1990.' Unpublished PhD dissertation, University of Toronto.

Falardeau, Louis. 1979. 'Le livre blanc sur la souveraineté.' *La Presse*, 2 November, 1.

Feyerabend, Paul. 1978. *Science in a Free Society*. London: New Library Books.

Fiske, John. 1989. *Understanding Popular Culture*. Boston: Unwin Hyman.

– 1987. *Television Culture*. New York: Methuen.

Fiske, John, and John Hartley. 1978. *Reading Television*. London: Methuen.

Fletcher, Frederick. 1987. 'Media and Parliamentary Elections in Canada.' *Legislative Studies Quarterly* 12: 341–72.

– 1984. *Canadian Politics Through Press Reports*. Toronto: Oxford University Press.

– 1981. *The Newspaper and Public Affairs*. Royal Commission on Newspapers. Vol. 7. Ottawa: Supply and Services Canada.

– 1981. 'Playing the Game: The Mass Media and the 1979 Campaign.' In *Canada at the Polls 1979 and 1980: A Study of General Elections*, edited by Howard R. Penniman, 280–321. Washington, DC: American Entreprise Institute for Public Policy Research.

Francoeur, Louis-Gilles. 1980. '*La Presse* refuse à un éditorialiste le droit de se prononcer pour le oui.' *Le Devoir*, 19 May, 9.

Franklin, Ursula. 1992. *The Real World of Technology*. Concord, ON: House of Anansi Press.

Fraser, Graham. 1984. *PQ: René Lévesque and the Parti Québécois in Power.* Toronto: Macmillan.

– 1979. 'PQ Spells Out Its "New Deal."' *Gazette*, 2 November, 1.

Fraser, Nancy. 1992. 'Rethinking the Public Sphere: A Contribution to the Critique of Actually Existing Democracy.' In *Habermas and the Public Sphere*, edited by Calhoun, 56–80. Cambridge: MIT Press.

Frizzell, Alan S., Jon H. Pammett, and Anthony Westell. 1994. *The Canadian General Election of 1993.* Ottawa: Carleton University Press.

Frye, Northrop. 1957 (1969). *Anatomy of Criticism: Four Essays.* 2nd ed. New York: Atheneum.

Gagnon, Lysiane. 1980. 'Un cadeau du ciel.' *La Presse*, 12 Janvier, C11.

– 1979. 'Reprise des thèmes de la campagne du "Oui."' *La Presse*, 2 Novembre, A18.

Gagnon, Yves. 1980. 'Les quotidiens québécois et le référendum: analyse commentée.' *Communication et Information* 3, no. 3: 170–81.

Gans, Herbert. 1979. *Deciding What's News: A Study of CBS Evening News, NBC Nightly News, Newsweek, and Time.* New York: Random House.

Geertz, Clifford. 1983. *Local Knowledge: Further Essays in Interpretive Anthropology.* New York: Basic Books.

– 1973. *The Interpretation of Cultures.* New York: Basic Books.

Genette, Gerard. 1982. *Figures of Literary Discourse.* New York: Columbia University Press.

Giddens, Anthony. 1990. *The Consequences of Modernity.* Oxford: Polity Press.

Gitlin, Todd. 1977. 'Spotlights and Shadows: Television and the Culture of Politics.' *College English* 38, no. 8 (April): 787–801.

Glasgow University Media Group. 1980. *More Bad News.* London: Routledge and Kegan Paul.

– 1976. *Bad News.* London: Routledge and Kegan Paul.

Godin, Pierre. 1981. *La lutte pour l'information. Histoire de la presse écrite au Québec.* Montreal: Le Jour.

– 1979. 'Qui vous informe.' *L'Actualité* 4, no. 5 (May): 39.

Goffman, Erving. 1983. 'Radio Talk.' In *Forms of Talk*, 127–327. Philadelphia: University of Pennsylvania Press.

– 1974. *Frame Analysis: An Essay on the Organization of Experience.* New York: Harper and Row.

– 1959. *Presentation of Self in Everyday Life.* Garden City, NJ: Doubleday Anchor.

Gougeon, Gilles, ed. 1993. *Histoire du nationalisme québécois: entrevues avec sept spécialistes.* Montreal: VLB Éditeur de la Société Radio-Canada.

Gouldner, Alvin. 1976. *The Dialectic of Ideology and Technology*. New York: Seabury Press.

Graber, Doris. 1980. *Mass Media and American Politics*. Washington, DC: Congressional Quarterly Press.

Guay, Jean-Herman. 1996. 'L'évolution de l'opinion publique.' In *La bataille du Québec: Troisième épisode*, edited by Denis Monière and Jean Guay, 181–202. Montreal: Fides.

Gusfield, Joseph R. 1981. *The Culture of Public Problems*. Chicago: University of Chicago Press.

Habermas, Jürgen. 1989. *The Structural Transformation of the Public Sphere*. Cambridge: Polity Press.

Hackett, Robert. 1991. *News and Dissent: The Press and the Politics of Peace in Canada*. Norwood, NJ: Ablex Publishing.

Hall, Stuart. 1980. 'Encoding and Decoding Television Discourse.' Revised edition of 1973 CCCS Stencilled Occasional Paper no. 7, in *Culture, Media, Language*, edited by Stuart Hall et al., 128–39. London: Hutchison.

– 1979. 'Culture, the Media, and the Ideological Effect.' In *Mass Communication and Society*, edited by James Curran, Michael Gurevitch, and Janet Wollacott, 315–48. Beverly Hills, CA: Sage.

– 1973. 'Encoding and Decoding the Television Message.' Stencilled Occasional Paper. Birmingham: University of Birmingham.

Hallin, Daniel C., and Paolo Mancini. 1991. 'Summits and the Constitution of an Interactive Public Sphere: The Reagan–Gorbachev Meetings as Televised Media Events.' *Communication* 12: 249–65.

– 1987. 'Speaking of the President: Political Structure and Representational Form in U.S. and Italian Television News.' In *Theory and Society* 13, no. 6: 829–50.

Hamilton, Richard, and Maurice Pinard. 1976. 'The Bases of Parti Québécois Support in Recent Quebec Elections.' *Canadian Journal of Political Science* 9: 2–26.

Hamilton, Roberta. 1995. 'Pro-Natalism, Feminism, and Nationalism.' In *Gender Politics in Contemporary Canada*, edited by François-Pierre Gingras, 135–52. Toronto: Oxford University Press.

Handler, Richard. 1988. *Nationalism and the Politics of Culture in Quebec*. Madison: University of Wisconsin Press.

Hardin, Herschel. 1974. *A Nation Unaware: The Canadian Economic Culture*. Vancouver: J.J. Douglas.

Hartley, John. 1982. *Understanding News*. London: Methuen.

Iyengar, Shanto. 1991. *Is Anyone Responsible? How Television Frames Political Issues.* Chicago: University of Chicago Press.

Iyengar, Shanto, and S. Kinder. 1987. *News That Matters: Television and American Opinion.* Chicago: University of Chicago Press.

Jamieson, Kathleen Hall. 1992. *Dirty Politics: Deception, Distraction, and Democracy.* New York: Oxford University Press.

Johnson, A.W. 1979a. 'The Canadian Broadcasting Corporation and the Referendum Debate.' Paper presented to the Parliamentary Committee on Broadcasting, Films, and Assistance to the Arts, November.

– 1979b. 'The CBC and Canada's Turning Points in 1980.' Speech delivered to the Canadian Club of Montreal, 12 November.

Johnson, William. 1994. *A Canadian Myth: Quebec between Canada and the Illusion of Utopia.* Montreal: Robert Davies Publishing.

Johnstone, John, Edward Slawski, and William Bowman. 1976. *The News People: A Sociological Portrait of American Journalists and Their Work.* Urbana: University of Illinois Press.

Katz, Elihu. 1995. 'Introduction.' In *Public Opinion and the Communication of Consent,* edited by Theodore L. Glasser and Charles T. Salmon, xxi–xxxiv. New York: Guilford Press.

Klapper, John T. 1960. *The Effects of Mass Communication.* Glencoe, IL: Free Press.

Kline, Stephen. 1982. 'The Rationality of the Reel: The Structure of Interpretation in Television News.' *Working Papers in Communications.* Montreal: McGill University.

Knight, Graham. 1989. 'Reality Effects: Tabloid Television News.' *Queen's Quarterly* 96, no. 1 (Spring): 94–108.

Knight, Graham, and Ian Taylor. 1986. 'News and Political Consensus: CBC Television and the 1983 British Election.' *Canadian Review of Sociology and Anthropology* 23, no. 2: 230–46.

Kress, Gunther. 1988. 'Language in the Media: The Construction of the Domains of Public and Private.' *Media, Culture, and Society* 8, no. 3: 395–419.

Kuhn, Thomas S. 1962/70. *The Structure of Scientific Revolutions.* 2nd ed. Chicago: University of Chicago Press.

Lachapelle, Guy, and Jean Noiseux. 1980. 'La presse quotidienne.' In *Québec, un pays incertain: réflexions sur le Québec post-référendaire,* edited by Edouard Cloutier. Montreal: Québec/Amérique.

Lapalme, Georges-Émile. 1988. *Pour une politique: le programme de la Révolution tranquille.* Montreal: VLB.

Laprise, Huguette. 1980a. 'Le leader du OUI suspendu avec solde à *The Gazette.*' *La Presse,* 23 April 1980: A12.

- 1980b. 'Deux journalistes en congé au *Nouvelliste.*' *La Presse,* 30 April 1980: A12.

Laurion, Gaston. 1987. 'La langue française en danger: Québec 1969 propos sur la loi 63.' In *Le Québec, 1967–1987. Le Québec du Général de Gaulle au Lac Meech.* Montreal: Guérin.

Leblanc, Gérald. 1981. 'Living with Concentration.' In *The Journalists,* Kent Commission, vol. 2, 111–33. Ottawa: Ministry of Supply and Services.

Lee, Robert Mason. 1989. *A Hundred Monkeys.* Toronto: Macfarlane Walter & Ross.

Lemieux, Vincent. 1988. *Les sondages et la democratie.* Quebec: Institut Québécois sur les recherches en communication (IQRC).

Lemieux, Vincent, and Jean Crête. 1981. 'Quebec,' In *Canada at the Polls, 1979 and 1980: A Study of General Elections,* edited by Howard R. Penniman, 208–25. Washington, DC: American Entreprise Institute for Public Policy Research.

Lévesque, René. 1986. *Memoirs.* Toronto: McClelland & Stewart.

Liberal Party (Quebec). 1980. Constitutional Committee. *A New Canadian Federation* (Beige Paper). Montreal: Liberal Party of Quebec.

Lichtenberg, Judith. 1991. 'In Defence of Objectivity.' In *Mass Media and Society,* edited by James Curran and Michael Gurevitch, 216–31. London: Edward Arnold.

MacDonald, Ian. 1984. *From Bourassa to Bourassa: A Pivotal Decade in Canadian History.* Montreal: Harvest House.

MacFarlane, Andrew, and Robert Martin. 1982. 'Le journaliste et ses droits politiques de citoyen.' *Communication et Information* 5, no. 1: 35–61.

Maillé, Chantal. 1990. *Primed for Power: Women in Canadian Politics.* Ottawa: Canadian Advisory Council on the Status of Women.

Marsolais, Claude-V. 1992. *Le Référendum confisqué. Histoire du référendum québécois du 20 mai 1980.* Montreal: VLB Éditeur.

McCabe, Colin. 1974. 'Realism and the Cinema: Notes on Some Brechtian Theses.' *Screen* 15, no. 2: 7–27.

McCombs, Maxwell, and Donald Shaw. 1977. *The Emergence of American Political Issues: The Agenda Setting Function of the Press.* St. Paul, MN: West Publishing.

McGee, Michael C. 1975. 'In Search of "The People": A Rhetorical Alternative.' *Quarterly Journal of Speech* 61, no. 3 (October): 235–49.

McLaughlin, Lisa. 1993. 'Feminism, the Public Sphere, Media, and Democracy.' *Media, Culture and Society* 15, no. 4 (October): 599–620.

Meisel, John. 1975. *Working Papers on Canadian Politics,* 2nd ed. Montreal: McGill-Queen's University Press.

Menaker, David. 1979. 'Art and Artifice in Network News.' In *Television: The Critical View,* edited by Horace Newcomb, 231–7. New York: Oxford University Press.

Mendelsohn, Matthew. 1993. 'Television's Frames in the 1988 Canadian Election.' *Canadian Journal of Communication* 18, no. 2: 149–71.

Meyrowitz, Joshua. 1985. *No Sense of Place: The Impact of Electronic Media on Social Behavior.* New York: Oxford University Press.

Miller, Mary Jane. 1987. *Turn Up the Contrast: CBC Television Drama since 1952.* Vancouver: UBC Press/CBC Enterprise.

Monière, Denis. 1980. 'Deux discours pour le choix d'un pays: les propagandes.' In *Québec, un pays incertain: réflexions sur le Québec post-référendaire*, edited by Edouard Cloutier, 89–109. Montreal: Québec/Amérique.

Monière, Denis, and Jean H. Guay. 1996. *La bataille du Québec: Troisième épisode: 30 jours qui ébranlèrent le Canada.* Montreal: Fides.

Monière, Denis, Andrea Perella, and Kim Thalheimer. 1996. 'La couverture référendaire aux informations télévisées,' In *La bataille du Québec: Troisième épisode: 30 jours qui ébranlèrent le Canada*, edited by Denis Monière and Jean H. Guay, 75–94. Montreal: Fides.

Morin, Claude. 1991. *Mes premiers ministres.* Montreal: Boréal.

Morley, David. 1986. *Family Television: Cultural Power and Domestic Leisure.* London: Comedia Publishing Group.

– 1980. *The 'Nationwide' Audience.* London: British Film Institute.

Murdock, Graham. 1993. 'Communications and the Constitution of Modernity.' *Media, Culture and Society* 15, no. 4 (October): 521–39.

Nichols, Bill. 1976–7. 'Documentary Theory and Practice.' *Screen* 17, no. 4: 34–48.

O'Neil, Brenda. 1995. 'The Gender-Gap: Re-evaluating Theory and Method.' In *Changing Methods: Feminists Transforming Practice*, edited by Sandra Burt and Lorraine Code. Peterborough, ON: Broadview Press.

Paletz, David L., and Robert Entman. 1981. *Media, Power, Politics.* New York: Free Press.

Park, Robert E. 1952. 'News as a Form of Knowledge.' In *Human Communities: The City and Human Ecology*, edited by Everett Hughes et al. Vol. 2. Glencoe, IL: Free Press.

Patterson, Thomas E. 1980. 'The Role of the Mass Media in Presidential Campaigns: The Lessons of the 1976 Election.' *Social Science Research Council* 34, no. 2: 24–30.

Payette, Lise. 1982. *Le pouvoir? Connais pas!* Quebec: Éditions d'Amérique.

Pelletier, Gérard. 1986. *Le temps des choix, 1960–1968.* Montreal: Les éditions internationales Alain Stanké.

Peters, John Durham. 1995. 'Historical Tensions in the Concept of Public Opinion.' In *Public Opinion and the Communication of Consent*, edited by Theodore Glasser and Charles T. Salmon, 3–32. New York: Guilford Press.

250   Bibliography

Pinard, Maurice. 1994. 'De Meech et Charlottetown au ... Quebec.' *Opinion Canada* 2, no. 3:2 (Juin).

Pinard, Maurice, Robert Bernière, and Vincent Lemieux. 1997. *Un combat inachevé.* Montreal: Presses de l'Université du Québec.

Pinard, Maurice, and Richard Hamilton. 1986. 'Motivational Dimensions in the Quebec Independence Movement: A Test of a New Model,' *Research in Social Movements, Conflicts and Change* 9: 225–80.

– 1984. 'The Class Bases of the Quebec Independence Movement: Conjectures and Evidence.' *Ethnic and Racial Studies,* 7 January: 19–54.

– 1983. 'Dimensions du vote référendaire.' *L'Analyste* no. 36 (autumn): 37–42.

– 1981. 'The Politics of Quebec Intellectuals: An Analysis and Some Perspectives.' Paper presented to a Joint International Seminar, After the Referenda: The Future of Ethnic Nationalism in Britain and Canada. Bangor, University of North Wales, November.

Quebec. Conseil exécutif. 1979. *Quebec–Canada: A New Deal: The Quebec Government Proposal for a New Partnership Between Equals: Sovereignty-Association* (White Paper). Quebec: Éditeur officiel.

Raboy, Marc. 1992. *Les médias québécois: presse, radio, télévision, câblodistribution.* Boucherville: Gaëtan Morin.

– 1983. *Libérer la communication. Médias et mouvements sociaux au Québec, 1960–1980.* Montreal: Nouvelle Optique.

Reiss, Timothy. 1982. *The Discourse of Modernism.* Ithaca, NY: Cornell University Press.

Renaud, Marc. 1987. 'Quebec's New Middle Class in Search of Social Hegemony: Causes and Political Consequences.' In *Quebec since 1945,* edited by Michael D. Beheils, 48–75. Toronto: University of Toronto Press.

Riley, Denise. 1988. *'Am I That Name?' Feminism and the Category of 'Women' in History.* Minneapolis: University of Minnesota Press.

Rinehart, Sue Tolleson. 1992. *Gender Consciousness in Politics.* New York: Routledge.

Rioux, Marcel. 1990. *Un peuple dans le siècle.* Montreal: Boréal.

Robinson, Gertrude J. 1987. 'Visuelle Präsentationsformen von Fernsehnachrichten.' In *Mensch und Medien: Festschrift in Honor of Hertha Sturm,* edited by Marianne Grewe-Partsch and Jo Groebel, 58–78. Munich: K. Saur.

– 1981. *News Agencies and World News.* Fribourg: University Press of Fribourg, Switzerland.

– 1975. 'The Politics of Information and Culture During Canada's October Crisis.' In *Studies in Canadian Communications,* edited by Gertrude J. Robinson and Donald Theall, 134–55. Montreal: McGill. Graduate Program in Communications.

Robinson, Gertrude J., Michael Bloom, and Denis O'Sullivan. 1982. 'Présentation et représentation visuelle dans l'information télévisée.' *Communication et information* 5, no. 1 (Autumn): 63–95.

Robinson, Gertrude J., and Kai Hildebrandt. 'West Germany: The End of Public Service Broadcasting as We Know it.' 1993. In *Public Service Broadcasting in a Multi-Channel Environment*, edited by Robert K. Avery, 53–74. New York: Longman.

Robinson, Gertrude J., and Armande Saint-Jean. 1997. 'Canadian Women Journalists: The "Other Half" of the Equation.' In *The Global Journalist*, edited by David Weaver et al., 349–70. Creskill, NJ: Hampton Press.

– 1991. 'Women Politicians and Their Media Coverage: A Generational Analysis.' In *Women in Canadian Politics: Towards Equity in Representation*, edited by Kathy Megyery, 127–69. Toronto: Dundurn Press.

Rose, Jonathan. 1993. 'Government Advertising in Crisis: The Quebec Referendum Precedent.' *Canadian Journal of Communication* 18, no. 2 (Spring): 173–96.

Rosen, Jay. 1991. 'Making Journalism More Public.' *Communication* 12: 267–84.

Roshco, Bernard. 1977. *News Making*. Chicago: University of Chicago Press.

Roy, Michel. 1980. 'L'évolution des pratiques journalistiques au Québec.' In *Les journalistes*, edited by Florian Sauvageau, Gilles Lesage, and Jean de Bonville, 15–42. Montreal: Québec-Amérique.

Sahlins, Marshall. 1976. *Culture and Practical Reason*. Chicago: University of Chicago Press.

Saint-Jean, Armande. 1993. 'L'évolution de l'éthique journalistique au Québec de 1960 à 1990.' Unpublished PhD dissertation, McGill University.

Salter, Liora. 1993. 'Weights and Measures: Issues of Balance in Media Content.' *Canadian Journal of Communication* 17, no. 1: 129–35.

Sauvageau, Florian. 1981. 'French-speaking Journalists on Journalism.' In *The Journalists*, Kent Commission, vol. 2, 43–52. Ottawa: Ministry of Supply and Services.

Savage, Philip, Bill Gilsdorf, and Robert Hackett. 1992. 'Questioning Balance: Struggles over Broadcasting Policies and Content.' *Canadian Journal of Communication* 17, no. 1: 7–12.

Scannel, Paddy, 1992. 'Public Service Broadcasting and Modern Public Life.' In *Culture and Power*, edited by Paddy Scannel, Philip Schlesinger, and Colin Sparks, 317–48. London: Sage.

Schudson, Michael. 1982. 'The Politics of Narrative Form: The Emergence of News Conventions in Print and Television.' *Daedalus* 3, no. 4: 97–113.

– 1978. *Discovering the News: A Social History of American Newspapers*. New York: Basic Books.

Searle, John. 1969. *Speech Acts*. Cambridge: Cambridge University Press.

Selnow, Gary W. 1994. *High Tech Campaigns: Computer Technology in Political Communication.* Westport: Praeger.

Shapiro, Robert, and Harpreet Mahajan. 1986. 'Gender Differences in Policy Preferences: A Summary of Trends from the Sixties to the Eighties.' *Public Opinion Quarterly* 50: 42–61.

Siegel, Arthur. 1982. *Politics and the Media in Canada.* Toronto: McGraw-Hill Ryerson.

– 1978. 'French and English Broadcasting in Canada: A Political Evaluation.' Paper presented to the 50th Annual Meeting of the Canadian Political Science Association, London, Ontario, May.

Siltanen, Janet, and Michelle Stanworth. 1984. 'The Politics of Private Woman and Public Man.' *Theory and Society* 13, no. 1: 91–118.

Sisto, Jean. 1980. 'La couverture du référendum dans *La Presse.*' *La Presse,* 19 April 1980: A9.

Smith, Dorothy. 1974. 'Theorizing as Ideology.' In *Ethnomethodology,* edited by Roy Turner, 41–4. Baltimore: Penguin.

Soderlund, Walter C., et al. 1984. *Media and Elections in Canada.* Toronto: Holt Rinehart and Winston.

Sorecom Inc. 1973. 'Les mass média, l'attachement à sa langue et les modèles linguistiques au Quebec.' Etude réalisée pour la Commission d'enquête sur la situation de la langue française et sur les droits linguistiques au Québec (Gendron Commission), E17. Quebec: Editeur officiel du Québec.

Sparks, Colin. 1995. 'The Media as a Power for Democracy.' In *Javnost: The Public.* Vol. 2: 45–59.

Stark, Frank. M. 1984. 'Rhetoric and Power: Paper Number 4.' Kingston: Queen's University, Department of Politics.

Sturm, Hertha, and Marianne Grewe-Partsch. 1987. 'Television – The Emotional Medium: Results from Three Studies.' In *Emotional Effects of Media: The Work of Hertha Sturm,* edited by Gertrude J. Robinson, 25–34. Montreal: McGill University, Graduate Program in Communications.

Taras, David. 1993. 'The Mass-Media and Political Crisis: Reporting Canada's Constitutional Struggles.' *Canadian Journal of Commuication* 18, no. 2: 131–48.

Tardy, Évelyne. 1980. 'Les femmes et la campagne référendaire.' In *Un pays incertain,* edited by Robert Boily, 185–203. Montreal: Québec-Amérique.

Tremblay, Gaëtan, Claude-Yves Charron, et al. 1981. 'Le Livre blanc et la presse francophone à Montreal.' Paper presented at the Canadian Association of Communication Conference, Halifax, 24–6 May.

Tuchman, Gaye. 1978. *Making News: A Study in the Construction of Reality.* New York: Free Press.

– 1972. 'Objectivity as Strategic Ritual: An Examination of Newsmen's Notions of "Objectivity."' *American Journal of Sociology* 77 (January): 660–79.

Van den Bulck, 1995. 'The Selective Viewer: Defining (Flemish) Viewer Types.' *European Journal of Communication* 10, no. 2 (July): 147–77.

Van Dijk, Teun. 1988. *News as Discourse*. Hillsdale, NJ: Lawrence Erlbaum.

– 1986. 'News Schemata.' In *Studying Writing: Linguistic Approaches*, edited by C. Cooper and S. Greenbaum, 155–86. Beverly Hills, CA: Sage.

Venne, Michel. 1996. 'Le déroulement del la campagne.' In *La bataille du Québec: Troisième épisode: 30 jours qui ébranlèrent le Canada*, edited by Denis Monière and Jean H. Guay, 31–62. Montreal: Fides.

Vipond, Mary. 1992. *Listening In: The First Decade of Canadian Broadcasting*. Montreal: McGill-Queen's University Press.

Wagenberg, Richard et al. 1988. 'Campaigns, Images and Polls: Mass Media Coverage of the 1984 Canadian Election.' *Canadian Journal of Political Science* 21: 117–28.

Weaver, David H.S. and Cleveland Wilhoit. 1991. *The American Journalist: U.S. News People and Their Work*. 2nd ed. Bloomington: Indiana University Press.

Williams, Raymond. 1974. *Television, Technology and Cultural Form*. London: Fontana.

Woodbury, Hanni. 1984. 'The Strategic Use of Questions in Court.' *Semiotica* 48, nos. 3/4: 197–228.

Wright, Charles R. 1975. *Mass Communication: A Sociological Perspective*, 2nd. ed. New York: Random House.

Zelizer, Barbie. 1989. '"Saying" as a Collective Practice: Quoting and Differential Address in the News.' *Text* 9, no. 4: 369–88.

Zisk, Betty. 1987. *Money, Media, and the Grass Roots*. Thousand Oaks, CA: Sage.

Author Index

Subject Index